The Wu-Tang Clan and RZA

The Wu-Tang Clan and RZA

A Trip through Hip Hop's 36 Chambers

Alvin Blanco

Hip Hop in America
Juleyka Lantigua Williams: Series Editor

 **PRAEGER**

AN IMPRINT OF ABC-CLIO, LLC
Santa Barbara, California • Denver, Colorado • Oxford, England

Library of Congress Cataloging-in-Publication Data

Blanco, Alvin.
  The Wu-Tang Clan and RZA : a trip through hip hop's 36 chambers / Alvin Blanco.
    p. cm. – (Hip hop in America)
  Includes bibliographical references and index.
    ISBN 978-0-313-38442-4 (hard copy : alk. paper) – ISBN 978-0-313-38443-1 (ebook)
1. Wu-Tang Clan (Musical group) 2. RZA (Rapper) 3. Rap musicians–United States–Biography. I. Title.
ML421.W8B53   2011
782.421649092′2—dc22   2011000023

ISBN: 978–0–313–38442–4
EISBN: 978–0–313–38443–1

15 14 13 12 11   1 2 3 4 5

This book is also available on the World Wide Web as an eBook.
Visit www.abc-clio.com for details.

Praeger
An Imprint of ABC-CLIO, LLC

ABC-CLIO, LLC
130 Cremona Drive, P.O. Box 1911
Santa Barbara, California 93116-1911

This book is printed on acid-free paper ∞

Manufactured in the United States of America

Contents

Acknowledgments   vii

Introduction   ix

1. A Family Affair   1
2. From Many There Is One Wu   7
3. Form Like Voltron   13
4. The Debut Chamber   17
5. The First Wave (Wu-Tang Clan Soloist) Splinter Cells   27
6. Wu-Tang Goes Worldwide   71
7. The Re-up: The Second Wave (More Wu-Tang Clan Solos)   85
8. Wu-Tang as a Brand, Music and Beyond   123
9. A New Millennium, Even More Wu   133
10. Chinks in the Clan's Armor   153
11. Group Hiatus, Solos Still Flow   163
12. Goodbye Ol' Dirty Bastard, Wu-Tang Marches On   173
13. Wu-Tang Redux   201
14. Shaolin Still Runs It   213

Index   229

Acknowledgments

Thanks to my beautiful wife Stacy for her patience, enthusiasm, and knack for proofreading.

Thanks to my entire family for their unyielding support, especially my sisters (Noelia, Christina), brother Justo (Freddy), and mommy and daddy (Roberto, Aquilina).

Thanks to Juleyka Lantigua for being an awesome editor and believing that I was capable of writing a book before I even did. Thank you to the staff at ABC-CLIO and Praeger.

Thanks to my dear friends and fellow journalists who kept me on my toes, assigned me stories or inspired me in some way or fashion along the way, if a name is missing, blame the brain, not the heart: Miguel Burke, Jerry Barrow, Vaughn Caldon, Hasan Stephens, Shawn Butler, Izell Blackwell, Tay Canacoo, Vernida Chaney, Damon Aulston, UVA Gambinos, Tonya Pendleton, Miles Marshall Lewis, Smokey Fontaine, Porscha Burke, *AllHipHop Gunshow*: Chuck Creekmur, Grouchy Greg Watkins, Jamilah Creekmur, Jake Paine, Jayson Rodriguez, Janna Zinzi, Steve Julien, Dove Clark, Kathy Iandoli, Odell Hall, Sidik Fofana, Martin Berrios, Michelle Berrios, *Scratch Magazine* Crew: Brian Coleman, Tony Gervino, Jesús Triviño Alarcón, R. Scott Wells, Dalmar James, Kaity Velez, Lizz Carroll, Yaminah Ahmad, Brook Stephenson, Bettina Goolsby, Nadiyah Bradshaw, Phylicia Fant, Whitney Benta, Manny Bella, Dwight Willacy, Serena Boyd, Elise Wright,

Dhanraj Maharaj, Audra Jackson, Oyama Caviness, Elon Johnson, Tracey Ford, Aliya S. King, Erik Parker, Carlito Rodriguez, Andreas Hale, Angela Bostick, Timeka Williams, Ben Osborne, Bonsu Thompson, Elliott Wilson, Kim Osorio, Vanessa Satten, Jack Erwin, Anslem Samuel, Brian Miller, Brolin Winning, Paul W. Arnold, Carl Chery, Celia San Miguel, Kim Cooper, Joshua Fahiym Ratcliffe, Alex Gale, Chloe Hilliard, Hillary Crosley, Mike Yi, Roberta Magrini, Juan Pablo, Chuck Eddy, Clover Hope, Dan Frosch, Datwon Thomas, Mahogany Browne, Timmhotep Aku, Gregory Johnson, Imani Dawson, Jason Newman, Jesse Serwer, kris ex, Leah Rose, Mark Allwood, Jermaine Hall, Matt Conoway, Maurice Garland, Deepa Shah, Mike Piroli, Miranda Jane, Rashaun Hall, Rob Markman, Rondell Conway, Roberto Santos, Ronin Ro, Russ Bengtson, Simone Kapsalides, Tomika Anderson, Tracy Hopkins, Wendy Day, Ebonie Jackson, Wes Jackson, Malik Buie, Omar Williams, Ruben Canales, Zenobia Simmons, Matt Caputo, Paul Cantor, Natanya Mitchell, and Alpha Phi Alpha Fraternity, Inc.

Introduction

In 1993, I discovered Wu-Tang Clan's first single, "Protect Ya Neck," on New York City's late night, underground radio dial. The specific show escapes me; it was probably the "Stretch Armstrong & Bobbito Show" on Columbia University's WKCR. But I clearly remember getting virtually sucker-punched by the dazzling display of rhyme energy from nine MCs, with no two sounding alike, moving as a cohesive unit over an epic beat. I didn't know it then, but I had found a group whose musical catalog would expand with more superb music to get lost in for more than a decade.

The South Bronx in the 1980s and early 1990s was defined by a near-blighted urban landscape. That was the backdrop to my childhood. Hip-hop was my escape, my paradise, my fantasy world. As the years went by, different artists came and went, though not necessarily ever disappeared, from my personal and the overall hip-hop enthusiast's playlist. Doug E. Fresh and the Get Fresh Crew gave way to Public Enemy and Big Daddy Kane, who gave way to N.W.A, De La Soul and A Tribe Called Quest, leading to Nas and OutKast, and so on and so on.

The degree to which the hip-hop artists affected the culture varied, but many acts have earned their place in the annals of hip-hop history. By 1993, being a hip-hop fan was getting easier. MTV was still playing videos, some of them occasionally from hip-hop acts, and more hip-hop oriented stations such as New York City's Hot 97 or the Bay Area's KMEL were becoming commonplace. By this time, Sean "Diddy" Combs, then called "Puffy," began his march to hip-hop supremacy while rapper/producer Dr. Dre (formerly of N. W. A) had already climbed to the top of the rap mountain.

The champagne dreams Combs's burgeoning Bad Boy artists articulated in their music were worthy aspirations, but they left a void for fans who were unable to relate. Enter the Wu-Tang Clan (pun intended), whose bomb-shelter-ready sonic aesthetics were more akin to my reality. Their videos were low budget, their sound was lo-fi, but the music was high-caliber. Their legion of devoted fans awarded the group a commercial success unheard of for what was, at least initially, an underground act. It also meant there were many fans seeking the music the Wu-Tang Clan was bringing and willing to deliver.

Though the Wu-Tang Clan's brand of hip-hop music has spread to all corners of the earth, its source can be traced back to one individual: Robert Fitzgerald Diggs, professionally known as RZA. Named by his mother after Kennedy brothers Robert and John Fitzgerald, RZA rose out of an impoverished background to become the sonic architect of the Wu-Tang Clan.[1] Under his guidance, the Wu-Tang Clan would release four albums between 1993 and 2007.

RZA is unequivocally the de facto leader of the nine (sometimes 10) member group. However, it is the latent talents of the GZA/Genius, Inspectah Deck, Masta Killa, Ghostface Killah, U-God, Method Man, Raekwon, the Chef and the late Ol' Dirty Bastard (ODB) that provided the raw materials to aid RZA in creating their musical masterpieces.[2] The different personalities also meant that listeners gravitated to some members more than others. Since individual projects had been a goal since Wu-Tang Clan's inception, its members were happy to oblige demands for solo material.

Four group albums is a modest number, but it becomes prolific when one considers that individual members have released 46 of their own albums, as of early 2011.[3] Over the years I've listened to and digested all things Wu-Tang Clan, first as a fan and then as a critic through my years as a contributing writer to publications including *XXL Magazine* and *The Source Magazine*, and editing the music review and features sections of AllHipHop.com. Wu-Tang Clan's music and members were inevitably topics long on discussion, debate, and dissection.

I have thus developed a keen and knowledgeable perspective on the group's sometimes-precarious, always-prominent station in hip-hop music and culture. While the Wu-Tang Clan is collectively known simultaneously for genre-bending and genre-defining music, verbally dense and challenging lyricism, along with a heavy inclusion of kung-fu mysticism and film dialogue, the mastermind behind the cultural phenomenon is RZA.

In late 1992 at RZA's behest, eight rappers (nine when including RZA—who is none too shabby at delivering rhymes as well) independently released a single called "Protect Ya Neck." As the song proliferated through the underground, record labels came calling for Wu-Tang Clan's services, but RZA chose to align with Loud Records, the only label willing to accept RZA's terms: the group signs to the label as long as individual members are free to sign elsewhere.

The first album, *Enter the Wu-Tang (36 Chambers)*, would be released in November 1993 and become a platinum-selling album the following year. By that time two individual stars from the group would emerge, Ol' Dirty Bastard and Method Man. Labels began seeking their individual services, as RZA planned, and Method Man and Ol' Dirty Bastard signed with Def Jam Records and Elektra Records, respectively. Method Man's debut, *Tical*, was released in November 1994 and would be certified platinum in July of the following year. In March 1995 Ol' Dirty Bastard would release his own debut, *Return to the 36 Chambers: The Dirty Version*, which would reach gold sales by that June.

Ol' Dirty Bastard's *Return to the 36 Chambers* album was the first of four critically acclaimed, commercially successful albums released between 1995 and 1996 that would cement Wu-Tang Clan's tremendous popularity and prestige as hip-hop trendsetters. Raekwon would release *Only Built 4 Cuban Linx . . .* in August 1995, GZA/Genius would release *Liquid Swords* in November 1995 and Ghostface would cap off this string of sonically scintillating albums with *Ironman* in October 1996.

Each of the five aforementioned albums, beginning with Method Man's *Tical*, would be lauded for their production, which was almost entirely handled by RZA. Critically acclaimed and commercially successful—each album would be certified at least gold, with Method Man's and Ghostface Killer's eventually reaching platinum status—the albums were the high-water mark in the Wu-Tang Clan's success. Name any ballyhooed hip-hop producer—DJ Premier, Dr. Dre, Pete Rock, Pharrell Williams—none have amassed the streak of undisputed classic albums RZA created almost single-handedly between 1993 and 1997. Since RZA was instrumental in Wu-Tang Clan's best work, this book will closely examine music and albums that carried RZA's influence. It is no coincidence that albums full of his fingerprints were the Clan's best, though it is not necessarily the rule.

RZA was also key in Wu-Tang Clan's success at expanding their brand beyond just music. While these albums were being rapidly purchased and digested by rabid fans, Wu-Tang Clan branded themselves beyond beats and rhymes with a Wu-Wear Clothing line, a video game, and even comic books. There were also a number of ancillary groups affiliated with Wu-Tang Clan (Killarmy, Sunz of Man, and others), chomping at the bit to release material. But RZA's five-year plan was still in effect, meaning another Wu-Tang Clan group album needed to be released first.

In June 1997, Wu-Tang Clan would release *Wu-Tang Forever*, a double album that would go on to reach quadruple platinum sales. The tremendous sales meant the Wu-Tang Clan was a commercial juggernaut despite critical reception—its length was often noted as a detriment—to the album being mixed. Nevertheless, with RZA handling the majority of the production his legend was only growing. The album's music featured a heavy amount of live instrumentation due to RZA beginning to learn music theory.

From Wu-Tang Clan's earliest demos, through their meteoric rise as a group and individual successes, RZA's hand was usually a guiding force during those artistic triumphs. Conversely, though not always, his contributions were lacking or even stymied during the Clan's inevitable musical and career missteps. RZA's five-year lordship over Wu-Tang Clan came to an end with the release of *Wu-Tang Forever*. Stepping back from his intrinsic involvement in all Wu-Tang solo projects freed RZA to pursue his endeavors as a solo artist, via an alter-superego called Bobby Digital.

RZA would still contribute production to the albums of Wu-Tang Clan solo members, and a number of their affiliates, but with mixed results. The second wave of Wu-Tang Clan releases began in 1998 with Method Man's *Tical 2000: Judgement Day* and RZA's *As Bobby*

Digital in Stereo. The year 1999 would see the most releases with GZA/Genius (*Beneath the Surface*), Inspectah Deck (*Uncontrolled Substance*), Ol' Dirty Bastard (*Nigga Please*), U-God (*Golden Arms Redemption*), and Raekwon (*Immobilarity*) all delivering albums.

The reaction to this second wave of albums was scattershot in terms of quality and focus. Method Man released a successful collaborative album with Redman (*Blackout!*) while Ol' Dirty Bastard, whose second album was released while he was incarcerated, ramped up his strange behavior and entanglements with legal authorities. GZA/Genius's *Beneath the Surface* managed to go gold and Method Man's *Tical 2000* went platinum, but they were not as well received as their previous efforts. Raekwon's sophomore album, *Immobilarity*, was panned for its lack of RZA beats and radically veering from the crime rap template he established with *Only Built 4 Cuban Linx . . .*

At the tail end of 1999 RZA would executive produce *Ghost Dog: The Way of the Samurai: The Album*, the soundtrack to the Jim Jarmusch film. Come January 2000 Ghostface would make up for the general malaise in recent Wu-Tang Clan music with the release of his sophomore album *Supreme Clientele* (notably, RZA was an executive producer on the project and instrumental in its beat selection).

Using the momentum of Ghostface Killah's *Supreme Clientele*, and perhaps as a way to affirm their wavering position in the exponentially growing hip-hop/rap landscape, the group reassembled to release *The W* (November 2000), which sold platinum plus units. RZA again played a prominent role in the production. Considering the Wu-Tang Clan's now sizeable musical catalog and eight distinct voices vying for time behind the microphone, the album was a surprisingly succinct 14 songs.

The group's subsequent album, *Iron Flag* (December 2001), which went gold, was released a relatively short year later. It received a lukewarm response and featured outside production from the Neptunes and Trackmasters, an attempt at more mainstream appeal. While their lyrics still revealed a propensity for street tales—"Y'All Been Warned"—and machismo—"Uzi (Pinky Ring)"—the former hunger and resulting work ethic of eight rappers desperate to have their voices heard was getting dampened by the complacency that can occur after millions of records are sold. Worth noting, ODB was on the run from authorities during the release of *The W* and in prison during the creation of *Iron Flag*.

While individual members including GZA/Genius (*Legend of the Liquid Sword*, 2002), Raekwon (*The Lex Diamond Story*, 2003), and even Masta Killa (*No Said Date*, 2004) remained active in the year following *Iron Flag*, there would not be another group album until late 2007. At this point releases had slowed to a relative crawl and group infighting and bickering led to concerns about the Wu-Tang Clan's future in an ever-evolving music space. RZA found success scoring films such as Quentin Tarantino's *Kill Bill Vol 1 & 2* and the *Afro-Samurai* anime cartoon. As RZA gained acclaim from his outside projects, Ghostface was the only other Wu-Tang Clan member to gain much critical success.

With fans questioning the splintering of what was once the strongest alliance in hip-hop, and a failed reunion tour in 2004, Wu-Tang Clan signed a one-album deal with SRC Records (run by Steve Rifkind, who signed the Wu-Tang Clan to their original record deal) in December 2006 and *8 Diagrams* was released in December 2007 after a six-year hiatus. However, to the album's detriment, certain members made public their discord over RZA's beat selection. The album would be Wu-Tang Clan's least commercially successful release, while RZA's continual experimentation with the Wu-Tang sound is a love it or hate it, with little in between, scenario.

In the wake of *8 Diagrams* the usual trickle of Wu-Tang solo efforts would continue. A number of fans, myself included, had faith that Wu-Tang Clan still had plenty of gas in their tank. Our prayers were answered and naysayers were silenced when Raekwon's years-delayed *Only Built 4 Cuban Linx . . . Pt. II* album was released in September 2009 to tremendous critical and commercial acclaim (debuting at number 2 on the *Billboard* R&B/Hip-Hop Albums chart). Appropriately, the album featured production from RZA.

The purpose of this book is not simply to chronicle Wu-Tang Clan's exploits. There have been artists and groups maybe as infamous, but none as influential. Incredibly, at the heart of their rise to prominence are ordinary men of relatively little means who with little more impetus than hoping to make good music, and earn an honest buck, realized their dreams off of sheer talent. Similar aspirations are no doubt shared by the innumerable artists who upload hundreds, if not thousands, of MP3s to the Internet every day hoping to make their own mark in hip-hop. The rise of the Internet has democratized the music industry playing field and more music from the Wu-Tang camp is in the works that will inevitably be added to this infinite stream of music.

In this book's case study of the Wu-Tang's catalog I hope to illustrate why the Wu-Tang Clan logo is still worthy of its Gibraltar status in a hip-hop world whose music seems to become more disposable—or deletable—by the day. With a new generation of listeners getting acquainted with RZA and company's music—like I did in 1993, except now via a blog post rather than a record spin—this book will illuminate why Wu-Tang Clan embodies all that is good in rap music, occasional warts and all. One of the reasons I became a music journalist is because I wanted my take on hip-hop to be properly documented, and here I hope to extend that courtesy to the magnanimous efforts of the Wu-Tang Clan.

NOTES

1. Ashon, Will. "RZA as Bobby Digital." *Trace Urban Magazine*, November 1998, 50 (48–56).

2. Cappadonna has been an on-again, off-again member of Wu-Tang Clan since first appearing on Raekwon's *Only Built 4 Cuban Linx . . .* album. Cappadonna has released three solo albums to date.

3. The number includes only albums billed as solo albums by the original nine Wu-Tang Clan members.

CHAPTER I
A Family Affair

Robert Fitzgerald Diggs, professionally known as RZA, was born in the Brownsville neighborhood of Brooklyn, New York, on July 5, 1969. While he occasionally spent summers with an uncle in North Carolina, RZA and the rest of his immediate family eventually settled in the Marcus Garvey Projects in Brooklyn before he and two of his 11 siblings moved to Staten Island to stay with his grandparents. There, he spent his formative years shuttling between Brooklyn and the borough that would eventually be dubbed "Shaolin."

With his two cousins, Russell Jones, professionally known as Ol' Dirty Bastard, and Gary Grice, professionally known as GZA/Genius, RZA would traipse New York City during the 1980s on the hunt for rhyme battles and block parties, seeking the hip-hop music that was quickly dismissing any notions the culture was a fad with every passing day. The story goes, GZA, who was the oldest and living in Staten Island's Park Hill Projects, taught RZA how to rhyme and, in turn, RZA taught Ol' Dirty Bastard how to rhyme.[1]

According to RZA, it was in the spring of 1980 that GZA/Genius began teaching him the art of MCing.[2] But before he delved fully into the world of rapping, the previous year in a theater of New York City's then grimy 42nd Street, RZA saw a kung-fu film called *The Five Deadly Venoms*. From then on he was hooked on the genre's high-flying action and entertaining stories that often involved a small, dedicated group or sole fighter taking on a larger faction and often overcoming overwhelming odds.

In 1983 he viewed a film called *The 36th Chamber of Shaolin* (it was originally released in 1978 by Shaw Brothers Films), and RZA credits it as resonating with his then-developing sense of purpose, going as far as to say the film "drew people like me into the truth of our own

1

history."[3] Lastly, in 1989 RZA would screen another Shaw Brothers film titled *Eight-Diagram Pole Fighter* to the various rappers that would come and go from his apartment, including GZA/Genius and Ghostface Killah. The film was about a family of fighters who were betrayed by a general who feared their power and influence. All the eventual traits of the Wu-Tang Clan—disciplined techniques, strong familial ties, and an us-versus-them mentality—could be traced back to these films.

The lessons gleamed from these films and other key kung-fu titles, including *Shaolin and Wu-Tang*, would also correspond with teachings his older cousin GZA/Genius began hipping him to in 1981. GZA/Genius had taken the name Justice because he had gained knowledge of self. Justice was a member of the Nation of Gods and Earths (often referred to as the Five Percent Nation). The Nation of Gods and Earths was founded by Clarence Smith (Clarence 13X), after he separated from Elijah Muhammad's Lost-Found Nation of Islam in 1964. A former student minister in the Nation of Islam—coincidentally, his duties included teaching members of the Harlem Temple No. 7 the martial art karate—the Nation of Gods and Earths lived by an ethos that there is no unseen "mystery God" to be worshipped in the heavens but that God is in every individual.

Whereas Christians have the Bible, Jews the Torah, and Muslims the Qur'an, the Nation of Gods and Earths has the Supreme Alphabet, Supreme Mathematics and the 120 Lessons.[4] GZA/Genius hipped RZA to Supreme Mathematics and the Supreme Alphabet, a system whose concepts supposedly unlock the mysteries of the universe and forms the tenets of the Five Percent Nation. The knowledge the required teachings of the Five Percent Nation bestowed its practitioners gave them a profound sense of self and self-confidence. This aided in its fast popularity among disenfranchised African American youth in the New York City and East Coast areas during the 1970s and 1980s.

Hip-hop has long been full of vernacular whose true or hidden meaning is only known to a select few. But beyond the basic urban street slang, the Wu-Tang Clan's lyrics were loaded with terms taken directly from the teachings of the Five Percent Nation. The Five Percent Nation's rhetoric that was eventually dispersed throughout Wu-Tang's lyrics was not new to hip-hop. Years earlier one of the first renowned MCs to use terms directly from the teachings was Rakim on Eric B. & Rakim's "Paid in Full" when he finished the song by saying "Peace."[5] Words and phrases taken directly from the lexicon of the Five Percent Nation also made their way into the rhymes of esteemed rappers such as Brand Nubian and Big Daddy Kane. RZA's memorization of the 120 Lessons is legendary. The Wu-Tang Clan liberally intermixed the jargon into their rhymes, granting them a natural affinity to listeners who were members of or at least familiar with the Five Percent Nation. It also would provide plenty of rhymes for their fans to decipher.

Christian Ex's article in *The Source Magazine* in 1997, "Whatever Happened to the Gods and Earths?," explains the movement's relationship with hip-hop:

> Hip-hop culture's inherent need for change, its birth as a rebellion against the vapid tendencies in popular music, and its focus on self-sufficiency made its marriage with the Nation of Gods and Earths a match made in heaven. But such romanticizing does not explain why a once powerful source of knowledge has apparently been reduced to cliché phrases and empty rhetoric.[6]

Beyond making for interesting and engaging audio on records, the kung-fu philosophy utilized in Wu-Tang Clan's music was applied to the group's overall philosophy. The original Wu-Tang (Wudang) sword style of ancient times was developed by former members of the Shaolin Temple in Dengfeng, China. The Wu-Tang sword style is symbolic of the tongue—ultimately the source of the rap group Wu-Tang Clan's lyrics. Also worth noting, it was their Staten Island slang for Old English malt liquor.

But before taking their neighborhood kung-fu and Five Percenter codes to the national stage, the trio of cousins—Bedford-Stuyvesant, Brooklyn, native GZA, going by the name Genius, RZA going by the Scientist, and East New York, Brooklyn, native Ol' Dirty Bastard calling himself the Specialist—would form a group called All in Together.[7] GZA/Genius explained to *Scratch Magazine* in 2006, "All In Together used to be a group with myself, RZA and Dirty many years ago in the '80s and we actually had a song called 'All In Together Now.' It was one of the first songs I ever recorded. . . . Dirty was doing the beatbox and I was rhymin', it was almost like some 'La Di Da Di' type thing."[8]

All In Together would make a little noise locally in Staten Island, but it would be RZA, who was then going by Prince Rakeem, and Genius who would eventually score recording deals with Tommy Boy Records and Cold Chillin' Records, respectively, in the late 1980s. RZA and GZA/Genius were at the time being managed by Melquan, a notable producer in hip-hop circles at the time, and under his watch the cousins signed their respective deals.[9]

GZA/Genius's stint on Cold Chillin' Records was initially filled with promise considering it was the same record label that housed renowned hip-hop producer Marley Marl's Juice Crew of top tier rappers (Big Daddy Kane, Kool G. Rap, MC Shan, et al.). The Juice Crew can be considered a precursor to the Wu-Tang Clan's template of a talented, and united, group of rappers.[10] "We ain't gon' front. We on some Juice Crew shit," RZA would admit to *The Source Magazine* in late 1993 in one of the group's earliest interviews.[11] However, after GZA/Genius recorded his debut album, *Words from a Genius*, which featured production from Easy Mo Bee (who in the future would produce music for the late Notorious B.I.G. and Miles Davis), it was released with little fanfare.

Words from a Genius's lead single was "Come Do Me," an R&B-influenced track that depicts GZA/Genius more like a playboy than a cerebral MC. According to GZA/Genius himself, he acquiesced to Cold Chillin' Records executives' demands for a more commercial song after he initially submitted the album.[12] Soon after, GZA/Genius found himself dropped from the label, whose past Juice Crew glory days were already fast fading. Cold Chillin' would rerelease *Words from a Genius* years later in the wake of the Wu-Tang Clan's success. Ironically the album is an underappreciated work that features GZA/Genius's succinct but impactful rhymes, his worry-free cadence already fully developed. One of the better songs on the album was "Pass the Bone," which features GZA/Genius and RZA trading rhymes over a rather laid-back guitar loop and drums.

While GZA/Genius's recording career was off to a stuttered start, RZA didn't have much better luck. As Prince Rakeem, he only managed to eke out a single called "Ooh, I Love You Rakeem" that portrays him as a happy-go-lucky rapper whose main focus is bagging "too many ladies." The song is produced by RZA (credited as "Prince Rakeem") and features a rather rote bass line and monotonous horn samples. Not surprisingly, "Ooh, I Love You Rakeem" gained little traction; it never charted. But hints of what was to be were beginning to be revealed. Also included on the "Ooh, I Love You Rakeem" 12″ single were two songs, "Deadly Venoms," produced by Prince Rakeem, and "Sexcapades," produced by Easy Mo Bee and coproduced by Prince Rakeem. "Deadly Venoms" featured a marching drum rhythm and RZA's rhymes are more boastful of his prowess on the microphone; it sounds more akin to the Wu-Tang Clan's musical aesthetic yet to be revealed, while its title is a nod to the film *Five Deadly Venoms*. The B-side "Sexcapades" is more in line with the sexual dynamo fantasies of "I Love You Rakeem" but worth mentioning is the included "Wutang Mix" [*sic*] of the song.

All the while, during the infancy of his recording career, RZA was recording demos for future Wu-Tang Clan members including Method Man and Ghostface. However, a proper Prince Rakeem album was never to be. RZA's deal with Tommy Boy was for a single with the possible option of recording an album. In 1991, Tommy Boy passed on picking up the album option on his contract and RZA's woes were compounded by a legal matter that threatened his freedom. With no money coming in from his recording contract, RZA was spending time dealing drugs in Steubenville, Ohio. After finding himself in the middle of a feud that led to a late-night shootout, the then 22-year-old was charged with felonious assault and faced the prospect of an eight-year jail term.[13] Claiming self-defense, RZA was acquitted of the charges. Having dodged the proverbial bullet, illegal routes to cash were no longer an option and music, even though his deal with Tommy Boy was kaput, became his focus.

Now back home, RZA knew Staten Island had plenty of MC talent; the cadre of part-time rappers who had been slowly and surely gravitating around him proved that. He just needed to convince them this super-rap-group concept formulating in his head was feasible. But before the code of the Wu-Tang Clan could be cracked, it had to be formed. With a core philosophy of principles in tow that essentially said putting the good of the group first would ultimately reap individual benefits with patience—no doubt co-opted from the teachings of the Five Percent Nation and the Shaolin philosophies depicted in kung-fu films—and a newfound dedication to the music he first started practicing with All In Together, RZA was ready to see his vision of affecting the hip-hop music business with the Wu-Tang brand go from theory to reality. He told *Vibe Magazine* in 1995, "The media says that Wu-Tang came from rags to riches. All we did was go from knowledge to born," which is a direct reference to going from 1 (Knowledge) in to 9 (Born) in the Supreme numbers.[14]

RZA had come full circle. What essentially amounted to an initial failure only sharpened his business acumen and sparked his determination to flip the record business's status quo onto its head. He couldn't do it alone.

NOTES

1. Dre, A. L., "Lyrical Blades," *The Source Magazine*, December 1995, 47 (47, 52).

2. The RZA and Chris Norris, *The Tao of Wu* (New York: Riverhead Books, 2009), 33.

3. Ibid., 53.

4. According the Nation of Gods and Earths its followers are the 5 percent of humanity who live righteously (have knowledge of self). Eighty-five percent of humanity is deaf, dumb, and blind (the uncivilized) while the remaining 10 percent have knowledge but are content with keeping the 85 percent ignorant to it.

5. Scientific, Sun-God, "All Praises Due," *The Source Magazine*, June 2005, 95.

6. Ex, Christian, "Whatever Happened to the Gods and Earths?," *The Source Magazine*, August 1997, 75.

7. Dre, A. L., "Lyrical Blades," *The Source Magazine*, December 1995, 47.

8. Aku, Timmhotep, "Across the Board," *Scratch Magazine*, January/February 2006, 64 (62–65).

9. Coleman, Brian, *Check the Technique: Liner Notes for Hip-Hop Junkies* (New York: Villard, 2005, 2007), 452.

10. Smith, R. J., "Phantoms of the Hip-Hopera," *Spin Magazine*, July 1997, 70 (68–74, 126).

11. Life, Matt, "Hittin' You From Every Angle," *The Source Magazine*, January 1994, 89 (87–89).

12. Watson, Margeaux, "Think Different," *XXL Magazine*, August 1999, p. 66.

13. Owen, Frank, "Wu-Tang Clan Is Sumthing Ta Fuck Wit," *The Village Voice*, May 30, 2000, 43.

14. Malone, Ambassador Bonz, "Deep Space Nine," *Vibe Magazine*, June/July 1995, 75.

CHAPTER 2
From Many There Is One Wu

The Wu-Tang Clan is Gary "GZA/Genius" Grice, Russell "Ol' Dirty Bastard" Jones, Clifford "Method Man" Smith, Dennis "Ghostface Killah" Coles, Cory "Raekwon" Woods, Jason "Inspectah Deck" Hunter, Lamont "U-God" Hawkins, and Elgin Jamal "Masta Killa" Turner. Each member would go on to release solo albums with varying degrees of commercial and critical success. But those solo endeavors would not have occurred without their initial team success as the Wu-Tang Clan, and the unit's origin is centered on Robert "RZA" Diggs.

The All In Together crew consisting of RZA, GZA, and Ol' Dirty Bastard should rightfully be considered a forerunner to the Wu-Tang Clan. The remaining members of Wu-Tang all were associated with RZA at some point during his youthful days and the embryonic stages of his recording career as Prince Rakeem. That common thread would bring together future members of Wu-Tang Clan that even in the best of circumstances would normally have been rivals. "[RZA] was the common denominator—we all gravitated to him," Inspectah Deck told Brian Coleman in 2005's *Check the Technique*.[1]

Ghostface and Raekwon met in junior high school and were soon friends despite hailing from contending Staten Island housing projects, Stapleton (after living in West Brighton Projects) and Park Hill, respectively. Method Man, Inspectah Deck, and U-God were also from the Park Hill Projects and, along with Raekwon, all hung out as teenagers.[2] RZA met Raekwon in the second grade and Method Man in the ninth grade. Method Man, who was originally from Hempstead, Long Island, had a rap group called the DMD (Dick 'Em Down) crew along with Raekwon and Inspectah Deck. Also, GZA had known Raekwon and Inspectah Deck since elementary school.

After two years at Staten Island's New Dorp High School (where he was classmates with the members of the aforementioned DMD Crew), Ghostface dropped out and started spending more time with RZA, GZA, and Ol' Dirty Bastard. During RZA's infamous stint as a drug dealer in Steubenville, Ohio, Ghostface and Ol' Dirty Bastard moved with the producer to the town, whose most notable achievement as the birthplace of Rat Pack member Dean Martin made it unnoticed by the greater hip-hop community. While in Steubenville, Ghostface survived a gunshot wound to the neck and arm, the result of a heated altercation fueled by alcohol.[3] As for RZA, after being found not guilty at his attempted murder trial in Steubenville, he made his way back to New York City in late April 1991. He moved into a two-bedroom apartment on 134 Morningstar Road in Staten Island with his girlfriend and daughter, Ghostface, his brothers Divine (Mitchell Diggs) and Born, and his sister Sherri.[4] The apartment at 134 Morningstar would become the first home of Wu-Tang Productions.

RZA soon began a campaign of convincing his loose consortium of rapping associates that the best way to break into the industry was to unify as one group under the Wu-Tang Clan banner. Solo opportunities would eventually arise out of their success. RZA's street credentials, stemming from his drug-dealing days, gained him an audience with the raw MCs. Also, his reputation as a learned individual because of his mastery of the 120 Lessons usually swayed anyone who needed convincing that his plan just might work. On what would become a seemingly mystic shroud that surrounded the Wu-Tang, RZA, as he told *Spin Magazine* in 2005, put it squarely on the group being a "strange mixture" of "ex-felons, self-taught men, tough guys, fashion guys, as well as deep thinkers."[5] Getting this motley crew of thugs with rap skills on the same page required their giving up something anyone making a living on the streets never wants to—control.

While in dramatized accounts, the Wu-Tang Clan was viewed as a democracy, it was actually a dictatorship, and RZA was the king of the castle. RZA had a five-year plan. In *The Wu-Tang Manual*, RZA wrote, "I told them, 'If y'all give me five years of your life, I promise you in five years I'm gonna take us to the top.' And so we gave each other our word. The Wu-Tang Clan was born."[6]

RZA convinced all of the future members of Wu-Tang Clan to sign contracts to Wu-Tang Productions—business is business, after all—and his five-year plan set sail. While Staten Island had never been considered a hip-hop hotbed, it proved to be a fertile ground for Wu-Tang Clan to bloom. Being centered in Staten Island, literally the borough on the outskirts of NYC proper, made for a unique opportunity. RZA wrote in his book *The Tao of Wu-Tang*, "A nine-man hip-hop crew based on Mathematics, chess, comics, and kung-fu flicks wasn't springing up in the middle of a Manhattan art scene. Only on a remote island can something like King Kong grow to his full capacity."[7]

All the lip service given to dreams of taking over the music industry would be for naught without a proper sonic introduction to the rap underground and eventually the masses. With all the rappers on board, RZA orchestrated the recording of "Protect Ya Neck." First impressions can easily make or break an artist and as the Wu-Tang Clan's first official single, "Protect Ya Neck" (recorded in October 1992) was an uppercut to a hip-hop world dominated by the gangsta, though backyard-barbecue-friendly, rap music of Death Row Records' Dr. Dre and Snoop Dogg.

"Protect Ya Neck" had a distinctly lo-fi, basement-demo quality to its production that was a stark contrast to the cleanly produced rap music dominating the charts at the time. Despite the homemade feel, the track's drums were strong in the mix and its marauding bass line set a spare but engaging stage for the rappers' lyrics to be presented front and center. In what is likely the first review of the single, *The Source Magazine* spotlighted the song as a Sure Shot Single in its April 1993 issue. "The Wu-Tang Clan is packed with flavor MCs, all bringing a unique style to the cutting edge of underground hip-hop," said the review.[8]

Each member (to that point, Masta Killa does not appear on the song) gets a verse to introduce himself on "Protect Ya Neck." The first rapper heard is Inspectah Deck, whose claim that he "smokes on the mic like Smoking Joe Frazier" reeled listeners in for a series of double entendres and insider references for the remainder of the song. The placement of all the verses was calculated, as Inspectah Deck was the second to rhyme in the original session but RZA went back and changed the order in post-production. "Once I heard the final [song], I knew to never doubt the RZA when it comes to this music," Inspectah Deck told journalist Brian Coleman in *Check the Technique*.[9]

Raekwon follows Inspectah Deck's lead-off verse with one of his own, chock full of slang, which would come to be one of his trademarks. Interestingly, Raekwon's rap was the only verse he had ever written down to that point, with all his other rhymes being spontaneous freestyles.[10] Method Man rhymes third and his smoky baritone with the distinct timbre is followed by a quick four-bar verse from U-God. According to Wu-Tang lore, U-God's short jab on "Protect Ya Neck" was a last-minute addition as he had just returned from a stint in prison. The verse's clipped length makes it sound like a segue into a bridge, leading directly into Ol' Dirty Bastard harmonizing of "Come on baby baby come on," before launching into his half singing, half rapping, all emoting delivery. Like Raekwon, Ol' Dirty's vocal styling first evidenced on this seminal Wu-Tang Clan song would also become his trademark.

Ol' Dirty Bastard's turn is followed by a merely adequate verse from Ghostface. While Ghostface would prove himself to be one of Wu-Tang Clan's most consistent artists, his verse on "Protect Ya Neck" didn't set him apart in what was quickly becoming an artfully varied band of rappers. RZA would follow, presenting his lines with an energized delivery that compares his rhyme flow to Christ speaking the gospel, speaks on the high rate of unemployment in the African American community, and interpolates "She'll Be Coming 'Round the Mountain." It would prove to be a small but substantial glimpse into the arsenal—rhyming, sampling, pop culture referencing—of RZA in one verse.

Capping off this rap free-for-all is a verse from GZA/Genius. Up to that point the Genius was the member of Wu-Tang Clan with the most renown thanks to his stint on Cold Chillin' Records and the release of his *Words from the Genius* album in 1991 (RZA only managed to release the quickly forgotten "Ohh We Love You Rakeem" single). GZA's verse was a verbal indictment on the treacherous label record treatment of rap musicians, a topic he was all too familiar with. Blithely naive A&Rs, underhanded record label deals, squeaky-clean rappers (the Wu-Tang Clan's antithesis); all felt the wrath of GZA's measured flow. The verse would be named The Dopest Rhyme of '93 in the January 2004 issue of *The Source Magazine* and was the perfect closer to Wu-Tang Clan's first volley into the hip-hop world.[11]

The initial pressing of the "Protect Ya Neck" 12″ single on Wu-Tang Records—funded by each member contributing $100—featured a song called "After the Laughter" on its B-side. While very rare—the initial vinyl run was about 5,000 copies—the song appears on a *Wu-Tang Clan Demo* that began making the Internet file-sharing rounds in the early 2000s. "After the Laughter" was recorded in 1992 before "Protect Ya Neck" and the song features RZA and Ghostface's crudely recorded and distorted vocals over the easily recognizable Wendy Rene "After Laughter (Comes Tears)" sample. The song is an early version of what would become "Tearz" on Wu-Tang Clan's debut album, *Enter the Wu-Tang (36 Chambers)*.

But it would be another year before Wu-Tang Clan would release *Enter the Wu-Tang*. Before then, DJ Kid Capri started playing "Protect Ya Neck" on his mix show on New York City radio station WBLS in early 2003. From there other DJs, including the highly influential DJ Funk Master Flex, quickly followed suit. Soon "Protect Ya Neck" was receiving major play on hip-hop mix shows, college radio, and, maybe more importantly, on the taste-making streets of New York City. There was also a self-funded video— shot mostly in black and white—that effectively relayed Wu-Tang Clan as average, everyday street toughs that happened to be blessed with star-ready rap talents. In turn, major record labels began showing interest in this new group not from Brooklyn, Harlem, the Bronx, or even Compton, but from Staten Island.

NOTES

1. Coleman, Brian, *Check the Technique: Liner Notes for Hip-Hop Junkies* (New York: Villard, 2005, 2007), 455.

2. Cockfield, Errol A., Jr., "Catching Red," *The Source Magazine*, March 1999, 124 (120–124).

3. Mao, Chairman, "Ghostface Killer: The Iron Man Cometh," *Ego Trip*, Vol. 2 No. 5 (1996), 28 (26–30).

4. RZA and Chris Norris, *The Tao of Wu* (New York: Riverhead Books, 2009), 104.

5. Aaron, Charles, "20 Years of Spin," *Spin Magazine*, November 2005, 64 (64–65).

6. RZA and Chris Norris, *The Wu-Tang Manual* (New York: Riverhead Books, 2005), 76.

7. RZA and Chris Norris, *The Tao of Wu*, 16–17.

8. "Sure Shot Singles: 'Protect Ya Neck,' " *The Source Magazine*, April 1993, 76.

9. Coleman, *Check the Technique*, 463.

10. Alvarez, Gabriel, "Spit Darts," *The Source Magazine*, December 1999, 172.

11. "The Dopest Rhyme of '93," *The Source Magazine*, January 2004, 25.

CHAPTER 3
Form Like Voltron

The name of Wu-Tang Clan's first single, "Protect Ya Neck," became an ironic title; Wu-Tang Clan managed to grab the recording industry by the throat. The enthusiasm for the song's stark, gritty basement groove matched by an assault of blistering battle raps not only won Wu-Tang Clan a legion of fans but a who's who of label suitors. Record labels were eagerly looking to align themselves, and score a payday, with the posse from Staten Island. By March 2003, "Protect Ya Neck" had sold 10,000 copies independently via RZA's Wu-Tang Productions. Despite taking meetings with labels, RZA wasn't going to be satisfied by resorting to the status quo—artist as a slave to the label—relationship that was the music industry norm. RZA told *Vibe Magazine* in 1995, "We ain't trying to come in here as new artists, we gonna come in as what? The new *industry*. If you want real hip-hop, you gotta come to this source."[1]

All of the offers the Wu-Tang Clan received sought to sign the group to a restrictive group contract. Then there was the inevitable reality of any advances having to be split between eight individual artists. The only label willing to play on RZA's terms was an independent label called Loud Records that boasted distribution by RCA. In exchange for their relatively low album advance of $200,000, Loud agreed to sign Wu-Tang Clan to a group deal that allowed individual members to sign solo deals with any competing record label of their choice, so long as Loud was granted the opportunity to sign the artist first. The move was unprecedented and would be seen, in hindsight, as a genius move by RZA.

The Wu-Tang Clan and RZA were also given more creative control of their music. After initially signing a single deal with Loud Records, the label pressed up copies of the "Protect Ya Neck" single, except that the original "After the Laughter Comes Tears" B-side was swapped out in favor of "Method Man." Although RZA's and GZA's voices can be heard at the beginning of "Method Man" (the latter name checks the entire Wu-Tang Clan roster), the song is ultimately a Method Man solo record as he is the only artist to rhyme on the track. While its position on the charts was modest—it peaked at #40 on the *Billboard* R&B/Hip-Hop Songs chart—the song was an unquestionable hit at hip-hop clubs and radio stations, and most importantly with the Wu-Tang Clan's growing legion of fans. Method Man's first verse on "Method Man" was granted a "Hip-Hop Quotable" in the August 1993 issue of *The Source Magazine.*[2]

Over cascading chords provided by RZA (he would be producing all of Wu-Tang's material), Method Man delivers his vocals with a voice that sounds like it has been made harsh by the copious amounts of the reefer smoke he derived his name from, while still maintaining a melodic quality. The song's hook, inspired by the chorus of Hall & Oates' "Method of Modern Love" (1984), simply spells out the name "M.E.T.H.O.D." while the word "Man" accentuates the end of each spelling, making for an easily remembered and repeated refrain. Method Man's sing-songy delivery kicks off with "Hey you, get off my cloud . . . ," (a nod to the Rolling Stones 1965 song "Get Off of My Cloud") presenting an easily understandable cadence that is as deft at supplying cartoon (Tweety Bird) quoting catch phrases ("Hold up wait, I thought a I saw putty cat.") as it is at possessing a key component in every great rapper's arsenal, witty similes ("The master of the plan wrapping shit like saran, wrap"). Add to the mix handsome looks that attracted him to the ladies despite his attempts to appear as grimy as any street hoodlum, and the Wu-Tang Clan found its first bankable solo star.

Interestingly, "Method Man" was one of Wu-Tang Clan's earliest songs, having been written in the summer of 1991 and recorded in November 1991.[3] According to RZA, "Method Man" and a song called "Wu-Tang Clan Ain't Nuthing to F' Wit' " were made with stolen electricity using eMU SP1200 and Ensoniq EPS 16 samplers and an 8-track recorder.[4] RZA says he learned how to fuse the four elements of hip-hop in his beats and that "Method Man" was for breakers, and it was the track's drums (which he won't reveal) that made you rhyme to it.[5]

With RZA's sound on the cusp of becoming hip-hop's next big thing thanks to the two singles already making the rounds, Wu-Tang Clan got down to the business of creating their debut, *Enter the Wu-Tang (36 Chambers)*. RZA would be the album's sole producer and his "instrument" of choice was the Ensoniq EPS sampling workstation. Keyboard based, the sampler boasts 12-bit technology, which made it a top-of-the-line sampler for the time. According to RZA, he borrowed the EPS from a producer called RNS (in exchange for allowing RNS to borrow his SP1200) who had found success producing for a Staten Island–based rap duo called the UMCs, and for an adolescent rapper, and eventual Wu-Tang affiliate, named Shyheim the Rugged Child.

"That changed my whole perspective," says RZA of the EPS in his book *The Wu-Tang Manual*.[6] Since it was a keyboard, instead of a drum machine, it allowed him more flexibility in manipulating the samples, playing them like notes and breaking them down into chords. The keyboard-based EPS allowed RZA to play with the melodies of his samples, which would become one of his trademarks and be imitated by his followers. It must be noted that at this point RZA did not possess any formal musical training. What he lacked in music theory, he made up for in curiosity and an engineer-like persistence in extending the capabilities of the tools he had.

While RZA became accustomed to using the EPS, Ensoniq soon released the EPS 16+, which boasted 16-bit sample quality, and added more sampling time. RZA also realized that by lowering the sample rates he was using, he would be able to extend his sample time. This would be to the detriment of the sound quality of the sample, but that gritty, lo-fi sound that would occur was music to RZA's ears. RZA gives credit to the EPS 16+ with launching his career production-wise while the release of the Ensoniq ASR-10 in 1991 would only further his development.[7]

Besides his tools of the trade, RZA had flesh-and-blood influences that guided his production. He told *Scratch Magazine* in 2006, "I think the classic producers Marley Marl and Prince Paul were influences to my sampling. If you put those two styles together with some Large Professor mixed in, you could find [my] foundations."[8] In a matter of a few years, RZA would trump these aforementioned producers in esteem and success. But before then, it would be the release of 1993's *Enter the Wu-Tang (36 Chambers)* that would first see the masterful sound manipulations RZA honed on samplers and sequencers broadcasted to the world. Hip-hop music would never be the same.

NOTES

1. Malone, Ambassador Bonz, "Deep Space Nine," *Vibe Magazine*, June/July 1995, 74 (70–75).

2. "Hip-Hop Quotable: Method Man," *The Source Magazine*, August 1993, 29.

3. Life, Matt, "Hittin' You from Every Angle," *The Source Magazine*, January 1994, 89 (87–89).

4. RZA and Chris Norris, *The Tao of Wu* (New York: Riverhead Books, 2009), 111–112.

5. Golianopoulos, Thomas, "Chain Reaction," *Scratch Magazine*, March/April 2006, 79 (76–82).

6. RZA and Chris Norris, *The Wu-Tang Manual* (New York: Riverhead Books, 2005), 197.

7. Ibid.

8. Golianopoulos, Thomas, "Chain Reaction," *Scratch Magazine*, March/April 2006, 79 (76–82).

CHAPTER 4
The Debut Chamber

ENTER THE WU-TANG (36 CHAMBERS)

Bring Da Ruckus/Shame on a Nigga/Clan in da Front/Wu-Tang: 7th Chamber/Can It Be All So Simple/Da Mystery of Chessboxin'/Wu-Tang Clan Ain't Nuthing ta F' Wit/C.R.E.A.M./Method Man/Protect Ya Neck/Tearz/ Wu-Tang: 7th Chamber, Pt. 2

The Wu-Tang Clan's debut album, *Enter the Wu-Tang (36 Chambers)*—the title a nod to the Shaw Brothers kung-fu film *Master Killer* aka *36 Chambers of Shaolin*—was released rather quietly on Tuesday, November 9, 1993. In a year's time, Wu-Tang Clan had gone from selling their first, independently released "Protect Ya Neck" single out of car trunks to releasing their album on a major label, via RCA Records' distribution of Loud Records.

Enter the Wu-Tang featured sparse and raw production by RZA, the perfect background beats for the cacophony of voices he had assembled. The album sold a modest 30,000 units its first week in stores, which is a resounding success considering it has been noted that the album only cost a mere $36,000 to record. The years of blood, sweat, and tears the Wu-Tang Clan managed to squeeze into only a dozen hardboiled hip-hop songs was priceless. The Wu-Tang Clan was finally here, and the world was ready to listen.

While hip-hop was birthed in the Bronx and for years the East Coast dominated the music charts, the West Coast had come to prominence. The rap charts of 1993 were being ruled by Dr. Dre's *The Chronic*, which was released in late 1992. That momentum would continue with

Snoop Dogg's debut album *Doggystyle*, which was released two weeks after *Enter the Wu-Tang*. Wu-Tang Clan would provide a decidedly underground counterpoint to Death Row Records' constant rotation on radio and MTV.

Enter the Wu-Tang Clan opens with "Bring the Ruckus." The album actually starts with a sample of dialogue from the film *Shaolin and Wu-Tang* with a portion saying, "If what you say is true, the Shaolin and the Wu-Tang could be dangerous." RZA's voice is heard first, beginning with the song's hook, yelling at no one in particular to "Bring the motherfucking ruckus!" The statement was purposefully vague to cover a wide variety of targets. Says RZA in *The Wu-Tang Manual*: "Whether we were talking to another crew from another hood, or an officer of the law, or the American government, or some MC who thought he could rhyme, we were just saying 'Bring it, motherfucker, Bring it on.' "[1]

The first verse heard on the album is from Ghostface Killah; apropos since he was the first person to formally join the Wu-Tang Clan fold with RZA. The rappers in order on the track are Ghostface, Raekwon, Inspectah Deck, and GZA. All of their lyrics are aggressive in nature— Raekwon notes that he brings "36 styles of danger" and Inspectah Deck says, "He'll scream on your ass like your dad"—and sets a high bar for the album's energy. The beat incorporates a sample of the late Melvin Bliss's 1973 song "Synthetic Substitution," a classic hip-hop breakbeat whose drums have been sampled by dozens of artists, though nearly indecipherably due to RZA's filtering of the snares and kicks.

The song immediately segues into samples of a few seconds of kung-fu fighting before launching into "Shame on a Nigga," which features Ol' Dirty Bastard, Raekwon, and Method Man. Since Ol' Dirty Bastard performs the chorus, along with help from Raekwon at the song's outset, and has two verses on the track, the song sounds decidedly like it belongs to Ol' Dirty Bastard. This is no easy feat considering Method Man unleashes a stringent verse delivered in a hurried intonation that differs from the one he displayed on his namesake song. The way Ol' Dirty delivers his rhymes could easily be mistaken for a strictly free-association style thanks to his bouncy, almost drunken cadence, but the words reveal them to be quite pointed. "I come with that ol' loco, couldn't see me with a pair of bifocals," he raps quite lucidly and wittily. Meanwhile, on his second verse he reveals having contracted gonorrhea. Dirty's illicit honesty would prove to be a constant in all of his future musical output.

The rumbling bass line and stuttered horn blasts on "Shame on a Nigga" (lifted from Syl Johnson's "Different Strokes" [1970]) and quick-hitting drums give the song the feel of a sprint, while the soft piano run (provided by a sample of Thelonious Monk's 1955 cover of Duke Ellington's "Black and Tan Fantasy") provides an interesting melodic counterpoint. Though "Shame on a Nigga" was never a proper single it is still one of Wu-Tang Clan's best songs, receiving play in Ol' Dirty Bastard tribute sets and spins from discerning DJs.

After the piano in "Shame on a Nigga" begins to fade, "Clan in da Front" begins with the voice of RZA bellowing, "Up from the 36 Chambers is the Ghostface Killer," with a sly laugh before proceeding to name check every member of Wu-Tang Clan including Masta Killa. Interestingly, on the album's back cover Masta Killa's name is not listed as a member of Wu-Tang Clan. The three-note loop heard during RZA's musing are from the intro portion of New Birth's "Honey Bee" (1971). The buzzing also heard in this track proved useful since the Wu-Tang Clan affiliates, including True Master (one of RZA's production protégés) and Shyheim the Rugged Child, were dubbed "Killa Beez." After one minute and 18 seconds, more sampled kung-fu dialogue ("Give him the sword") gives way to the start of the proper song.

Starting with the refrain "Clan in the front, let your feet stomp, Niggas on the left, brag shit to death, hoods on the right, wild for the night, Punks in the back, c'mon and attract to," is how one of *Enter the Wu-Tang*'s best examples of rhyme dexterity begins. The song is really a GZA solo since he is the only rapper who performs with two short but intense verses. In this case the bare-bones track—the drums should be familiar since they are once again from Melvin Bliss's "Synthetic Substitution"—lets GZA's lyrics be clearly heard and understood. The second verse ends with GZA using baseball as a metaphor to describe his dismantling of another rapper. "How ya sound B? You're better off a quitter, I'm on the mound G, and it's a no-hitter," raps GZA. GZA's extensive use of metaphors, as well as an expert ability to tell vivid stories with relatively few words, would endear him to his fans and be cited as evidence of his elevated status among his rapping peers.

"Wu Tang: 7th Chamber" kicks off with more audio samples of kung-fu fighting. But before the song begins, listeners hear a skit where Raekwon is chastising Method Man for not returning a copy of the film *The Killer* (1989) he loaned him.[2] Shortly after this occurs an animated Ghostface is heard relaying a story about how, while heading to the store to get a "culture cipher," he witnessed their friend Shamik get ambushed and shot.[3] "Wu-Tang: 7th Chamber" is a generally underappreciated posse cut—all members rhyme on the track save for Masta Killa—that gets lost due to the success of *Enter the Wu-Tang*'s numerous singles.

While the previous songs feature most of the Clan's players, on the following track, "Can It Be All So Simple," only Ghostface and Raekwon are accounted for, besides RZA's nostalgic musings about his favorite year—1987, coincidentally the year he got his hands on a 4-track recorder—at the beginning of the song, though he doesn't actually rap on the song.[4] Ghostface's performance on "Can It Be All So Simple" brought him into higher regard as a lyricist. The chemistry shown between him and Raekwon also set the stage for future, more formal, collaborations between the pair. On the track, the rappers reminisce in rhyme about the easier days of their youth, just as the beat's sample of Gladys Knight and the Pips's 1974 "The Way We Were/ Try to Remember" dictates. RZA paid only $2,000 to clear the liberal use of the sample.[5] "Can It Be All So Simple" was made with an Ensoniq ASR-10 sampler, and RZA notes that via lowering sample rate frequencies he was able to extend the length of the sample; the once four-bar loop barrier of a several seconds of sample time was greatly extended.[6] The beauty of the song is clearly heard as the instrumental is allowed to play out for almost a minute after the verses have been completed.

After the proper track concludes, a radio interview is heard where Method Man is naming and describing each member of the Wu-Tang Clan's unique abilities. Method Man notes RZA as being "the sharpest motherfucker in the whole clan . . . razor sharp with the beats, with the rhymes *and* he DJ." When asked by the interviewer of their goals, Raekwon passionately chimes in that "Right about now, the Wu got something that I know everybody want to hear," with Method Man adding, "We trying to make a business out of this." Those words would become reality.

On the vinyl version of the album "Protect Ya Neck" is the following track, but in all other versions (i.e., CD) it is "Da Mystery of Chessboxin'." "Chessboxin' " begins with sampled dialogue from *Shaolin and Wu-Tang* that equates the game of chess to sword fighting. This is followed by dialogue from the kung-fu film *The Five Deadly Venoms*.[7] The song commences with U-God's only verse on the album, besides his four-bar cameo on "Protect Ya Neck." U-God was in four prisons in two years before returning from Bear Hill Penitentiary in time to participate on only two tracks.[8] Following U-God's lead (he brings it "raw like cocaine straight from Bolivia") the song is a relentless onslaught of battle rhymes over charging drums and melodic accents that sound similar to the tone of a sitar. Method Man chimes in with the hook after the first three verses from U-God, Inspectah Deck, and Raekwon, again after Ol' Dirty Bastard's and finally after Ghostface and Masta Killa's. RZA and GZA are the only members without a verse on the song. Being granted the closing verse on a Wu-Tang Clan song with so many players was no easy feat but Masta Killa earned it with an exacting verse, his debut and only contribution to the album.

On "Da Mystery of Chessboxin' " the sampled kung-fu movie quote at the track's beginning says, "The game of chess, is like a sword fight." True to the ancient game, the Wu-Tang Clan's record moves were made with the second and third steps, and beyond, already in mind.[9] The following song in the sequence is "Wu-Tang Clan Ain't Nuthing ta F' Wit," which RZA placed late on the album's track list exactly because of its punchy rhythm and frenetic pace.[10] Beginning with a slow build before the back track explodes, RZA is the lead-off rapper on the song, which is the B-side to *Enter the Wu-Tang's* "C.R.E.A.M." single, though the latter follows on the album's track list. Inspectah Deck drops a typically assertive verse while Method Man closes out the song with a nursery rhyme ("Whatever you say bounces off of me sticks to you") with rugged angst.

Before "C.R.E.A.M." kicks in, Raekwon can be heard feigning as if he's back on the streets of Staten Island selling drugs. Long regarded as the only option many urban, disenfranchised youth had to make money, the flashback is fitting considering the song is an acronym for Cash Rules Everything Around Me. "What we mean by that is 'Cash rules everything around me,' but cash don't rule *me*," RZA told *Vibe*

Magazine in 1996.[11] "C.R.E.A.M.," which RZA has stated was one of the first beats he ever created, was *Enter the Wu-Tang*'s second single and would be its most successful, peaking at #32 on the Billboard R&B/Hip-Hop Songs chart.

"Leave it up to me while I be living proof, to kick the truth to the young Black youth," rhymes Inspectah Deck. Considering he himself had been in jail for selling drugs, the message he was sending was sincere. Utilizing a somber piano loop, morose vocals, and swelling strings from a sample of the Isaac Hayes and David Porter–penned "As Long as I've Got You" (1967), performed by the Charmels, matched to a plodding drum track, Raekwon and Inspectah Deck go on to deliver some of the most poignant recollections of ghetto nihilism ever recorded in hip-hop. Raekwon was granted "Rhyme of the Month" for his verse on "C.R.E.A.M." in the April 1994 issue of *The Source Magazine*.[12] The song heard on the album is a shortened version of a song called "Lifestyles of the Mega-Rich" that featured extended verses from Inspectah Deck and Raekwon. RZA took the best of each MC's rhymes and pieced them together to create "C.R.E.A.M.," similarly to his machinations with the order of the performances on "Protect Ya Neck."

A vulgar exchange between Method Man and Inspectah Deck imagining torture techniques is added to the beginning of the former's namesake song. "Method Man" was Wu-Tang Clan's second hit and set the rapper Method Man on the path to becoming a household name, first in hip-hop circles and then in the mainstream via his acting in films such as *How High* and television roles including HBO's *The Wire*. Because of his stature as one of the more recognizable members of the nine-man Wu-Tang Clan, Method Man would be the first member to sign a solo recording contract with Def Jam Records in 1994. Even if the success of Method Man's solo record on *Enter the Wu-Tang* is removed from the equation, his verse on "Protect Ya Neck," which is the next song, already was a favorite among fans and critics.

After "Protect Ya Neck" is "Tearz," one of the first songs recorded by Wu-Tang Clan. Featuring rhymes from RZA and Ghostface, the song is a refined recording of the "Protect Ya Neck" original B-side track "After the Laughter." It would be years later when a Wu-Tang Clan demo began making the Internet file-sharing rounds before more listeners would be privy to this early version. RZA's verse recounts the senseless killing of a close friend in a robbery while Ghostface's verse has him sharing a tale about a friend whose unsafe sex practices led to his acquiring of the HIV virus. The latter would become known for his movie script–worthy tales in rhyme and this early song reveals his raw talents.

Closing the album is "Wu-Tang: 7th Chamber, Pt. 2," which is little more than a remix version of the original that keeps the lyrics unchanged while swapping in a different beat. The original is the more memorable of the pair with the remix containing some vocal inflections and what sounds like a filtered kudzu, paling in comparison. The album closes abruptly with kung-fu dialogue barking "It's a secret!," after the host of the show the Wu-Tang is being interviewed on dares to ask what is the Wu-Tang's style.

But the Wu-Tang Clan's style was no secret at all. The Clan's musical aesthetic of brash abrasive rhymes over spare, industrial beats was now on vinyl, CD, and cassette for listeners to digest. *Enter the Wu-Tang* was awarded with a four and a half out of five mic rating in the February 1994 issue of *The Source Magazine*, which at the time was regarded as the bible of hip-hop music and culture. Being that a five-mic review meant an album was a "classic," *Enter the Wu-Tang*'s rating was stellar. In the review, writer The Ghetto Communicator said the album harkens back to a time when "Beats concentrated on raw dopeness instead of slick production and beauty. Never since *Criminal Minded* has an album been so stripped down and pure."[13] *Rolling Stone Magazine* didn't review the album until its April 7, 1994, issue, five months after its release, with writer Toure describing the album as "hip-hop you won't find creeping up the Billboard charts but you will hear booming out of Jeep stereos in all the right neighborhoods."[14] Acclaim for the album has only increased with each passing year. *Enter the Wu-Tang* was eventually retrofitted with a five-mic rating in *The Source Magazine*'s March 2002 issue, citing its influence in the years since its release.[15] The album is included in *Rolling Stone's 500 Greatest Albums of All Time*, while numerous publications cite it as one of the most important hip-hop records of the 1990s.

On *Enter the Wu-Tang*'s album cover the group members were anonymous thanks to their faces being obscured with stockings. Not a bad idea considering some members, such as Method Man who had been arrested for weed possession and U-God who was in jail, were not present for the album cover photo shoot.[16] But Wu-Tang Clan's anonymity was about to end. The succeeding couple of years would see the Wu-Tang Clan release a string of albums both commercially and critically accepted, with many now deemed classics of the hip-hop genre. Somehow, someway, RZA would be the conductor of this raucous rap train, steering it into a Grand Central Station of Wu-Tang Clan mania.

NOTES

1. RZA and Chris Norris, *The Wu-Tang Manual* (New York: Riverhead Books, 2005), 201.

2. Audio snippets from *The Killer* would be prominently used in Raekwon's debut album, *Only Built 4 Cuban Linx . . .* two years later.

3. Culture Cipher corresponds to the numbers 4 and 0, respectively, in the Supreme Numerals used by Nation of Gods and Earths. Hence, Culture Cipher is slang for a 40 ounce of malt liquor. Coded terms such as this example are found throughout Wu-Tang Clan lyrics, skits, and dialogue heard on their albums.

4. Strauss, Neil, "What Do You Do When You're One of Hip-Hop's Most Creative Producers?," *Rolling Stone*, September 4, 1997, 38.

5. Newton, Matthew, "Is Sampling Dying," *Spin Magazine*, December 2008, 32 (31–34).

6. RZA and Chris Norris, *The Wu-Tang Manual*, 198.

7. Specifically the Toad style in which its practitioner's skin was nearly invincible.

8. Valdes, Mimi, "Right and Exact," *Vibe Magazine*, September 1997, 116 (114–118).

9. RZA and Chris Norris, *The Wu-Tang Manual*, 76.

10. Coleman, Brian, "Classic Material: Enter the 36 Chambers," *XXL Magazine*, 208.

11. Mao, Chairman, "Next Chamber," *Vibe Magazine*, September 1996, 114.

12. "Rhyme of the Month: 'C.R.E.A.M.,' " *The Source Magazine*, April 1994, 25.

13. The Ghetto Communicator, "Record Report: Enter the Wu-Tang (36 Chambers)," *The Source Magazine*, February 1994, 73–74.

14. Toure, "Rap up—Enter the Wu-Tang (36 Chambers) by Wu-Tang Clan/ Enta da Stage by Black Moon/Constipated Monkey by Kurious Jorge," *Rolling Stone Magazine*, April 7, 1994, 73.

15. "Got Five On It," *The Source Magazine*, March 2002, 176

16. DeCurtis, Anthony, "Wu Tang Family Values," *Rolling Stone Magazine*, July 10, 1997–July 24, 1997, 86.

CHAPTER 5
The First Wave (Wu-Tang Clan Soloist) Splinter Cells

A key part of Wu-Tang Clan's master plan was always for its individual members to become solo stars in their own right. Their unique recording deal with Loud/RCA Records made doing so possible without the bureaucratic red tape of restrictive group recording contracts and competing record labels. The first member to spark chatter about a potential solo album was Method Man, who had stood out on "Protect Ya Neck" and proved he was capable of recording a successful solo song with "Method Man."

RZA still maintained control in the house of Wu-Tang Clan by delegating which labels individual members would sign solo deals with. RZA encouraged, sometimes forcefully, the Clan members to sign to an assortment of labels, which would inevitably spark tensions. Method Man signed to the storied Def Jam label, and Ol' Dirty Bastard wanted to sign to the label as well. But RZA urged ODB to sign with Elektra Records, the two men even getting into a physical altercation over the matter before his late cousin finally relented.

While Def Jam (LL Cool J, Slick Rick) and Elektra (Brand Nubian, Pete Rock & CL Smooth) had a reputation for possessing successful and well-regarded hip-hop acts, RZA also persuaded members to sign with labels not known for a strong presence in the hip-hop market. GZA/Genius would sign with Geffen Records, whose biggest artist was Kurt Cobain's Nirvana and didn't even have a proper Black music department at the time. "I chose those labels because they didn't have anybody we'd have to compete with. At the time, nobody could see the value of it," RZA told the *New York Times* in 1996.[1]

RZA's foresight would prove the value of the Wu-Tang Clan's individual members, as well as his musical production imprint, thoroughly obvious over the few years after *Enter the Wu-Tang*'s 1993 release. The first solo albums from Method Man (*Tical*), Ol' Dirty Bastard (*Return to the 36 Chambers: The Dirty Version*), Raekwon (*Only Built 4 Cuban Linx . . .*), GZA/Genius (*Liquid Swords*), and Ghostface Killah (*Ironman*) would all go gold, with Method Man and Ghostface eventually reaching platinum sales. All would feature RZA's distinct production techniques, yet manage to sound musically distinct from each other. Worth mentioning is the critically acclaimed Gravediggaz project titled *6 Feet Deep* that was released in August 1994. The Gravediggaz consisted of RZA, Prince Paul, a renowned producer in his own right, and rappers Fruikwan and Too Poetic. All of the member were previously signed to Tommy Boy Records and though RZA contributed a handful of tracks to *6 Feet Deep*, his role in the group—he went by the moniker "The Rzarector"—was more of a rapper.[2]

The base of RZA's operations for creating the majority (*Tical* was already completed) of this first wave of Wu-Tang solo albums was a two-bedroom apartment at Mitchell's Court in Mariner Harbor that he moved into in 1994. All the recording equipment was in the basement and it would be dubbed 36 Chambers Studio. Unfortunately, a flood shortly after the completion of GZA's *Liquid Swords* album would destroy the studio. RZA says he lost at least 300 beats in the flood, including at least 15 individual beats for each member's solo album that had been organized shortly after the release of *Enter the Wu-Tang*.[3]

RZA has said that each album was to be like a movie and the first feature film would come from Method Man.[4] The Wu-Tang Clan collective was about to get two resounding thumbs up.

METHOD MAN, *TICAL*

Tical/Biscuits/Bring The Pain/All I Need/What the Blood Clot/Meth vs. Chef/Sub Crazy/Release Yo' Delf/P.L.O. Style/I Get My Thang in Action/Mr. Sandman/Stimulation/Method Man (Remix)

Method Man's debut album, *Tical*, is named after a slang term for a marijuana cigarette (or blunt) dipped in a sweetener, not the currency of Thailand. RZA was lauded for the lo-fi quality of the sounds on

Enter the Wu-Tang and on *Tical* he accomplishes an even grungier sound. The album can sound so muddled and distorted that listeners have to turn up the volume since its audio levels were noticeably low. *Tical*'s murky music would prove to be the best setting for Method Man's witty, off-kilter yet on point rap flow. The album opens with a haunting sample of melancholy tones, directly from the film *Master Killer*, that could easily set the stage for an epic kung-fu showdown. Sounds of a martial arts fight follow and mark the commencement of the battle about to take place between RZA's beats and Method Man's rhymes, with the only clear winner being the listener.

The first song is the title track and its refrain features Method Man playfully asking/calling "What's that shit that they be smoking?" The answer is "Tical." This, in turn, is answered with "Pass it over here then!" While smoking marijuana would presumably help listeners greater appreciate RZA's filtered bass line and snappy drums, it isn't a requirement. Method Man's rhymes center around the bluster of his being one of the best at what he does—rapping.

Right after comes "Biscuits," whose beat is a series of cascading tones with more snappy drum kicks that serve to anchor the track. What sounds like a distorted vocal wail runs throughout the track, prominently at times and completely disappearing at other intervals. Method Man's voice is so deep in the mix that sometimes his voice sounds like it's just another subservient element of the beat. This is not the case with the subsequent song, and the album's lead single, "Bring the Pain."

"Bring the Pain" is based on a haunting, one-bar loop of a vocal sample of soul singer Jerry Butler's "Mechanical Man," from his 1974 album *Sweet Sixteen*, that gives the track a sinister tone. Parts of the opening piano tinkles are used throughout the track as well. Considering Method Man's opening lines—"I came to bring the pain hardcore from the brain, let's step inside my astral plain"—the rapper and the rest of the song's lyrics are in accord with the instrumental's ominous and otherworldly nature. Only two verses, the song's choruses appear after each verse and consist of Method Man chanting, "Is it real son, is it really real son, let me know it's real son, if it's really real. Something I could feel son, load it up and kill one, want it raw deal son, if it's really real." Heard only after the first chorus, an artist named Booster chimes in with an interpolation of dancehall artist

Ninjaman's opening chants on "Test the High Power" (1991). As the song begins to fade, Method Man is heard delivering more torturous threats, in the same vein as those delivered with Inspectah Deck right before the start of "Method Man" on *Enter the Wu-Tang*.

"Bring the Pain" certified Method Man as a worthy selection as first in line of Wu-Tang solo acts, and it would peak at #45 on the *Billboard* Hot 100 chart, but it was not *Tical*'s biggest hit. That distinction belongs to a pair of remixes to the next song on *Tical*'s track listing, "All I Need." But before getting into details of "All I Need" it must be understood why it was remixed in the first place. *Tical*'s second official single was "Release Yo' Delf," a highly charged song that features a frenetic track filled with lively, upbeat horns and passionate singing from R&B artist Blue Raspberry, a future Wu-Tang Clan affiliate. While "Release Yo' Delf" was popular among devoted Wu-Tang fans, it did not perform well on the charts or radio. Though "Release Yo' Delf" reached #28 on the *Billboard* Hot Rap Singles chart, it only managed to peak at #98 on the *Billboard* Hot 100 chart. But radio play had never been substantial when it came to the Wu-Tang Clan's music, despite their solid sales and popularity.

What these numbers meant to Def Jam Records was that Method Man needed a radio hit to help spur sales of *Tical*, which after its November 15, 1994, release debuted at #4 on the *Billboard* 200 chart and #1 on the *Billboard* R&B/Hip-Hop Albums chart, selling over 120,000 units its first week. Lyor Cohen, then COO of Def Jam, urged Method Man to record a version of "All I Need," which was a dedication to his longtime girlfriend Tamika (the "Shortie" in the song's lyrics), with platinum recording artist Mary J. Blige. Although Blige was in the middle of recording her sophomore album, *My Life*, she jumped onboard.[5]

Two remixes dubbed "I'll Be There for You/You're All I Need to Get By" were made, a gruffer "Razor Sharp Mix" by RZA and a polished "Puff Daddy Mix" by Sean "Puffy" Combs with "additional programming credited to Jean 'Poke' Olivier of TrackMasterz." Both versions, particularly Mary J. Blige's vocals, liberally interpolated Marvin Gaye and Tami Terrell's 1968 hit "You're All I Need to Get By." The Razor Sharp Mix was used for the song's video. The song became a big hit on The Box, a former Miami Beach–based cable company that allowed viewers to request which videos they wanted to watch.[6] It also became a radio smash. Most, if not all, of a 6,000-plus word *New York Times* article on the Summer of 1995's #1 love song was about "You're All I Need/I'll Be There for You" and specifically noted: "The song went up against "Scream," Michael Jackson's excruciatingly hyped comeback single. "I'll Be There" received 200 requests in one weekend to Michael Jackson's 30."[7]

"I'll Be There for You/You're All I Need to Get By" hit #1 on the *Billboard* R&B/Hip-Hop Songs chart in late May, reached #3 on the *Billboard* Hot 100 chart in early June 1995, and by July 1995 *Tical* had sold one million copies. Not bad for a song Method Man originally had no intentions of making until Cohen gave him money to buy a new Lexus.[8] RZA was in agreement with the need to create a record that would cater to the ladies, in spite of Method Man's opposition at being viewed as a sex symbol. "He make a thug nigga smile, he gets all the women, and the children are into him, too. They look at him as a super-hero," RZA told *Spin Magazine* in 1998.[9] Thankfully, RZA and Cohen's pressure, Mary J. Blige's participation, and a new Lexus convinced Method Man to make the remix.[10]

Ironically the rest of the album is the polar opposite of the rap love song that is "I'll Be There for You/You're All I Need to Get By." Its original form "All I Need" boasts men gutturally singing, "You're all that I need, I'll be there for you," and it may sound sincere but doesn't exactly evoke tender thoughts. Method Man probably does not have a problem with that. In 1995, the rapper told *Vibe Magazine* the album was "Going into the mind of a nigga that done had enough, man."[11] That sentiment is heard throughout *Tical*'s songs where the structure may be minimal, yet his rhymes come in nonstop waves. Thankfully, as *Spin Magazine* put it in a 2007 analysis of Wu-Tang albums, Method Man possesses the ability to "turn every line into a catchphrase."[12]

Witty turns of phrase dominate "What the Blood Clot," which is littered with tumbling drums and a three-note chord loop engaging enough to keep anyone paying attention to Method Man's words. The song closes with shout-outs to a number of incarcerated friends. The conclusion of "What the Blood Clot" serves as the close of the first act before the listening audience is brought back to life with "Meth vs. Chef."

Kicking off with the same sonic motif heard on the album's intro, Method Man and guest MC Raekwon the Chef reenact the Wu-Tang

Clan legend that stipulated any member seeking a RZA beat for themselves had to lyrically battle for rights to the track.[13] "Meth vs. Chef" consists of ballistic drums swiped from 1966's "Papa Was Too" by Southern soul singer/songwriter Joe Tex and a ray beam sounding tone that is accented with a two-note piano loop. A fight bell is heard as an un-credited voice is heard introducing the song's two sparring partners, boxing match style.

While their verses could be aimed at any general MC rival, Method Man's conclusion of his rhyme with the line, "Slobbin' on my knob like an all day sucker, bitch," could be taken as a personal strike. Raekwon pulls no punches either, delivering a tight battle verse of his own. But the victor is clearly Method Man because Raekwon stumbles halfway through his rhyme, saying "Tack the boards like chess moves," seemingly losing his place. He then says, "Yo, yeah, yo," and "Tack tack tack," to stay on beat, and finally restarts with, "Tack them boards like chess moves," and finishes his verse. Keeping the verbal missteps in the song adds to "Meth vs. Chef's" authentic rap battle vibe. While giving *Tical* a four out of five mics rating in its January 1995 issue, *The Source Magazine* wrote " 'Meth vs. Chef' is the aural equivalent of Marvel's Hulk vs. Thing epics."[14]

"Sub Crazy" is credited as being coproduced by 4th Disciple, one of RZA's production apprentices that would go on to produce tracks for both Wu-Tang Clan group and solo albums. While all of *Tical*'s instrumentation can be considered spare, "Sub Crazy" is particularly so with a running, filtered clap dominating the production. "Release Yo' Delf" follows and is the previous track's opposite in musical layers. The song contains at least three samples and an interpolation of Gloria Gaynor's 1978 disco hit "I Will Survive" for its Blue Raspberry sung chorus.[15]

"P.L.O. Style" is coproduced by Method Man and features a guest verse from rapper Carlton Fisk, who notably quotes Sir Walter Scott's poem "Marmion." The track is a pretty standard rap song where every rapper takes a turn rhyming over the beat. Immediately after is "I Gets My Thang in Action," one of *Tical*'s, and Method Man's, best songs. Over what could be theme music for a night raid by mercenaries in a warzone, the track's menacing groove, thanks to a gloomy, filtered bass line courtesy of Bo Diddley's "Hit or Miss" (1974), is a perfect backdrop for Method Man's lyrical barbs aimed at would-be competitors and detractors. Only two verses, the chorus from "I Gets My

Thang in Action," as well as its title, is an interpolation of the "Verb!" lesson/song from the *Schoolhouse Rock* educational cartoon that aired on Saturday morning in the 1970s and 1980s.

The borderline paranoia at potential foes leads to Method Man dropping lines filled with double entendres and witty sarcasm, all peppered with his distinct vocal inflections. The opening of the second verse is a good example: "Fresh out the toilet, I got my shit together . . . I'll be the stormy weather rain comin' down, so weatherproof your leather."

After "I Get My Thang in Action" is the Chordettes sampling "Mr. Sandman." While the Chordettes were a female pop quartette from the 1940s and 1950s, RZA uses their vanilla "Mr. Sandman" (1954) refrain like choruses to separate the jarring posse cut's verses from himself, Method Man, Carlton Fisk, Streetlife, and Inspectah Deck. RZA leads off the opening verse by shouting, "Lyrical shots from the glock!," and he sets the tone that there will be no sleeping while this song is being played. The song's brash chords seem to be sourced from a heavily filtered sample of Lyn Collins's 1972 cover of "Ain't No Sunshine"[16]

The rather upbeat "Stimulation"—surely because it samples strings from Jazz songstress Sarah Vaughn's "Snowbound" (1963)—features Method Man delivering a sing-song flow and more singing from Blue Raspberry on the chorus. The album then closes with "Method Man (Remix)," which was making the mix-show and mix-tape rounds before the album's release. Method Man would feel that *Tical* was rushed and too "off the head."[17] But at a comfortable 13 tracks, the album nevertheless reveals Method Man to be an artist learning his way around song formats and structure.

Tical has no "theme" such as future releases from Raekwon (*Only Built 4 Cuban Linx . . .*) would, but its combination of RZA's beats and Method Man's rhymes—made engaging by his nuance when delivering his rhymes—made an overbearing topic for the album unnecessary. In many ways Method Man represented the average street hustler with ambitions of becoming a star rapper. There was no need for elaborate drug kingpin machinations since he was more of a hand-to-hand, low-level dealer anyway. In 1995 he told *The Source Magazine* so: "I never really got mine in the drug game, that's why it didn't influence my rap style. You never hear me say that in my rhymes. That part of my life right there? That was traumatic. That whole fucking era, I hated it."[18]

While *Tical* may not have been deemed an immediate classic as other Wu-Tang releases, it was a sound album that inaugurated Method Man's promising solo career and began the Wu-Tang Clan's string of successful solo albums. The East Coast rap world certainly needed a new star as *Vibe Magazine* relayed in its 1994 review of the album: "The East is looking hard for a hero who, with verbal dexterity and mad rhyme skills, will make Snoop, Cube, Warren G and the rest just shut the fuck up—out of sheer respect. In this contest to recite the best reality, Redman is the contender, but Wu-Tang's Method is the man who would be king."[19]

If Method Man was king, then Wu-Tang Clan's court jester surely wanted to show off his exceptionally entertaining abilities. And that clown prince of the Wu-Tang Clan would be none other than Ol' Dirty Bastard.

OL' DIRTY BASTARD, *RETURN TO THE 36 CHAMBERS (THE DIRTY VERSION)*

Intro/Shimmy Shimmy Ya/Baby C'mon/Brooklyn Zoo/Hippa to da Hoppa/Raw Hide/Damage/Don't You Know/The Stomp/Goin' Down/Drunk Game (Sweet Sugar Pie)/Snakes/Brooklyn Zoo II (Tiger Crane)/Protect Ya Neck II The Zoo/Cuttin' Headz/Dirty Dancin'/Harlem World

---

Trouble seemed to follow Ol' Dirty Bastard wherever he went. Before his debut, *Return to the 36 Chambers (The Dirty Version)* was released on March 25, 1995, he had already been charged with burglary in Queens, New York. ODB insisted that being chased is the reason why he jumped out of a second-story window, which landed him in the hospital. Ol' Dirty would check himself out of the hospital a week later after claiming he was receiving death threats. A couple of days after leaving the hospital, he was shot in Bedford-Stuyvesant, Brooklyn, via either a robbery or beef over the name of his Brooklyn Zoo rap crew. With the swirl of strange behavior and occasional violence, usually done upon him, it is no wonder *Return to the 36 Chambers* is such a cacophony of disparaging styles and sounds, all lassoed to fluidity by RZA, who served as executive producer and produced the majority of the album's tracks.

Return to the 36 Chambers begins with an "Intro" track that is almost five minutes long and features Ol' Dirty Bastard thanking everyone for attending the show they are about to hear. Along the way he manages to compare himself to James Brown, tearfully admits that he contracted gonorrhea, and croons a crass ditty about receiving fellatio. Faux clapping and the occasional organ chords are played for added effect. All of the many facets of the intro are akin to Ol' Dirty Bastard's personality, which correlates to the plethora of styles he will utilize on *Return to the 36 Chambers*.

While *Return to the 36 Chambers* alludes to it being a sequel to Wu-Tang Clan's *Enter the Wu-Tang (36 Chambers)*, this is not the case. The last 13 seconds of the intro are a vocal sample of the San Te character in *The 36th Chamber of Shaolin* film when he speaks his intention to create a new, 36th chamber of Shaolin. Considering Ol' Dirty Bastard's boisterous presence, a new chamber, with nods to the old, was necessary. At the conclusion of the dialogue, the staccato keys of "Shimmy Shimmy Ya" kick in, and *Return to the 36 Chambers* is off to a flying start.

The shimmering key hits of "Shimmy Shimmy Ya" made it instantly recognizable from the moment the record started playing. The track's murky bass line is from Stax vocalists The Emotions' 1972 hit "I Like It," while the drums are from Booker T & The MG's' "Hip Hug-Her" (1967). Ol' Dirty Bastard rap/sings the song's refrain "Ooh baby I like it raw, yeah baby I like it raw," before launching into his sing-song delivery. Less than three minutes long, in the song Ol' Dirty Bastard provides only one verse, which is repeated after the first verse is played in reverse, literally. RZA had figured out how to replay music he recorded backwards with his ASR-10 beat machine.

"Baby Come On" follows and features straight-forward battle raps. The succeeding song in the sequence is the album's lead single, "Brooklyn Zoo." "Brooklyn Zoo" is not produced by RZA, but by True Master (Ol' Dirty Bastard also receives coproduction credit). RZA's student had come into his own. The marauding tones of "Brooklyn Zoo" were created on RZA's own Ensoniq EPS 16 Plus sampler.[20] It was the machine RZA walked True Master through and the same one used to create Wu-Tang Clan's "Protect Ya Neck," "Cream," and "Method Man." "Brooklyn Zoo" is an example of Ol' Dirty at his rhyming best. While the free-flowing delivery may confuse the casual listener into thinking he is merely spitting gibberish, his rhymes are thoroughly coherent. When Ol' Dirty Bastard raps—"Ason, I keep planets in orbit"—he's referring to his Five Percent Nation name (Ason Unique) and the movement's tenet that the Black man created the earth, moon, and stars. As for rap superego bluster, see: "Introducing . . . yo, fuck that niggas name, my Hip-Hop drops on your head like rain." The "rain" is delivered with his prototypical half-sung, half-rapped, fully emphasized vocal inflection. More examples of Ol' Dirty Bastard's woefully underappreciated skills as an MC follow on "Hippa to Da Hoppa."

Ol' Dirty delivering battle rhymes on "Hippa to Da Hoppa" is a requirement considering that the track's drums are sampled from the Skull Snaps "It's a New Day" (1973), one of the most frequently sampled records in hip-hop music over the years. "Hippa to Da Hoppa's" track ends with kung-fu fighting, including a quick snippet of a character saying "Dragon Fist," and serves as a reminder that his is a Wu-Tang Clan record after all. Up to this point Ol' Dirty Bastard has been rhyming solo but the ensuing song, "Raw Hide," features assistance from Method Man and Raekwon. Apropos, since the former released his solo album previously while the latter's would follow after Ol' Dirty Bastard's. While many outlets cited the "Raw Hide" couplet about Ol' Dirty Bastard being born into and still receiving welfare assistance as a look into his comical nature, the line before that infamous statement is more revealing. In it Ol' Dirty rhetorically asks, "Who the *fuck* wants to be an MC if you can't get paid, to be an MC." Cash and high levels of paranoia certainly ruled everything around Ol' Dirty Bastard, who would demand payments from magazines that wanted to feature his image on their covers. He figured if he helped sell the magazine, he should be duly compensated.

It was clear in his interviews before and after the release of *Return to the 36 Chambers* that ODB was becoming increasingly mistrustful and sheltering himself from his associates as a response to it.[21] His music at times seemed to thrive on this witty unpredictability, one could say. It was also seen as a liability. "It's this same wild side that occasionally derails the album's momentum in a flurry of self-indulgent concepts," said *Vibe Magazine* in its review of *Return to the 36 Chambers*.[22]

On "Damage" Ol' Dirty Bastard and GZA rehash their All In Together days, trading spirited rhymes back and forth over dirty drum kicks. The self-indulgence referred to by *Vibe* can be applied to the X-rated "Don't U Know." The lyrics are a fantasy in rhyme about Ol' Dirty Bastard being late to class but nevertheless managing to seduce his schoolteacher. Killah Priest, a Wu-Tang Clan affiliate who was also a member of an affiliate group called Sunz of Man, contributes an articulate verse about seducing a girl named Chandra. At the conclusion of Killah Priest's verse, Ol' Dirty Bastard returns not rapping, but speaking about how he prefers "nasty bitches." Needless to say, the Wu-Tang Clan had garnered, and earned, criticism for their misogynistic lyrics. After Dirty's short rant he starts his third verse, which concludes his narrative about carrying on with his teacher, who's now teaching him about oral sex. Near the end of the verse, Ol' Dirty's cadence is more like spoken-word poetry—by now the beat's drums have been removed, leaving a raving vocal loop—as he recounts his escapades with the teacher in graphic detail. While sexually suggestive lyrics were nothing new in hip hop, combined with Ol' Dirty's near delirious ravings when rhyming, it made the artist seem all the more unique in the Wu-Tang Clan.[23]

"The Stomp" was more in line with the Wu-Tang Clan aesthetic with Ol' Dirty Bastard dropping braggadocious rhymes over a marching drum beat (Ol' Dirty shares production credit for the song with RZA). It's a shame the tightly wound song is only a little over two minutes long. This is more apparent when listening to the overly indulgent "Goin' Down," which meanders. Ol' Dirty doesn't start rhyming until a couple of minutes into the track's ethereal synth, thanks to RZA's sampling of Bel Canto's "Time Without End" (*Birds of Passage*, 1989). By the song's end, Ol' Dirty kicks into a fairly credible rendition of "Somewhere Over the Rainbow." Ol' Dirty continues to flex his vocal chops on "Drunk Game (Sweet Sugar Pie)," which is essentially an R&B song—or a hip-hop flavored torch song—since it includes no rhyming from the artist over the track's warm chords. Production is credited to only Ol' Dirty Bastard and Ethan Ryman (though, for Wu-Tang Productions) and throughout the song Ol' Dirty's vocals can also be heard in the background shouting out R&B artists who influenced him, including Luther Vandross, Gladys Knight, and his mother Cherry Jones, who taught him to sing.

With his R&B vocalist dreams out of his system for now, "Snakes" is a return to Wu-Tang Clan rapping mode. The posse cut features lyrical contributions from Killah Priest, RZA, Masta Killa, and Buddha Monk, a longtime friend of Ol' Dirty Bastard. Again, dialogue from *Five Deadly Venoms*—an explanation of the "Snake" style—sets the stage for the song. RZA's track features an early use of the sped-up vocal sample—Joe Tex's vocals from "I'll Never Do You Wrong" (1968) sounds like they are being sung by chipmunks—that would become popular in the early 2000s. The drums are from another Joe Tex song, "Papa Was Too," and all is combined by RZA to make a jarring track. Ol' Dirty Bastard's verse, fourth after Killah Priest, RZA, and Masta Killa, is clipped, almost as if he was drunk and RZA used enough of what was bearable before Buddha Monk closes with a short verse of his own. RZA's verse is a highlight of the song, dropping a narrative about neighborhood toughness with doses of Five Percent Nation rhetoric.

"Brooklyn Zoo II (Tiger Crane)" can best be described as bizarre. Ghostface and Ol' Dirty Bastard (who is warming up by singing "Blue Moon") are heard speaking at the beginning of the track, and the latter kicks things off by ferociously—after starting once, stopping, and starting again—rhyming the same lyrics heard on "Damage," including GZA's parts, on his own. Ol' Dirty kicks about half of the rhyme before Ghostface delivers a new verse. Ghostface's impassioned verse offers a hint of what is to come from him musically (he also refers to himself as Tony Stark, his Wu-Gambino moniker, to be discussed later). After Ghostface concludes his verse, samples of the *Return to the 36 Chambers* songs "Baby C'mon," "Brooklyn Zoo," "Drunk Game (Sweet Sugar Pie)," and "The Stomp" are heard in succession, sounding like radio stations being rapidly searched through on a car radio. Things settle again with RZA's rugged instrumental until audio from an un-credited announcer introduces the Brooklyn Zu, Ol' Dirty's personally helmed crew of rap artists.

Brooklyn Zu members (Buddha Monk, Zu Keeper, Murdoc, 12 O'Clock, Shorti Shit Stain) are heard on "Protect Ya Neck II The Zoo" as well as Prodigal Sun, Killah Priest, and 60 Second Assassin of Sunz of Man. While the song is notable for RZA's buzz saw of beat, considering the only official Wu-Tang Clan member on the song is Ol' Dirty Bastard, it lags in comparison to other Wu-Tang Clan posse cuts heard so far. "Cuttin' Headz" follows and is another All In Together reunion of sorts. This time Ol' Dirty Bastard and RZA are rhyming back and forth over drums lifted from Melvin Bliss's "Synthetic Substitution" and a piano sample from Thelonious Monk's "Ba-Lue Bolivar Ba-Lues-Are" (1957). The song's green, almost playful nature, as well as RZA saying, "There's nothing new in '92," reveals its early placement in the Wu-Tang Clan discography's timeline. A rawer sounding version of "Cuttin' Headz" is heard on a *Wu-Tang Clan Demo Tape* that wouldn't begin circulating until years later.

A pair of cuts, the Method Man–assisted "Dirty Dancin' " (which was originally credited as a Wu-Tang Clan song called "Dirty Dancing" that appears on the *Jerky Boys Original Soundtrack* released in early 2005), and the lethargic but funky "Harlem World" (produced by Big Dore, which along with "Drunk Game" are the only non RZA-produced songs on the album), close out the CD and digital versions of the album, but they were not on the vinyl or cassette tape releases of *Return to the 36 Chambers*. Neither of the songs are too memorable.

But no one would ever forget Ol' Dirty Bastard. Listeners to *Return to the 36 Chambers* were privy to the mind of part musical genius, part madman, all Russell Jones. He told *Billboard Magazine* in 1995, "I'm dirty because when I step to a mike I come uncut, I speak my mind from the heart. The ol' comes from the fact that I was influenced by the old school—everybody from Al Green and Millie Jackson to the Sugar Hill Gang. And the bastard part is these because there is no father to my style."[24] Ol' Dirty Bastard continued, "For the first time, [fans] are gonna see inside my whole . . . head. They're gonna see all sides of me; a cool side, a happy side . . . everything. My album is just entertainment. I wouldn't say my shit is New York; I wouldn't say it's West Coast. I'd just say it's Ol' Dirty."[25]

Elektra Records' and RZA's plan was to take ODB from the hip-hop world to the mainstream world at large. The album, along with scene-stealing cameos on songs with Mariah Carey ("Fantasy Remix") in 1995 and the Fugees member Pras ("Ghetto Superstar") a few years later, would eventually help make Ol' Dirty Bastard an international star. But while *Enter the 36 Chambers (The Dirty Version)* was fresh in CD players of the hip-hop nation, Ol' Dirty was the latest example of the musical consistency that would come to be a hallmark of Wu-Tang Clan and its leader and production impresario, RZA.

The general consensus is that it takes three examples of a phenomenon before it constitutes a trend. With two solo albums down, the third individual album from the Wu-Tang Clan core would be critical in proving they weren't a flash in the pan hip-hop act. An unlikely Staten Island rapper who went by Shallah Raekwon and Raekwon the Chef, but that would soon begin answering to Lex Diamond, delivered a Wu-Tang hat trick, and then some.

RAEKWON THE CHEF FEATURING GHOSTFACE KILLAH: *ONLY BUILT 4 CUBAN LINX . . .*

Striving for Perfection/Knuckleheadz/Knowledge God/Criminology/Incarcerated Scarfaces/Rainy Dayz/Guillotine (Swordz)/Can It Be All So Simple (Remix)/Shark Niggas (Biters)/Ice Water/Glaciers of Ice/Verbal Intercourse/Wisdom Body/Spot Rusherz/Ice Cream/Wu-Gambinos/Heaven & Hell/North Star (Jewels)

Thanks to their boisterous personalities on wax, fans were quick to seek out solo music from Method Man and Ol' Dirty Bastard. Those same fans were slower to come around to the prospect of a solo effort from Raekwon the Chef. But stand-out appearances on the albums of Method Man and Ol' Dirty Bastard, on "Meth Vs. Chef" and "Raw Hide," respectively, warmed casual Wu-Tang Clan listeners to the possibility. Raekwon's solo deal was via Wu-Tang Clan's label home, Loud Records, and despite the relatively lesser buzz in the run up to its release, *Only Built 4 Cuban Linx . . .* is now considered a classic hip-hop album.

While *Only Built 4 Cuban Linx . . .* is technically Raekwon's solo album, it is often referred to in interviews and songs as Ghostface's debut album as well. The album's cover clearly says "Guest starring Tony Starks [Ghost Face Killer]" and Ghostface appears on 13 of the album's 16 proper songs. The fine musical chemistry Raekwon and Ghostface share on the album can be traced back to their schoolboy days in Staten Island personally and musically when the two formally connected in song with "Can It Be All So Simple" from *Enter the Wu-Tang (36 Chambers)*.

A constant point of admiration in the nearly universal praise for the album is RZA's use of music from the score and dialogue from John Wu's hardboiled Chinese cinema classic *The Killer* to clearly define the album's theme. In *The Killer*, an assassin decided to take on one last hit while a detective, who also admires him, pursues him for arrest. In parallel, on the opening track of *Cuban Linx*, "Striving for Perfection," Raekwon and Ghostface are overheard discussing plans for one last score as drug dealers so they can get out of the game and move on with their lives. The bed of music heard as Raekwon and Ghostface reveal their intentions are from soft, eerie chimes heard in *The Killer*'s score by Hong Kong's Lowell So.

RZA has noted that John Woo sent a letter thanking him for his use of *The Killer*. Good thing, since the samples were never formally cleared.[26] So begins the album's intense, cinematic, and authentic tales of back-alley dealings in audio form. Raekwon discussed *Cuban Linx* with *The Source Magazine* in 2003: "That album right there is a street novel. When I made it, I was living that every day, but I was also having a dream. The sounds of that album made it official because we were on some movie shit. I was already a movie in my mind."[27]

While a unifying theme helped thread together the album's various tales of criminal enterprise, RZA's beats to this "soundtrack" are consistently masterful. No instrumental sounds like the other yet they are all enthralling and match the rappers' sentiments and topics. "Rza's production sensibilities, sometimes minimal, other times symphonic, pull the listener in despite the chaos," said the *Los Angeles Times* in 1995 about *Only Built 4 Cuban Linx* ...[28]

The album was written in South Beach, Miami, and was recorded in RZA's Staten Island basement.[29] But Ghostface and Raekwon originally headed for the island of Barbados for inspiration.[30] The dynamic duo intended to write the album in Barbados but they got into an argument with the owners of the resort they were staying at, and claiming racism, they left for Miami.[31] Considering Miami's reputation as a hub for drugs in the 1980s and 1990s, there was no better place, besides maybe Colombia, for Raekwon and Ghostface to lyrically codify their tales. The album's title was originally to be *Only Built 4 Cuban Linx Niggaz*. The N-word was inevitably removed from the title to avoid issues at retail, likely the only case of censorship related to the album when considering its content. The Cuban link chains Raekwon favored at the time were also supposed to be the strongest jewelry to don. Raekwon told *XXL Magazine* in 1998, "We came up with the shit because it symbolized the strength of family. We wasn't trying to be Italians because we *ain't* Italians."[32]

Cuban Linx's first official single was "Glaciers of Ice," the "ice" referring to diamonds, and was released in the early summer of 1995 and featured guest verses from Ghostface and Masta Killa. The song was a "Sure Shot Single" in *The Source Magazine*, which described the beat as containing "illified watery keyboards."[33] Despite the assistance of two of his Clan members, Raekwon nevertheless continued to assert himself as a solo artist, building excitement for his debut album.

While recording *Cuban Linx*, Raekwon wasn't worrying about creating radio-friendly records. He didn't even listen to anything on the dial. Again, in 1998 he told *XXL Magazine*, "I cut myself off from everything around me when I'm writing. I don't listen to radio or nothin' . . . I like to come original."[34] The album's packaging was also innovative in that the CD case and cassette were tinged purple in color, hence the album being referred to often as "The Purple Tape." In part of a retrospective of the album, "The Documentary," Raekwon told *XXL Magazine* in 2005, "I wanted to portray an image that if I was selling cracks or dimes on the street, [you would] recognize these dimes from other niggas' dimes," said Raekwon.[35]

After Ghostface and Raekwon relay their intentions to make one final move before going legitimate on "Striving for Perfection," the album kicks off with jumpy guitar strings plucked from The Dramatics "Get Up & Get Down" (1972) over dusty drums that is "Knuckleheads." The song's order of rappers is Raekwon, Ghostface, and U-God. Raekwon's verse relays imagery of life on the streets while Ghostface's verses are a tale of robbing rival dealers; "Who's the knucklehead wanting respect," barks Ghostface at the start of his verse. U-God's verse is off topic; his rhyme is more about self-posturing. Originally U-God was supposed to be killed in the narrative but U-God, shortly after recording his verse, would violate his parole and return to prison.

The sequence continues with "Knowledge God," which is the first time we hear Raekwon on a song by himself. At the track's onset he can be heard sniffing his nose and the urban legend was that he was actually snorting cocaine in the studio. However, Raekwon insists it was just a sensitive mic. The effect was fitting considering "Knowledge God" is a vivid rhyme about fantasies that include the high price of drugs purchased from Colombians, buying kilos in Greece, and project dope fiends. The imagery is only heightened by RZA's use of operatic strings, secured with solid, underlying drums and chords.

The following song is "Criminology," which at the time of the album's release was familiar to some because it was the B-side of "Glaciers of Ice" and is considered *Only Built 4 Cuban Linx*'s second single. Ghostface told RZA he wanted a beat that sounded similar to a breakbeat. The resounding horns and strings are from a sample of Black Ivory's "I Keep Asking You Questions" (1972), slowed down and punched up for added thump. The sharp keys are sampled from the beginning of 1973's "Why Marry" by The Sweet Inspirations (whose founder was Cissy Houston, Whitney Houston's mother). Ghostface says "Criminology" was recorded in San Francisco and he might have been drunk off Ballantine Ale. The brand manages to turn up in a number of Wu-Tang Clan's rhymes. The track begins with sampled audio from a film, this time Brian DePalma's *Scarface*, perfectly in line with the album's drug-dealing adventures with the character Alex Sosa threatening Al Pacino's Tony Montana character for failing to go through with a hired hit.

Despite murderous tones set by the dialogue at the beginning of "Criminology," both of the verses from Ghostface and Raekwon are more about flexing their lyrical skills, particularly the former who delivers one of the most passionate verses of his early career. Raps Ghostface, "Extravagant, RZA bake the track and it's militant, then I react, like a convict, and start killin' shit/It's manifested, the Gods work like appliances, dealin' in my cipher I revolve around sciences." The particular lines stand out for their bravado, lithe use of simile, and inclusion of Five Percent rhetoric ("the Gods work"). "Criminology/ Glaciers of Ice" would peak at #43 on the *Billboard* Hot 100 chart and #32 on the R&B/Hip-Hop Songs chart.

While "Criminology" hits the listener like a punch to the gut, "Incarcerated Scarfaces" is a glancing blow that eventually results in the knockout. Before the proper track begins, dialogue from *The Killer* is heard where the officer charged in the film with tracking down the hired assassin delivers his profile ("He looks determined, without seeming ruthless, something heroic in his manner."). This assessment of the film's protagonist in regard to its antagonist could be thinly applied to Raekwon and Ghostface who hailed from rival housing projects. Immediately after the sampled dialogue, the enthralling drum pattern RZA lifted from 1973's "You're Getting Too Smart" by the Detroit Emeralds kicks in. A soothing guitar note is also heard—a miniscule sample from the late Koko Taylor's "Wang Dang Doodle" (1966). The resulting beat was unlike any other hip-hop instrumental track heard before, while Raekwon delivers on his end of the bargain with two slickly delivered verses dedicated to "niggas locked up."[36]

Purportedly, RZA was already finished with Raekwon's album and happened to have the instrumental, which was intended for GZA's album, playing in the studio. GZA would get his own set of provocative beats for *Liquid Swords*, while "Incarcerated Scarfaces," the B-side to *Only Built 4 Cuban Linx*'s third single "Ice Cream," would become one of Raekwon's trademark tracks. It contains Raekwon's vivid imagery, wrapped in a dense mélange of slang. One song that sums up Raekwon's style and motivation is "Incarcerated Scarfaces." On his wordplay, in 1997 Raekwon told *Rolling Stone Magazine*, "You can never get it no fresher, comin' up out the projects, 20 or 21 years old, and you start rhymin', and that's how you make your money—by speaking your lingo. Rap, to me, is slang poetry. It answers your questions: why young kids is doin' bad, why they turn to drugs to get away from their misery. This is the shit we talk about—and how to escape it."[37]

The ensuing track was never a single but is nevertheless recognizable to fans of Wu-Tang Clan. "Rainy Dayz" finds Raekwon and Ghostface detailing the tribulations of a man who makes his living on the streets, which puts a strain on the relationship with his mate who nervously awaits his nightly return home. The song features the singing of Blue Raspberry, who RZA signed to his Razor Sharps Records with intentions of releasing a solo album that never manifested. RZA heard Blue Raspberry singing Barbara Streisand and Donna Summer's solemn, 1979 duet "No More Tears (Enough Is Enough)." Instead, it was interpolated and given a more street appeal; the "It's raining, it's pouring, it's raining, it's pouring, my love life is boring me to tears" heard in the original tune became, "It's raining, he's changing." Blue Raspberry's soulful vocals are just as key to the track as the elements of Michael Jackson's 1972 version of "Ain't No Sunshine" that RZA samples (by speeding up the strings) to create the track. "Waiting on these royalties takes too long, it's like waiting on babies," laments G, detailing the real strain Wu-Tang Clan members faced between their quick-fix street past versus the slower music industry grind.

Fortunately for rap fans, instead of slinging dope, Raekwon and Ghostface decided to focus on slinging rhymes. The tongue was necessary to say these rhymes, and in Wu-Tang parlance the tongues were the sword. That said, "Guillotine (Swords)" was a sharp barrage of rhymes from, in order, Inspectah Deck, Ghostface, Raekwon, and GZA. The track is familiar to attentive Wu-Tang Clan fans because the beat is a loop of a beat first heard on *Tical*'s "Meth vs. Chef" (as well as the album's intro track). Raekwon had told RZA he wanted to use the beat ever since he first heard it.[38] A song in the style of "Guillotine (Swords)" where four or more MCs jump on a searing, RZA-produced track and rap their hearts out is a staple of all Wu-Tang Clan albums, whether group or solo efforts. And like "Guillotine (Swords)" when Inspectah Deck is the first rapper heard on the song, it's usually a standout.[39]

The following track is "Can It Be All So Simple (Remix)," a worthy successor to the original heard on *Enter the Wu-Tang (36 Chambers)*, which also appears on the soundtrack to the film *Fresh* (1994), which was released the previous year. It too prominently utilizes the same Gladys Knight and The Pips' "The Way We Were/Try to Remember" sample heard on the original. Ghostface uses his verse to rap about his own true-to-life story of being shot in the neck during his drug-dealing days. Though Ghostface expresses remorse for his way of life and its consequences, an extended skit titled "Shark Niggas (Biters)" follows; here, he and Raekwon show no such compassion for rival MCs who they suspect of biting (mimicking) their musical styles. Ghostface declares, "They hear you say one word then here they come with the word, tryin' to flip it and bounce it on some bullshit, not sounding right first of all."

The aforementioned dis could have been applied to a number of contemporary rap artists. But Ghostface then goes on to say a certain artist bit off of Nas's album cover. This was a clear shot at the Notorious B.I.G. whose album cover for his debut *Ready to Die* (released in September 1994) featured a picture of a young baby boy while the cover of Nas's debut *Illmatic* (released in February 1994) featured a picture of him as an adolescent. Despite the Notorious B.I.G. being a fan of the group (Method Man appeared on "The What" on *Ready to Die*), it would be a point of contention between the two factions (Notorious B.I.G. & Bad Boy Records vs. Wu-Tang Clan). "Shark Niggas (Biters)" closes out the first side of "the purple tape." Ghostface made peace with the Notorious B.I.G. while both were coincidentally in Los Angeles, a couple of days before his murder on March 9, 1997.

Despite the barely subtle jabs at the Notorious B.I.G., Raekwon maintains that he never had any problem with the late rapper.[40] In hindsight, Ghostface says he would have worked with him and thought about it even before the rapper's death.[41]

In an album full of captivatingly sublime tracks there may not be a beat as innovative as "Ice Water." RZA melds a haunting vocal moan—it sounds like the tail end of a soprano voice singing "aha"—with a succinct drum program. The resulting emotion elicited by the productions melody fittingly cradles Ghostface's, Raekwon's, and Cappadonna's cocksure rhymes about dealing drugs. Ghostface would reuse his opening line—"Ayo check out the rap kingpin, the black Jesus"—on his own debut, *Ironman*, about a year later.

The previously discussed "Glaciers of Ice" follows after, but added to the track's beginning is a skit that features Ghostface discussing Clarks footwear. While most rappers at the time of Wu-Tang Clan's rise to prominence in the early to mid-1990s stuck to a general uniform of either sneakers or Timberland boots, Ghostface chose to prominently wear Clarks Wallabee shoes, lauding them for their style, comfort, and relative uniqueness since the only substantial population to wear the shoes in New York City were West Indians in Brooklyn. The contagious energy Ghostface revels in while detailing his plans to dye the shoes unique colors made it one of hip-hop's most popular skits. Credit RZA with having the wherewithal to make spontaneous moments on inspiration recordable by provided Wu-Tang Clan members with a portable DAT recorder.

After "Glaciers of Ice" arrives "Verbal Intercourse" featuring the renowned Queensbridge, New York, rapper Nas. Besides his gifts as a lyricist—his lead-off verse earned him a "Hip-Hop Quotable" in the September 1995 issue of *The Source Magazine*—Nas also holds the title of the first non–Wu-Tang Clan affiliated artist to appear on one of their albums.[42] With no hook, "Verbal Intercourse" is a relentless stream of rewind-worthy rhymes, earning it great renown despite only being an album cut. RZA's haunting use of a string-laden vocal sample of the Emotion's "If You Think It (You May As Well Do It)" (1972) didn't hurt either.

"Wisdom Body" follows and has the distinction of being Ghostface's lone solo song on the album. As Raekwon matter of factly told *XXL Magazine*, "It was his album too."[43] Opening with a sample of the pimp

Pretty Ricky's explanation of how he keeps his prostitutes in line from cult favorite Blaxploitation film *The Mack*, the song features Ghostface describing his street-savvy version of courting a beautiful woman ("Wisdom" being a slang term of endearment for a woman in the Nation of Gods and Earths). The song was originally called "Fly Bitch Shit." Ghostface has also admitted that some words had to be punched in later during postproduction since he was drunk and slurring some of his lines when it was initially recorded.[44]

With "Verbal Intercourse" and "Wisdom Body," their downtempo rhythms bring a calming effect to the album and the listener. This continues immediately, albeit momentarily, on the beginning of "Spot Rusherz." We hear Ghostface and Raekwon anticipating that something is about to go down ("Yo, tonight feel like a nigga gon' get burnt, right?," rhetorically asks Ghostface). While Raekwon and Ghostface are holding their conversation a St. Ides Malt Liquor commercial featuring rhymes from Method Man (the tail end of his rhyme), Raekwon, Ghostface, U-God, and RZA can be heard in the background. "Spot Rusherz," which only features rapping from Raekwon, kicks off with snappy drums and cascading five-note piano sample. The song details a rival drug dealer getting set up for a robbery (hence his "spot" getting "rushed"). At the track's conclusion two gunshots are heard, which RZA claims were intended to bring the listeners to attention.

Any gimmick to regain a listener's attention wasn't needed as soon as "Ice Cream" was heard. The track's beat is a sped-up sample of Earl Klugh's acoustic guitar from the 1980 song "A Time to Love." Method Man is heard on the intro announcing that "the Ice Cream Man is coming!," as Eddie Murphy did in his stand-up comedy film *Eddie Murphy Delirious* (1983), and handles the song's chorus: "Watch these rap niggas get all up in your guts/French-vanilla, butter-pecan, chocolate-deluxe/Even caramel sundaes is getting touched, and scooped in my ice cream truck, Wu tears it up."

The ice cream flavors name dropped in the song correlated to the complexions of women (Butter Pecan Rican denoted Puerto Ricans, for example) and was no mere coincidence. RZA saw the song's hook, which he had to convince Method Man to perform, as an opportunity for more Wu-Tang Clan merchandise (women were seen in the "Ice Cream" video wearing Wu-Wear branded T-shirts with the ice cream flavor spelled out on the front) and branding. The song's MCs in order are Ghostface, Raekwon, and Cappadonna.

Though Cappadonna was already heard on *Cuban Linx* via the song "Ice Water," the sometime Wu-Tang Clan member's first official recording with the group is actually "Ice Cream." Cappadonna jumped on "Ice Cream" after visiting RZA's studio with Ghostface and hearing the track.[45] Cappadonna, who was working as a security guard at the time, said he was only joking about getting on the track, until RZA said to go ahead.[46] Cappadonna's situation as a new, unique voice in the Wu conglomerate, as well as the cockiness revealed in lines of his like, "I love you like I love my dick size," garnered the Staten Island resident fairly rapid popularity. Ironically, Raekwon saw the song as too much of a play for radio airplay and didn't want it to be a single.[47] Needless to say, to this day it is one of his most popular songs.

Another popular song of Raekwon and Wu-Tang Clan in general is "Wu-Gambinos." *Cuban Linx* ... was the official debut of the Wu-Gambinos; Wu-Tang Clan members take on mafia-inspired alternate names. Since the album's narrative unravels like a story out of a John Woo film, directed by Martin Scorsese, it was only right that the Wu-Tang Clan take on monikers fitting of criminals with honor. RZA became Bobby Steels, GZA became Maximillion, Method Man became Johnny Blaze (actually a Marvel character, for those keeping up), U-God became Lucky Hands, Inspectah Deck became Rollie Fingers, Master Killa became Noodles, Ghostface became Tony Starks, and Raekwon became Lou Diamonds. As for Ol' Dirty Bastard, he doesn't appear on *Only Built 4 Cuban Linx* ..., while Cappadonna (aka Cappachino) makes his debut as an on-again, off-again Clansmen. Said writer dream hampton in *Vibe Magazine*'s 1995 review of *Only Built 4 Cuban Linx* ...: "That Wu-Tang Clan should plunge deeper into the moniker abyss and further away from the names their mamas gave them is only appropriate. ... Black boys finding freedom in cultural appropriation is sweet vindication."[48]

On the proper "Wu-Gambinos" song only Method Man, Raekwon, RZA, Masta Killa, and Ghostface, in said order, appear. The song's tremendous drums and yearning string samples make it another classic Wu-Tang Clan posse cut. While "Wu-Gambinos" finds the album's players full of gusto and bravado, "Heaven & Hell" stumbles on Raekwon and Ghostface in an introspective mode. The song, entirely written by

Raekwon, though Ghostface also performs on the record, is one of the earliest tracks recorded for *Only Built 4 Cuban Linx* ... (in contrast to "Wu-Gambinos," which was one of the last) and previously appeared on the soundtrack for the film *Fresh*. RZA lifted the beats melody from Syl Johnson's beautifully lush "Could I Be Falling In Love?" (1974) and Blue Raspberry provides strong background vocals.

"Heaven & Hell" closes the *Cuban Linx*'s "purple tape" and vinyl versions. On CD and digital version, however, the album's closer is "North Star (Jewels)." RZA liberally lifts portions of Barry White's "Mellow Mood, Part 1" for the beat while Ol' Dirty Bastard can be heard singing background vocals as Papa Wu (aka Freedom Allah) gives Raekwon advice inflected with teachings of the Nation of Gods and Earths. Raekwon then drops a succinct, crime-laden but thoughtful verse. Papa Wu closes the album saying, "For no man is good and bad at the same time, Either you good, or you bad," a statement that sums up the dichotomy of the album.

Only Built 4 Cuban Linx ... was universally considered a classic hip-hop album almost immediately. In 1995 the album was originally given a four and a half out of five mic rating in *The Source Magazine*, with writer Nicholas Poluhoff opining, "Production wise this may be the RZA's most impressive feat yet," though he oddly adds, "The beats are all solid, and while many aren't as catchy as those on previous Wu solo joints," before adding, "The end result is one of the best rap LPs of the year (if not ever), and another success for Shaolin's finest."[49] *The Source Magazine* would eventually bestow *Cuban Linx* with a classic five out of five mic rating in its March 2002 issue.[50] A five-mic rating from *The Source* was the ultimate honor, and Raekwon's work was deserving of accolades.

Praise for the album was not limited to traditional hip-hop press. "Never before have the Scarface fantasies of young black men, the dreams of transforming giant bricks of pharmaceuticals into giant stacks of dead presidents, been portrayed with so much precision, poetry and pathos," said writer Toure in his 1999 *Rolling Stone Magazine* review of *Only Built 4 Cuban Linx* ...[51]

Cuban Linx ... vaulted RZA to the top of the list of hip-hop producers. The album also advanced Raekwon's and Ghostface's positions in the overall rap artist hierarchy and in turn boosted the Wu-Tang Clan's already esteemed reputation as a collective. " 'Cuban Linx' is actually a Wu-Tang album disguised as a Raekwon solo," said the *Los Angeles Times* in its 1995 review of the album.[52] The Wu-Tang Clan's growing commercial success also elevated East Coast rap's presence in a hip-hop world that had been dominated by the West Coast as of late. Said the *Los Angeles Times*, again in its 1995 review of the album, "In terms of rhyme content, cadence and sonic complexity, the debut solo effort by one of the strongest vocalists of the nine-member, Staten Island-based Wu-Tang Clan single-handedly resurrects East Coast-based hip-hop, much the same way Dr. Dre's 'The Chronic' altered the West Coast rap sound."[53]

Raekwon's and Ghostface's masterpiece would go on to inspire narrative albums from the likes of Jay-Z (*Reasonable Doubt* [1996]) and 50 Cent (*Get Rich or Die Trying* [2003]), and others. "We tried to make every song a single," said Ghostface.[54] That mission was accomplished with albums cuts such as "Verbal Intercourse" and "Ice Water" being revered as much as the official singles. The onus for this New York rap renaissance rested squarely on the shoulders of RZA. "When we worked on *Cuban Linx*, there was no engineer. Not a single knob was twisted by anyone but me," says RZA in his second book, 2009's *Tao of Wu*.[55] RZA would again chair the recording boards of the latest Wu-Tang solo endeavor, GZA's *Liquid Swords*.

GZA/GENIUS, *LIQUID SWORDS*

Liquid Swords/Duel of the Iron Mic/Living in the World Today/ Gold/Cold World/Labels/4th Chamber/Shadowboxin'/Hell's Wind Staff/Killah Hills 10304/Investigative Reports/Swords-man/I Gotcha Back/B.I.B.L.E. (Basic Instructions Before Leaving Earth)

Liquid Swords is GZA's second album, but due to the limited distribution, and critical malaise, of his debut, *Words from the Genius*, many mistook it for his debut. But GZA's cool and deliberate delivery—he only uses as many words as he needs to get his point across, never more—and the respect the Wu-Tang Clan gave him (as Method Man stated on *Enter the Wu-Tang*, "He's just the genius") betrayed his status as a grizzled rap veteran. In a 1995 *The Source Magazine* feature,

"Lyrical Blades," GZA said it best: "I just paint pictures. What they say in ten lines, I might say in one or two lines."[56]

RZA and GZA began formally working on *Liquid Sword* in 1994. The album's title signifies sharp tongues. With the tongue symbolic of the sword, the sword style on display through the album is clearly lyricism. The album's iconic cover art was designed by Denys Cowan, a renowned comic book artist. The concept—a battle taking place on a chessboard—was all GZA's, who is an avid and accomplished chess player. Actor Seth Rogen famously wore a T-shirt emblazoned with the *Liquid Swords* album cover in the 2005 film *The 40-Year-Old Virgin*. As for the sequence of the album, fans were thrown for a loop when they realized the track listing on the back cover didn't match the order of songs on the actual album. What GZA did was rearrange the song titles to form a story. To his credit, "Song Titles Do Not Appear in Order" is clearly printed below the story, but that didn't help in initially figuring out what song is what on listening to the album.

Like its predecessor *Only Built 4 Cuban Linx* . . ., sampled dialogue from a film was used to cement the *Liquid Swords'* narrative. In this case it was the Japanese *jidaigeki* film *Shogun Assassin* (1980). The version of *Shogun Assassin* sampled throughout the album is a film that is actually a combination of the first two films (*Lone Wolf and Cub: Sword of Vengeance* and *Lone Wolf and Cub: Baby Cart at the River Styx*) in the Lone Wolf and Cub series of Japanese films. The film's plot is centered on a samurai warrior named Lone Wolf who is feared by the Shogun, and bloody conflict, encompassed by vengeance, naturally ensues. Worth noting is that the decision to add the *Shogun Assassin* samples to *Liquid Swords* was made at the last minute while the album was already completed and being mastered. Over $100,000 was paid to use the dialogue from *Shogun Assassin*, a hefty amount considering that the dialogue used from *The Killer* for *Only Built 4 Cuban Linx* . . . was never cleared.

The album opens, after a monologue from Lone Wolf's child detailing why the Shogun turned on Lone Wolf, with the title track, "Liquid Swords." RZA samples the stuttering riff that dominates the song from the late Willie Mitchell's "Groovin' " (1968). The baseline is a slowed and muffled sample from Willie Mitchell's 1968 version of "Mercy, Mercy, Mercy." RZA also adds his vocals on the hook and backing vocals. GZA's lyrics are typically succinct jabs. "Now come aboard, it's Medina bound, enter the chamber, and it's a whole different sound/ It's a wide entrance, small exit like a funnel, so deep it's picked up on radios in tunnels." Considering radio waves don't penetrate, say, train tunnels, that's pretty deep. The "Liquid Swords" single—its B-side was "Labels"—peaked at #48 on the *Billboard* Hot 100 chart and peaked at #33 on *Billboard* R&B/Hip-Hop Songs chart.

Right after, Ol' Dirty Bastard makes a rare appearance on a Wu-Tang Clan solo project when he performs the chorus on "Duel of the Iron Mic." "Duel of the iron mic, it's the fifty-two fatal strikes!," barks Ol' Dirty Bastard. For the beat RZA uses a small portion of key notes from David Porter's "I'm Afraid the Masquerade Is Over" (1971). The song has been sampled many times over in hip hop (Notorious B.I.G.'s "Who Shot Ya?" is one of the most popular), but RZA uses a not-so-obvious portion of the record. After GZA rhymes first (but not before listeners hear more sampled dialogue from *Shogun Assassin*), Masta Killa and Inspectah Deck deliver verses over the purposeful, though melodic, beat.

Next comes "Living in the World Today," an homage to The Ranch Crew, who RZA shouts out in the intro. The Ranch Crew was a group of MCs, in the mode of the call-and-response styled hip hop of the Cold Crush Brothers, who were from Staten Island and predate the Wu-Tang Clan. GZA would alter their sing-songy rendition of "If you living in the world today" for the more direct approach of contemporary rap. Method Man assists on the hook (adding "punk niggas shatter like a glass jaw" to complete the chorus) and provides a back-and-forth dialogue with GZA between the first and second (and last) verse. RZA samples chords from Ann Sexton's "I'm His Wife, You're Just a Friend" (1977) for the main melody while the wailing horns heard during the hook are from 1969's "In the Hole" by The Bar-Kays, which appears on the *WattStax* album.

Five Wu-Tang Clan members (Method Man, RZA, Ol' Dirty Bastard, Inspectah Deck, Masta Killa) appear on the album so far. It is not until "Gold" that listeners hear a true GZA solo record. The song is written from the perspective of a ruthless drug dealer, and rather than cash ruling all (a la "C.R.E.A.M.") GZA figuratively replaces it with "gold." GZA may have taken poetic license with the events he describes in the song, but his storytelling places the listener in the moment. "I'm deep down in the back streets, in the heart of Medina, about to set off something more deep than a misdemeanor, Under the subway, waiting for the train to make noise, So I can blast a nigga and his boys." The song's chorus only reiterates the tyranny of the dealer he's rhyming on behalf of, particularly its first portion: "Yo, the fiends ain't comin fast enough, There is no cut that's pure enough, I can't fold, I need gold, I re-up and reload, Product must be sold to you." RZA's track, a sample of "Aries" from Cannonball Adderley's *The Soul Zodiac* (1972) soul jazz album, is filtered and boosted to the point where it sounds like a buzz saw yet nevertheless complements GZA's rhymes.

Cold and calculating, is a good descriptor of GZA's rhyme technique. After that in the *Liquid Swords* storyline is "Cold World," which features Inspectah Deck aka Rollie Fingers if you are following the Wu-Gambino nicknames. Though its chart position betrays its popularity (the song peaked at #97 on the *Billboard* Hot 100 chart and at #57 on the *Billboard* R&B/Hip-Hop Songs chart), in hip-hop circles it is one of GZA's biggest hits. The two MCs on the song each get a verse to relay their high-definition tales of ghetto pathos. RZA skillfully chops up samples of The Dramatics's "In the Rain" (1971) and Stevie Wonder's "Rocket Love" (1980) for the main melody. As for the chorus, the original chorus of "Rocket Love" is liberally interpolated by a singer named Life, who happens to be GZA's cousin. GZA has noted that Life was so off beat that RZA had to correct recording in postproduction.[57] Perhaps to show off how incredibly his music had improved, the song's haunting groove is allowed to play for over a minute after the MCs have completed their verses.

"Cold World" was *Liquid Swords*' second single and its B-side was "I Gotcha Back," which was released about a year earlier on the *Fresh* soundtrack. "I Gotcha Back" appears again on *Liquid Swords* toward its tail end but the next song on the track list is another early B-side. "Labels" appeared on the flip to "Liquid Swords" but was also released earlier than the first single as a buzz/street record. On "Labels" GZA creatively incorporates the names of numerous records labels into one long verse. When GZA rhymes, "I death row an MC with mic cables, the epic is at a rush associated labels, from east west to atco, I bring it to a next plateau, but I keep it phat though," he has wittily and seamlessly name-dropped Death Row Records, Epic Records,

Rush Associated Labels, East/West Records, ATCO Records, and Next Plateau Records. "Labels" was granted "Hip-Hop Quotable" of the month in the August 1995 issue of *The Source Magazine*.[58] Though production of the track's mechanized rhythms and belligerent drums are credited to RZA, GZA has stated that he created the beat himself on an eMu SP-1200 and the most he divulged about the samples source is that it is only two records.[59]

After "Labels" arrives the bombastic "4th Chamber." Although "Shadowboxin' " is the next song on *Liquid Swords*, "4th Chamber" was the song's B-side. "4th Chamber" features guest verses from Ghostface, Killah Priest, and RZA. The apocalyptic sounding track's main melody is courtesy of "Assassin With Son" from the 1980 *Shogun Assassin* soundtrack while its drums (particularly the snares) come from Willie Mitchell's "Groovin'." All of the "Chamber" tracks (i.e., *Enter the Wu-Tang*'s "Wu-Tang: 7th Chamber") feature Wu-Tang Clan members essentially showing off their skills at rapping. That is the case with "4th Chamber," whose verse from Ghostface helped spark more interest in his soon to be released debut album. The written words fail to demonstrate the panache with which they are delivered, but Ghostface famously raps, "Why is the sky blue? Why is water wet? Why did Judas, rat to Romans while Jesus slept? Stand up, you're out of luck like two dogs stuck, Iron Man be sipping rum, out of Stanley Cups, unflammable." RZA too gets from behind the boards and delivers his own verse steeped in almanac worthy science—"fortified with essential, vitamins and minerals," he raps before closing with a veiled acronym for the word *peace* ("Protons electrons always cause explosions").

"Shadowboxin' " follows and is as much a Method Man songs as it is GZA's. Method Man, or Johnny Blaze in Wu-Gambino speak, handles the first and third verses while GZA anchors the middle. Method Man's opening verse on "Shadowboxin' " was given "Hip-Hop Quotable" in the December 1995 issue of *The Source Magazine*.[60] The first traditional kung-fu flick sample ("Allow me to demonstrate the skill of Shaolin, the special technique of shadow boxing," taken from *Shaolin vs. Lama* [1983]) is heard being scratched (DJ style) at the beginning of the song and at different moments throughout the song. A sped up sample of 1972's "Trouble, Heartaches & Sadness" by Memphis Soul singer/songwriter Ann Peebles is the basis of RZA's beat. Peebles's distorted voice saying "old man" becomes a prominent part of the track while the song's soft chords become the abrasively funky melody of "Shadowboxin'."

For "Hells Wind Staff/Killa Hills 10304" the latter portion of the title is a reference to Staten Island's Park Hill Projects, nicknamed Killa Hills and residing in the 10304 zip code. According to GZA "Hells Wind Staff" was the name of another Wu-Tang Clan song, though he doesn't confirm that it is the "Hellz Wind Staff" that appears on the Wu-Tang Clan's sophomore album, *Wu-Tang Forever*, which wouldn't be released for another five years. "Killa Hills" has an extended intro where RZA, as Bobby Steels, is having an illicit meeting with a contact named Grey Ghost before GZA begins the song's single, yet dense verse. GZA manages to smoothly tell a tale that includes stakeouts, Afghani hit men, bribed judges, and money laundering. All, as he says, "the life of a drug dealer" in Killa Hills 10304.

"Investigative Reports" comes after, which could fit comfortably on *Only Built 4 Cuban Linx . . .* as it features verses from Ghostface and Raekwon, along with U-God performing its chorus. Over a sample of the opening strings of Three Dog Night's "I'd Be So Happy," the MCs (in order: Raekwon, GZA, Ghostface) "report" on what they observe in the ghetto. Akin to their typical viewpoints, Raekwon's verse revolves around a fast-living gangster wanting to turn a new leaf, GZA recounts a detailed tale of a robbery gone wrong, and Ghostface reminisces about the good ol' days and the fly clothing he wore.

GZA holds down the following two songs, "Swordsman" and "I Gotcha Back," on his own. "Swordsman" is composed of a morose, almost melancholy, hodgepodge of drums and bass reverb for GZA to rhyme about his "knowledge of self" as a member of the Nation of Gods and Earths. "I Gotcha' Back," whose drums are courtesy of "As Long As I've Got You" by The Charmels (another portion of the song was used for Wu-Tang Clan's hit "C.R.E.A.M."), shows GZA's knack for throwing acronyms ("What is the meaning of crime? Is it criminals robbing innocent motherfuckers everytime?") into his rhymes.

The album's last song, "B.I.B.L.E.," is another acronym (Basic Instructions Before Leaving Earth) but is actually a Killah Priest song. GZA had Killah Priest signed to his GZA Productions company at the time and used the opportunity to showcase his artist. "B.I.B.L.E." is produced by RZA protégé 4th Disciple and did not appear on vinyl and cassette versions of the album. It wouldn't be the last time the marquee name on a Wu-Tang Clan–affiliated album wouldn't appear on one of its songs.

Liquid Swords peaked at #9 on the *Billboard* 200 chart and peaked at #2 on the R&B/Hip-Hop Albums chart, remaining on the chart for 37 weeks. *Liquid Swords* put the capstone on an incredible wave of solo material from the Wu-Tang Clan in 1995 with its release that November. *Liquid Swords* was given a four out of five mic review in the December 1995 issue of *The Source Magazine*.[61] Reviewer Selwyn Seyfu Hinds wrote, "1995 will go down as the signature year of the Clan," while adding, "*Liquid Swords* contains all the elements of RZA's increasingly sophisticated style."

RZA's imprint was profound, purposefully. In 2005 he told *XXL Magazine*, "The only two albums I did with nobody fucking with me was *Linx* and [GZA's] *Liquid Swords*. I was on a mission. To make all those early albums took three and half years of my life. I didn't come outside, didn't have too many girl relations, didn't even enjoy the shit. I just stayed in the basement."[62] There was one more album that was spawned in RZA's basement, Ghostface's *Ironman*. Though Ghostface's debut would arrive in 1996, it was only appropriate GZA close out the Wu-Tang Clan's most critically successful year since it was his verse that sealed "Protect Ya Neck," the single that marked the start of the Wu-Tang Clan's musical explosion and reign.

Immediately clear after listening to *Liquid Swords* is its near total lack of radio-friendly songs. The closest case would be "Cold World," mostly due to its Stevie Wonder sample and disregarding its rather bleak subject matter. Unlike his first venture with Cold Chillin' Records, Geffen Record granted GZA total creative autonomy to record his album. He told *The Source Magazine* in 2005, "I wouldn't make songs if I had to try to make 'em for the people, 'cause you never know what they're gonna like."[63] RZA was also in accord with his cousin's sentiments. "Other producers may have thought about club hits, radio, selling records. The only thing I thought about was MCs sounding aggressive," says RZA.[64] *Liquid Swords* is included in *The Guardian* (UK) series "1000 Albums to Hear Before You Die," which in its description of the album calls it "The best Wu-Tang solo album."[65]

Considering the near universal praise *Liquid Swords* received critically and at stores (the album has been certified gold by the RIAA),

GZA's, along with RZA's, instinct to do what he felt like regardless of radio demands paid off. Ghostface would go off instinct, and sound aggressive, to great effect and success, as well.

GHOSTFACE KILLAH, *IRONMAN*

Iron Maiden/Wildflower/The Faster Blade/260/Assassination Day/Poisonous Darts/Winter Warz/Box in Hand/Fish/Camay/Daytona 500/Motherless Child/Black Jesus/After the Smoke Is Clear/All That I Got Is You/The Soul Controller/Marvel

---

After Wu-Tang Clan's epic 1995 albums from Ol' Dirty Bastard, Raekwon, and GZA, there was one more solo project in the chamber before the group would reunite for 1997's *Wu-Tang Forever*. Ghostface was instrumental in *Only Built 4 Cuban Linx*'s success, since he was a guest star, but his own debut, *Ironman*, would be released in October 1996. Ol' Dirty Bastard's *Return to the 36 Chambers* showcased a raw, unfiltered Wu-Tang disciple, Raekwon's *Only Built 4 Cuban Linx* . . . embodied the Mafioso inspired street dreams of the ghetto, while GZA's *Liquid Swords* relayed the precise storytelling of a ghetto griot. Ghostface's *Ironman* would expand on what was begun on *Cuban Linx* but drench it in a soul music–inspired litany of hood fabulousness and ghetto righteousness.

In July 1996 it was announced that Ghostface had signed to RZA's Razor Sharp Records, distributed by Epic, a subsidiary of Sony.[66] Now a Wu-Tang Clan member was signed, at least partly, to a Wu-Tang Clan–owned imprint. Also worth noting is that Dennis Coles (Ghostface) was credited as one of the executive producers of *Enter the Wu-Tang*. The additional credit Ghostface receives makes it a safe bet he was more assertive in choosing the beats RZA presented to him for use. On *Ironman* the samples used by RZA—who would handle all of *Ironman*'s production with the exception of the True Master produced "Fish"—lean heavily toward 1960s and 1970s soul records. RZA has used samples from that musical era in all previous Wu releases, but they were considerably more pronounced on *Ironman*, at Ghostface's behest.

Ghostface claims he was in a sad and emotional state while recording the album, hence some of the relatively melancholy samples he rhymes over.[67] Tumultuous might be a better descriptor since he also recalled getting into a gunfight while in the company of the Philadelphia Soul singers the Delfonics, who appear on "After the Smoke Is Clear." But before getting ahead of the track list, let's start at the beginning of the album, where once again sampled movie dialogue marks the start of a Wu-Tang Clan solo album. In the case of *Ironman*, it is from the film *The Education of Sonny Carson* (1974), a relatively rare Blaxploitation-era film about the coming of age of Sonny, an African American male in Brooklyn, New York. The sampled conversation involves the main character seeking entry into a street gang called The Lords after delivering a message from its imprisoned leader, and despite the behest of a certain member. Sonny's fearlessness in spite of the gang member's resistance mirrors that of Ghostface and the creation of *Ironman*.

While Ghostface was not an immediate choice for solo work, his album would be last in the first wave of Wu-Tang solo albums; his efforts on previous releases raised his profile in a famously talented group of rappers. Now was Ghostface's chance to "shine on his own shit," to paraphrase his words from the infamous "Shark Niggas (Biters)" skit from *Cuban Linx*. After a tense exchange of words heard at the track's onset, "Iron Maiden" starts with a robust horn loop taken from the intro of Al Green's "Gotta Find a New World" from his *Green Is Blues* (1969) album. *Green Is Blues* marked the first time Al Green worked with Willie Mitchell, a favored sample source of RZA. The *Ironman* album's cover clearly notes that it is "Ghostface Killah featuring Raekwon and Cappadonna" while "Iron Maiden," which likely takes its title from a torture device seen in kung-fu movies such as *Five Deadly Venoms*, features rhymes from the album's aforementioned key players. Full of bluster—"We sit back on Malayan islands, sippin' mix drinks out of boat coconut bowls, we whylin'!," is how Ghostface closes his verse—the track is a strong lead-off record.

On "Wildflower" Ghostface kicks rap music's well-documented history of misogyny up a notch. The song is a relentless verbal tongue lashing of a woman who stepped out on her partner. Ghostface snorting "Then you had to go ahead and fuck this lobsterhead nigga" is close to the only vitriol spewed at the other man. Choice quotes from Ghostface's verbal acid include, "You sneaky fuck bitch, your ways and actions told it all/I fucked you while you was bleeding, held you down in malls," or, "You dumb bitch, horny hot fuck from out the mountains." While Ghost-face earns no points from the feminist crowd the angst heard in his rhymes is one of the traits that earns him praise from his fans, particularly when applied to more palatable topics heard later on in the album (i.e., "All That I Got Is You").

After "Wildflower" we get yet another example why at least early individual albums from group members were really Wu-Tang Clan albums in disguise. "Faster Blade" is a Raekwon solo record. In a song that clocks in at a shade under two and half minutes, RZA supplies diesel drums and a couple of hard chords for Raekwon's rhymes to create a song that could easily have fit into the previous year's *Only Built 4 Cuban Linx* . . . Before listeners forget whose album it is, Ghostface returns, albeit along with Raekwon, on "260." After more dialogue snatched from *The Education of Sonny Carson* is heard, the song's instrumental finds RZA utilizing little more than a thick three-note horn loop and a vocal run from the intro of Al Green's "You Ought to Be with Me" from his *Call Me* (1972) album (also another Willie Mitchell production). As Ghostface rhymes go on they unfold an intricate story about sticking up a rival drug dealer and Raekwon immediately continues the story in his second, and concluding, verse. While Ghostface gets plenty of credit for his storytelling, often being compared to hip-hop legend Slick Rick, Raekwon is just as gifted a hip-hop bard. At the tail end of Raekwon's verse Ghostface jumps in for some nice back-and-forth rhyming and the song concludes with the story's robbers realizing there were no drugs to steal.

At the start of the next song dialogue (in accord with the previous song since it is a character exhorting "There is no coke!") from the cult film *The Usual Suspect's* is heard.

However, before listeners get too used to Ghostface's storytelling, he is again completely absent from "Assassination Day." Instead listeners are privy to a Wu-Tang Clan song from Inspectah Deck, RZA, Raekwon, and Masta Killa. The song uses morose, synthesized organ chords and solid drums. Worth noting is RZA contributing a relatively rare verse, filled with his normal bluster and references to esoteric knowledge; "MC's upon their axis, their body has a tactic, lactic acid, desert drop cactus, practice. You can never master, it's invincible, Wu-Tang indispensable," he rhymes.

Ghostface returns, for good this time, on "Poisonous Darts." In Wu-Tang Clan's lexicon "darts" are rhymes, and as billed Ghostface's lyrics are more about showboating than sticking to a particular topic, besides how fly he is. Although "Poisonous Darts" has the classic aesthetics of a RZA produced Wu-Tang track—driving drums and a slice of kung-fu dialogue (from *Mystery of Chessboxing* [1979])—the next song is a better example of the only thing in the producer's toolkit that can be considered a formula. While RZA's beats were totally unpredictable thanks to the myriad of genres he samples from and his various production tricks, if there is one procedural that could be pegged to all Wu-Tang albums, it is the inclusion of a posse cut. The posse cut would contain at a minimum four different MCs taking turns rhyming over the same base track. "Wu-Gambinos" from *Cuban Linx* is an example while *Ironman*'s is "Winter Warz" (as is the previously discussed "Assassination Day").

While every MC on "Winter Warz" (in order of appearance, U-God, Ghostface, Masta Killa, Cappadonna, with Raekwon handling the chorus) delivers sharp verses, the best of the bunch is the enigmatic Cappadonna's. Going way past the typical 16 bars per verse allotment, Cappadonna delivers powerful punch lines such as, "I'm too ill, I represent Park Hill/See my face on the twenty dollar bill." The masterful technique Cappadonna displays had many wondering when his solo album would drop in lieu of original Wu-Tang Clan members such as U-God and Inspectah Deck, who had yet to release solo material. In fact, Cappadonna's debut, *The Pillage*, was released in March 1998 via RZA's Razor Sharp imprint, before the debuts of official Wu-Tang Clan members U-God, Inspectah Deck, Masta Killa, and even RZA.

After "Winter Warz" comes "Box in Hand," which is not really "Box in Hand." The actual "Box in Hand" is an old-school hip-hop inspired song that features Ghostface with Method Man and Streetlife. When *The Source Magazine* reviewed *Ironman* this is the version that was heard by the critic.[68] However, sometime before *Ironman* was finally mastered, the original "Box in Hand" was replaced by the version labeled "Box in Hand" on the album, though there is no reference to the title in the song. A song called "Deadly Darts" eventually began to be sold online and in record stores and is actually the true "Box in Hand" considering part of its chorus features the participants singing, "If you walking down the street with your box in your hands, and you're hearing the music of the Wu-Tang Clan."

The song erroneously labeled "Box in Hand" on *Ironman* is not too bad a tradeoff. The Force MD's are heard singing an interpolation of The Jackson 5's "Never Can Say Goodbye" with a Wu-Tang twist before RZA's mélange of morose chords and creeping keys, all anchored by sturdy drums, kick in for Raekwon, Ghostface, and Method Man to exploit as their backdrop.

The next few songs ("Fish," "Camay," "Daytona 500") should be considered the heart of the album because they are three of its strongest records, and *Ironman*'s starring trio—Ghostface, Raekwon, and Cappadonna—are their only participants. "Fish" is the only non-RZA production on the album. Produced by True Master (who coproduced Ol' Dirty Bastard's hit "Brooklyn Zoo"), the song's instrumental is a masterful reworking of sampled elements from Otis Redding's 1965 rendition of "A Change Is Gonna Come" into a new composition. Despite Ghostface's, Raekwon's, and Cappadonna's rhymes being top notch, the star of this show is the mesmerizing track. The soothing chords segue right into "Camay," a hip-hop torch song of sorts where RZA samples the late Teddy Pendergrass's "Can't We Try?" (1980). The trio keys in on the song's theme of seduction, dedicating each verse to a woman they are trying to woo, no pun intended.

After the lava lamp grooves of "Fish" and "Camay," listeners are ratcheted back to breakbeat-flavored hip-hop with "Daytona 500." The Force MD's, who hail from Staten Island, are again heard singing a stylized intro and on the chorus: "Them niggaz was older than us. In '81, '82—that's when them niggaz was flippin' shit. They was representin' Shao Lin," said Ghostface to *Vibe Magazine* in 1996 of the Force MD's appearance on his album.[69] As for the beat, RZA samples Jazz keyboardist Bob James's "Nautilus" (1974), long a classic hip-hop breakbeat sampled by the likes of Run-DMC and Eric B & Rakim. DJ scratches at the beginning of each loop mimics the feel of an actual DJ going back and forth between two copies of the record to create one continuous loop. Precise scratching of previous Raekwon songs that include "Ice Water" and "Incarcerated Scarfaces" add texture to the chorus as well. The frenetic pacing of the beat, and its rhymes, makes the song being named after a prestigious NASCAR race fitting. "Camay"/"Daytona 500" was *Ironman*'s lead single but failed to chart.

After the frenzied "Daytona 500," the album's pace is once again slowed down with "Motherless Child." The song was previously released earlier in the year as part of the *Sunset Park Original Soundtrack* (1996). For its instrumental, RZA samples heavily from O. V. Wright's version of "Motherless Child," a derivative of a Negro spiritual from his *(If It Is) Only Tonight (*1965).[70] The aching "I never will," also heard on the song, is from the title track of another O. V. Wright album, *Into Something (Can't Shake Loose)* (1977). Raekwon's contribution to the song is a four-bar intro ("Rich man, poor man, read the headlines," he begins) that sets off a prolonged Ghostface verse that is a detailed story about a Staten Island hustler who gets robbed in Brooklyn's Albee Square Mall (since demolished).

While "Motherless Child" acts like an urban fable where the listener is provided with an example to take heed of, the lesson is more direct on "Black Jesus." The song contains more knowledge and teachings of the Five Percent Nation being dropped by Papa Wu (previously heard on *Only Built 4 Cuban Linx*'s "North Star (Jewels)"). Despite the title, the song is more about slick, slang-heavy rhymes. All is forgiven thanks to the beat's gripping choral singing—culled from the Donald Byrd helmed Blackbyrds's "Riot" from the *Cornbread, Earl & Me Soundtrack* (1975)—matched to galloping drums and brooding keys from the original source being used as a murky bass line.

Earlier labeled "Wu-Delfonics" before the *Ironman* album's official release, "After the Smoke Is Clear" features live vocals from the Delfonics.[71] "After the smoke is done, Wu-Tang Delfonics number one," sing the Delfonics at the track's commencement and on its chorus. Yet another beat dripping with soul, it inspired RZA to get on the track with the third (last) verse after Ghostface and Raekwon have their turn. RZA's verse touches on the Wu-Tang's rise. He begins the track rapping about his upbringing—"Underprivileged, grew up in a Stapleton house village"—before mentioning the variety in the Wu-Tang Clan with, "My ninjas run wild like Shaka Zulu, some play peace like Donny the guru, Others live to be wise and old like Desmond Tutu." Also, Ghostface says, "Sharper than cuts laced on hardly scratched supreme clientele, my cartel," which is notable since *Supreme Clientele* would be the name of his second album.

As the album nears its close we finally get to Ghostface's biggest hit, "All That I Got Is You," featuring the vocals of R&B songstress Mary

J. Blige. "All That I Got Is You" chronicles Ghostface's sordid upbringing in Staten Island's Stapleton Projects. The emotive rapper was not kidding when he told *Rolling Stone Magazine* in 1997, "I got a song 'All I Got Is You.' I wrote that from the heart. My father left me when I was 6. My mother tried to take care of all of us on public assistance. . . . I took that as inspiration."[72] The song is dedicated to his mother, whose playing of old soul records influenced his taste in music and beats considering the sounds that dominate *Ironman*.

Ghostface certainly took creative license with his many coke-dealing tales, but on "All That I Got Is You" the sincerity of his words are only heightened since they are unequivocally true to life. Ghostface indeed has two brothers (Dion and Davon) with muscular dystrophy who both passed away.[73] The song's candidness—"Grab the pliers for the channel, fix the hanger on the TV, rocking each other's pants to school wasn't easy, We survived winters, snotty nosed with no coats, We kept it real, but the older brothers still had jokes."—was relatable to underprivileged listeners everywhere.

The beat to "All That I Got Is You" is just as endearing as its words, as RZA liberally samples The Jackson 5's ballad "Maybe Tomorrow" from the 1971 album of the same name. Mary J. Blige's contribution again was no doubt essential in the song getting a significant amount of airplay by Wu-Tang Clan standards. The song extends for over five minutes with Mary J. Blige singing an abridged verse ("I sit and think about all the times we did without," she coos) and Popa Wu following with more of his science that includes him saying, "If you forget where you come from . . . you're never gonna make it where you're going."

After the emotional peak of "All That I Got Is You" is another somber track called "The Soul Controller." In the song the Force MD's sing an interpolation of Sam Cooke's "A Change Is Gonna Come" (1964) with RZA providing an eerie flute sample that weaves in and out of the track. On only his second true solo song on the album, Ghostface waxes poetic about the lure of streets on the first verse, while the second verse is more about putting words together that sound fly. The described style of rhyme becomes more profound when Ghostface prepares his second album, *Supreme Clientele*, but for now it is only a taste of what is to come. Unfortunately, "The Soul Controller" was deleted from the 2001 reissue of *Ironman*, likely due to sample clearance issues.[74] This is debilitating to the album since the song closes with samples of dialogue from the films *Carlito's Way* and *The Usual Suspects* that seal the album's conclusion.

The last song is "Marvel" and plays out like a tamer version of "Wildflower." RZA contributes a verse where he manages to say, "You want it raw, let me plant my dynamite bitch deep inside your core." Again, no points are scored by Wu-Tang Clan with feminist rap fans. Being that "The Soul Controller," or "All That I Got Is You" on the reissue, would be a better closer, "Marvel" ends up being a lackluster finale to an otherwise stirring album. Nevertheless, praise for Ghostface's *Ironman* was universal. It earned a four out of five mic rating in *The Source Magazine* in 1996, with writer Warren Coolidge noting, "RZA does another masterful job ... [and] Ghost has created a soulful chamber."[75]

The album's biggest critic was Ghostface himself. "The album was rushed ... I couldn't really give it that good 200 percent," he told *Vibe Magazine* in 1997.[76] Ghostface also contends that engineers sequenced the songs improperly, while the levels on a couple of the songs were low.[77] In spite of the personal nitpicking, *Ironman* was yet another home run for RZA. Said *Rolling Stone Magazine* of RZA's work on *Ironman*, "After defining the music's rhythm in his dusted, offbeat, signature style, the RZA emphasizes simple, precise percussion and bass thuds that are augmented by moody traces of lush strings, baroque riffs and samples from '60s soul records."[78] *Ironman* marked an unprecedented sixth critically acclaimed album in a row where RZA was at the helm, steering the musical direction. No small feat when considering none of the albums sounded alike. Said *Vibe Magazine* in 1998, "Though the basic boom-boom-bap (kick-kick-snare) is RZA's favored template, the sonic layers he puts on top are tailor-made to fit each MC's style and flow to a tee, giving each Wu-Tang production its own unique signature."[79] With the first wave of solo releases finished, now was the precise time for the Wu-Tang Clan to reform and deliver a proper Wu-Tang Clan group album.

Because of their success, Wu-Tang Clan was no longer the underdog. When they arrived in 1993, hip hop was dominated by the sounds of the West Coast, behind the sales of Dr. Dre's *The Chronic* and Snoop Dogg's *Doggystyle*. Said *Time Magazine* in a 2000 story,

"Searching for the Perfect Beat," "At a time when West Coast gangsta rap was dominating the hip-hop scene, the arrival of Wu-Tang Clan of Staten Island, N.Y. announced that the East Coast was not to be ignored."[80] By constantly innovating and tinkering with his sound, RZA's production blueprint was coveted and copied by rival hip-hop producers. For example, RZA rarely quantized his beats—the quantize feature on samplers locks in a groove so it does not stray off beat—giving his drums a live feel since they would occasionally slip off beat.

Even while the Wu-Tang Clan and its particularized acts began asserting themselves with solo releases in the few years since their *Enter the Wu-Tang* debut, their gritty music remained a counterpoint to the commercial friendly hip hop of East Coast rivals such as the Notorious B.I.G., the Fugees, and Nas. Also, the West Coast was still thriving with acts such as the Dogg Pound and Tupac Shakur while acts such as OutKast, Scarface, and Bone Thugs-N-Harmony began establishing all the regions in between. With hip hop's landscape getting more crowded, Wu-Tang Clan had something to prove, and fans were anxious to see if RZA and his band of street toughs turned MCs could keep up their achievements. Considering 1997's *Wu-Tang Forever* would be a double album, their fans, and critics, would get plenty of music to listen to and digest.

NOTES

1. Diehl, Matt, "Brash Hip-Hop Entrepreneurs," *The New York Times*, December 8, 1996, 34.

2. The Gravediggaz would release *6 Feet Deep* on August 9, 1994. A second album, *The Pick, The Sickle and the Shovel*, would be released on October 14, 1997 with RZA, along with Tru Master and 4th Discilple, handling more production duties. By the group's third album, *Nightmare in A-Minor*, the RZA had left the group.

3. Mao, Chairman, "Next Chamber," *Vibe Magazine*, September 1996, 112 (112–14).

4. RZA and Chris Norris, *The Wu-Tang Manual* (New York: Riverhead Books, 2005), 108.

5. Chery, Carl, Jesse Gissen, Anslem Samuel, and Taiia, Smart Young, "Duets," August 2008, 65 (64–67).

6. Talty, Stephen, "The No. 1 Summer Song of Love," *The New York Times*, August 13, 1995, 32.

7. Ibid.

8. Ibid.

9. Norris, Chris, "Ghetto Superstar," *Spin Magazine*, December 1998, 146 (144–46).

10. Chery et al. "Duets."

11. Levine, Josh, "Method's Madness," *Vibe Magazine*, March 1995, 81 (80–81).

12. Ryan, Chris, "Across the Wuniverse," *Spin Magazine*, December 2007, 92 (91–94).

13. Ambassador Bonz, "Return of the Dark Knight," *The Source Magazine*, January 1995, 72.

14. Pierce, Mitchell, "Record Report: Method Man *Tical*," *The Source Magazine*, January 1995, 85.

15. "I Will Survive" by Gloria Gaynor is interpolated in the chorus, the bass line is samples from "The Jam" by Graham Central Station, the horns are sampled from "Treasure of San Miguel" by Herb Alpert, the sampled drums are from "Vicious" by Black Mamba.

16. http://kevinnottingham.com/2009/01/27/tical-original-samples/.

17. Seyfu Hinds, Selwyn, "Toxic Methods," *The Source Magazine*, December 1998, 196 (192–97, 233).

18. Bonz, "Return of the Dark Knight."

19. Gonzales, Michael, "Revolutions: Method Man; The Tical; Redman; Dare Is a Darkside," *Vibe Magazine*, November 1994, 125 (125–26).

20. Trivino, Jesus, "Wu to the Game," *Scratch Magazine*, March/April 2005, 57 (56–57).

21. Brodeur, Scott, "Ol' Dirty Business," *The Source Magazine*, April 1995, 52.

22. Mao, Chairman, "Revolutions: Return to the 36 Chambers: The Dirty Version," *Vibe Magazine*, May 1995, 97.

23. See Slick Rick's "Indian Girl" (*The Great Adventures of Slick Rick*) for an example.

24. Havelock, Nelson, "To Elektra, he's not just another," *Billboard Magazine*, February 2, 1995, 30.

25. Ibid.

26. Arnold, Paul W., Cantor, Paul, Caramanica, Jon, Duncan-Mao, Andrea, Kondo, Toshitaka, Mao, Chairman, Matthews, Adam, and Satten, Vanessa, "The Documentary," *XXL Magazine*, 102 (98–114).

27. Slay, Kay (moderated by Thomas Golianopoulos), "Ear to the Street: Back Talk," *The Source Magazine*, May 2003, 40.

28. Coker, Cheo H., "Record Rack: Raekwon the Chef has the Hip-Hop Recipe," *Los Angeles Times*, August 20, 1995, 58.

29. Kondo, Toshitaka, "Understanding," *XXL Magazine*, May 2005, 102–3.

30. Hinds, Selwyn Seyfu, "The Wu-Gambinos," *The Source Magazine*, October 1995, 87–88 (84–88).

31. Hester, Larry "The Blackspot," "Rae's Light," *XXL Magazine*, Vol. 2, No. 2, 184.

32. Hester, "Rae's Light," 103

33. Charles, Joe, "Sure Shot Singles: Raekwon," *The Source Magazine*, July 1995, 78.

34. Hester, "Rae's Light," 103

35. Mao, Chairman, "The Documentary," *XXL Magazine*, May 2005, 100.

36. Coleman, Brian, "Classic Material: Raekwon," *XXL Magazine*, May 2003, 148.

37. DeCurtis, Anthony, "Wu-Tang Family Values," *Rolling Stone*, July 10, 1997–July 24, 1997, 86.

38. Coleman, "Classic Material."

39. See Wu-Tang Clan "Protect Ya Neck," Raekwon "Wu-Gambinos," Wu-Tang Clan "Triumph," and Raekwon "House of Flying Daggers."

40. Mao, Chairman, "Why Wouldn't I?," *XXL Magazine*, April 2003, 134 (130–34).

41. Brannan, Eddie, "Phantom of the Opera," *Trace Urban Magazine*, Issue 22 ~1999, 54 (50–55).

42. "Hip-Hop Quotable: Nas 'Verbal Intercourse,' " *The Source Magazine*, September 1995, 40.

43. Coleman, Brian, "Classic Material: Raekwon," *XXL Magazine*, May 2003, 148.

44. XXL Cuban Linx Feature.

45. Ratcliffe, Joshua Fahiym, "A Stranger in the Clan," *The Source Magazine*, June 2001 (140–42, 212).

46. XXL Only Built 4 Cuban Linx feature

47. Coleman, "Classic Material."

48. hampton, dream, "Revolutions: Raekwon the Chef," *Vibe Magazine*, September 1995, 180.

49. Poluhoff, Nicholas, "Record Report: Only Built 4 Cuban Linx ... ," *The Source Magazine*, September 1995, 97.

50. "Got Five On It," *The Source Magazine*, March 2002, 177 (174–78).

51. Toure, "Raekwon: Only Built 4 Cuban Linx ... ," *Rolling Stone*, May 13, 1999, 74.

52. Coker, Cheo H., "Record Rack: Raekwon the Chef has the Hip-Hop Recipe," *Los Angeles Times*, August 20, 1995, 58.

53. Ibid.

54. Kondo, Toshitaka, "Understanding," *XXL Magazine*, May 2005, 103.

55. RZA and Chris Norris, *The Tao of Wu* (New York: Riverhead Books, 2009), 114.

56. Dre, A. L., "Lyrical Blades," *The Source Magazine*, December 1995, 52.

57. Blanco, Alvin, "Classic Material: Liquid Swords," *XXL Magazine*, April 2006, 173.

58. "Hip-Hop Quotable: GZA 'Labels,' " *The Source Magazine*, August 1995, 29.

59. Blanco, "Classic Material."

60. "Hip-Hop Quotable: Method Man 'Shadowboxin,' " *The Source Magazine*, December 1995, 40.

61. Seyfu Hinds, Selwyn, "Record Report: Liquid Swords," *The Source Magazine*, December 1995, 108.

62. Caramanica, Jon, "My Philosophy," *XXL Magazine*, May 2005, 106–7.

63. Dre, A. L., "Lyrical Blades," *The Source Magazine*, December 1995, 52.

64. RZA and Chris Norris, *The Wu-Tang Manual* (New York: Riverhead Books, 2005), 209.

65. "1000 Albums to Hear Before You Die," *The Guardian*, November 19, 2007, http://www.proquest.com.dmvgateway.nysed.gov/ (accessed July 22, 2010).

66. "Sony's Razor Sharp," *Billboard Magazine*, July 7, 1996, 6.

67. Brannan, Eddie, "Phantom of the Opera," *Trace Urban Magazine*, Issue 22, 1999, 53 (50–55).

68. Coolidge, Warren, "Record Report: Ironman," *The Source Magazine*. December 1996, 124.

69. Mao, Chairman, "Next Chamber," *Vibe Magazine*, September 1996, 112.

70. Allmusic.com credits the date as 1965, others have 1968.

71. The Blackspot, "Revolutions: Ghostface Killah Iron Man," *Vibe Magazine*, December 1996/January 1997, 186

72. DeCurtis, Anthony, "Wu Tang Family Values," *Rolling Stone Magazine*, July 10, 1997–July 24, 1997, 86.

73. In *Ironman*'s thank-yous it reads: "This album is dedicated to the memory of Davon Coles 1971–1994. I'll always love you—rest in peace."

74. http://allmusic.com/cg/amg.dll?p=amg&sql=10:fvftxqr0ldae.

75. Coolidge, Warren, "Record Report: Ironman," *The Source Magazine*. December 1996, 124.

76. Valdes, Mimi, "Enter the Ironman," *Vibe Magazine*, February 1997, 56.

77. Ibid.

78. Fernando Jr., S. H., "Recordings: Ironman," *Rolling Stone Magazine*, December 12, 1996, 82.

79. Fernando, Jr., S. H., "Beat You Down," *Vibe Magazine*, September 1998, 147 (146–49).

80. Farley, Christopher John, "Searching for the Perfect Beat," *Time Magazine*, December 11, 2000, 83.

CHAPTER 6
Wu-Tang Goes Worldwide

WU-TANG FOREVER

Disc One: Wu-Revolution/Reunited/For Heaven's Sake/Cash Still Rules/Scary Hours (Still Don't Nothing Move But the Money)/Visionz/As High as Wu-Tang Get/Severe Punishment/Older Gods/Maria/A Better Tomorrow/It's Yourz
  Disc Two: Intro/Triumph/Impossible/Little Ghetto Boys/Deadly Melody/The City/The Projects/Bells of War/The M.G.M./Dog Shit/Duck Seazon/Hellz Wind Staff/Heaterz/Black Shampoo/Second Coming/The Closing
  International Version: Sunshower/Projects (International Remix)

Though individual members gained solo success (while touting the greatness of Wu-Tang Clan), the time was ripe for Wu-Tang Clan to reunite and record a new group album. But much had changed since 1993. Egos had grown with their clout and RZA, despite still being within his five-year plan, was not able to administer as much creative control as he had in the past. *Wu-Tang Forever* was released after the untimely deaths of the Notorious B.I.G. (March 9, 1997) and, six months prior, Tupac Shakur (September 16, 1996). Perhaps as an influence from the latter, whose *All Eyez on Me* (1996) was one of the first commercially released hip-hop double albums, *Wu-Tang Forever* was made a double disc as well. Wu-Tang Clan was in Los Angeles recording at the time of Notorious B.I.G.'s murder.[1]

Hip-hop was losing heroes and gaining martyrs. In a 1997 *Rolling Stone Magazine* article, Masta Killa, by this time an official Wu-Tang Clan member, said, "I feel the world is in a state of confusion. We lost two great heroes: Biggie Smalls and Tupac Shakur. The world needs guidance. We the gods that gotta come through with the mathematics to see everything straight, to give condolence to the world."[2]

Influencing the world is an ambitious goal, but considering the wave of popularity Wu-Tang Clan was riding, it was feasible. Wu-Tang Clan had already begun shoring up their brand, for example, launching Wu-Wear clothing in 1995. But while most anything with the Wu logo attached to it sold well, it was first and foremost the music that made such influence possible. *Wu-Tang Forever* was originally given a February 2007 release date, which already had been shifted to April 1997 by the time a *The Source Magazine* cover story that followed the group as they were recording the album hit newsstands. Citing too many distractions in New York City, Wu-Tang Clan moved to California's Oakwood Apartments.[3] In California they recorded at Ameraycan Studios in West Hollywood.[4]

The first song sent to radio, though it wasn't an official single, was the sprawling "Triumph," which clocks in at more than six minutes and features every Wu-Tang Clan member, including Cappadonna, and lacks any semblance of a chorus. Ten MCs on one song is daunting but it was a welcome salve for Wu-Tang Clan fans awaiting the group's return (though they never really left). After a short, spoken intro from Ol' Dirty Bastard—then going by the moniker of Osirus—Inspectah Deck delivers the first, and probably most applauded, rhymes of *Wu-Tang Forever*. Kicking "I bomb atomically, Socrates' philosophies and hypothesis can't define how I be dropping these mockeries, lyrically perform armed robbery" to start, the rhyme would earn Inspectah Deck a "Hip-Hop Quotable" in the June 1997 issue of *The Source Magazine*, which featured a Wu-Tang Clan cover.[5]

By the time of *Wu-Tang Forever*'s release on June 3, 1997, the Wu-Tang Clan's popularity was at a fever pitch. Said *Entertainment Weekly* in its review of the album: "*Forever* is rap's event movie of the summer. A sprawling sequel to a hip-hop benchmark, the 27-track double CD is destined to 'sell more copies than Kinko's,' as Wu-Tang mastermind, the RZA, forecasts on *Forever's* 'Reunited.' "[6] Before getting to hear "Reunited," *Wu-Tang Forever*'s second track, one must first sit through its longwinded opening track, "Wu-Revolution." The first song of the album's first disc finds Popa Wu preaching principles of the Five Percent Nation. When RZA famously said kids should buy *Wu-Tang Forever* instead of going to summer school, few took it literally, but the overbearing sermonizing heard on "Wu-Revolution" is enough to fool the casual listener into believing his earnestness.

Credit RZA's savvy because a three-year hiatus between *Enter the Wu-Tang* and about a year since the last solo effort from an original member (Ghostface Killah's *Ironman*) meant fans were guaranteed to listen to the entire track, at least the first time they play the album, for fear of missing anything. While Popa Wu surely drops jewels, it is nothing even the casual Wu-Tang fan would not have heard before. Those hotly anticipating new Wu-Tang music would have been better off skipping to the last 20 seconds of the nearly seven-minute track when sampled kung-fu film dialogue of a monk asserting that in order for the Shaolin kung-fu he teaches to survive, "We must expand, get more pupils . . . so that the knowledge will spread."

The lessons officially begin with the first proper song, "Reunited." The song is a good example of some of the inconsistencies many outlets cited when reviewing *Wu-Tang Forever*. For the track, RZA matches violin strings and shimmering synth sounds to a staid drum track. GZA sets things off with a true-to-form and precise verse that describes Wu-Tang's position in the hip-hop hierarchy. "Reunited, double LP, we're all excited, struck a match to the underground, industry ignited," he unworriedly raps. But then Ol' Dirty Bastard follows with a belligerent verse that seems to only be included for the sake of having ODB on the album. RZA returns to the song's focus, declaring, "We return like Jesus, when the whole world need us," before Method Man closes out the song.

For a track with four Wu-Tang Clan MCs, "Reunited" is rather stoic, lacking any samples. On *Wu-Tang Forever*, RZA noticeably begins straying from the sample-heavy imprint that permeated his production discography thus far. In 1996, RZA began studying music theory. Depending on who you ask, this was either prudent or puzzling. For the former, exorbitant sample fees were eating into recording costs. The Gladys Knight sample heard on "C.R.E.A.M." cost a relatively cheap $2,000 in 1993. In comparison, clearing the samples of the film *Shogun Assassin* on GZA's *Liquid Swords* just two years later cost $10,000. In a few years, with the increasing expense of samples as a root cause, many producers including RZA started relying on keyboards to create wholly original beats.[7] While RZA may not have been hurting for money as other producers may have, it nevertheless affects a project's bottom line.

The faction questioning RZA's newfound taste for wholly original recordings on the other hand cried foul due to their aversion to accepting change. Now instead of bending and stretching samples to his will, RZA was bringing in musicians to play the music live. RZA was now a musical conductor in the literal sense. Another reason for RZA's altering his approach to his production was all the imitators of his sound popping up. RZA told the *New York Times* in 1998, "After five years and more than 250 songs, my sound is a common trait. I realized two years ago people were going to jump in my world and start imitating it. That's when I started studying the music. Because they can't do that, they can't imitate that."[8]

The change in dynamics of the beats' creation does not adversely affect the next pair of songs, "For Heaven's Sake" and "Cash Still Rules/Scary Hours (Still Don't Nothing Move But the Money)." "For Heaven's Sake" is standard battle rap fare and features the soon to be imitated, sped up vocal sample, from King Floyd's "Don't Leave Me Lonely" (1971), for its hook. "Cash Still Rules" is one of the first disc's highlights. Raekwon, Method Man, and Ghostface, a trio that would release their own formal album called *Wu-Massacre* 13 years later, over a somber, looped vocal hum deliver rhymes about robberies, hand-to-hand drug sales, and two-faced cops. Ghostface in particular gets so focused in his delivery that the song's beat drops out while he continues to rhyme. The inspiring beat is provided not by RZA but by 4th Disciple. While on previous Wu-Tang Clan albums RZA would usually handle all the beats save for one or two, of the 27 total tracks on the domestic version of *Wu-Tang Forever*, seven of the tracks were produced by others including True Master, Inspectah Deck, and 4th Disciple.

"Visionz" follows and is produced by Inpectah Deck, and features rhymes from Method Man, Raekwon, Masta Killa, Deck, and Ghostface. It is pretty standard Wu-Tang fare with the beat's synth chords leaning toward monotony. Ol' Dirty Bastard returns and his energy is better channeled by providing the chorus for "As High as Wu-Tang Get": "As high as Wu-Tang get, Allah allow us pop this shit, Just like black shoe fit, If you can't wear it, well don't fuck with it!," barks ODB between and after single, but potent, verses from GZA and Method Man. By the seventh song, "Severe Punishment," all of the Wu-Tang Clan's members have appeared on the album as U-God provides the lead-off verse.

"Severe Punishment" possesses the makings of a classic Wu-Tang Clan posse cut. The kung-fu dialogue heard at its start—a character tells another that he must be punished—sets the tone for the song. The virtual receivers of retribution are potential rivals who are the targets of the battle rhymes unleashed by the song's participants (in order of appearance: U-God, GZA, Raekwon, RZA, and Masta Killa). RZA, who deliberately rhymes on *Wu-Tang Forever* much more than on previous Wu-Tang Clan albums, uses the moment to mention needing to "muscle the industrial to make a hustle and politic with Lyor and Russell." RZA is referring to Lyor Cohen and Russell Simmons, longtime hip-hop recording industry moguls that the producer/rapper was becoming on par with thanks to the growth of the Wu-Tang Clan brand and businesses.

On "Older Gods" Raekwon and Ghostface reunite with a closing verse from GZA. Ghostface's stream-of-consciousness rhymes are front and center. Again, rhymes such as "Got these vegetable lasagna niggas in they whips jumping out they seats, 18 Bronzeman Part II, we like Dorothy Hamill on ice" are done no justice written down on paper.[9] The cadence and playful intensity of Ghostface's delivery is simply best heard rather than read. Raekwon's rhymes are just as dense thanks to his ceaseless use of slang but they are a tad bit more decipherable than Ghostface's. After their respective verses, the duo shares the chorus: "Yo, the older God put me on and had to rock this, maintain three sixty Lord live prosperous/It only takes a lesson a day, just to analyze life, one time in the respectable mind." The hook alludes directly to teachings of the Five Percent Nation since members calling themselves "Gods" and "living 360" refers to a complete circle or cipher of knowledge, an important concept for Five Percenters. The GZA verse feels almost like an addendum since it arrives after the lone hook, but is nevertheless a welcome addition.

However, on "Maria," Ol' Dirty Bastard once again manages to mention having contracted gonorrhea in his rhyme but not before declaring, "This is for the bitches!" The song is evidence to the Wu-Tang's contradictions in regards to espousing righteousness but still dropping misogynistic lyrics. Those who paid attention to "Wu-Revolution" heard Popa Wu showing disdain for those "calling my Black woman a bitch." Cappadonna drops a salacious verse in between ODB's first two X-rated verses and RZA devotes his bars to castigating a loose woman over a muddy bass line lifted from versatile rock band Blood, Sweat & Tears' "I Love You More Than You'll Ever Know" (1968) and drums from Lee Dorsey's "Get Out of My Life, Woman" from his *Ride Your Pony* (1966) album. The moral dichotomy of the Wu-Tang is plainly illustrated again with "A Better Tomorrow."

"A Better Tomorrow" finds Inspectah Deck, Masta Killa, U-God, RZA, and Method Man delivering a teach-the-kids-to-do-right song in the realm of Slick Rick's "Hey Young World." All of the song's participants deliver heartfelt verses on the topic but its theme is readily summed up in the hook (handled by Masta Killah and Inspectah Deck): "You can't party your life away, drink your life away, smoke your life away, fuck your life away, dream your life away, scheme your life away, cause your seeds grow up the same way." While the song can be deemed rote and preachy, Wu-Tang Clan doesn't take the easy way out— wrapping hidden lessons amid the usual sex and violence—and instead deliver an unfiltered message. RZA possesses renown for being Wu-Tang Clan's de facto leader and Method Man, who delivers the closing verse, is a superstar thanks to his platinum-selling *Tical*; the rest of the track's participants didn't enjoy as much clout. Nevertheless, Inspectah Deck, Masta Killa, and U-God deliver poignant verses over producer 4th Disciple's sublime keys, sampled from pianist Pete Nero's "A Time for Us" (1969), and prickly drums. "A Better Tomorrow" is one of Wu-Tang's most tragically unheralded songs.

The first disc of *Wu-Tang Forever* closes out with "It's Yourz," the album's lone official single. Produced by RZA, it samples Gaz's "Sing Sing," a popular breakbeat, and bassist Wilbur "Bad" Bascomb's "Black Grass" (1973) for its meandering, but funky, drum track. The title is a subtle homage to rapper T-La Rock's "It's Yours." There are no overreaching themes here; "It's Yourz" is strictly Wu-Tang Clan declaring their continued dominance. This is brought home in the RZA-rapped hook whose opening line declares, "It's yours! The world in the palm of your hand," and eventually closes with "It's yours, double LP from Wu-Tang Clan!" "It's Yourz" would only peak at #75 on the *Billboard* R&B/Hip-Hop Songs chart.

RZA begins the second disc of *Wu-Tang Forever* with a short diatribe where he asserts that Wu-Tang Clan is "true Hip-Hop in its purest form." RZA also makes sure to mention that producers who merely take a familiar R&B loop to create a hit (a technique Bad Boy Records artists were successful at) are not the "sound of the culture." RZA also goes as far as to admonish MCs for not paying their proper dues, biting styles Wu-Tang Clan used first ("We told you on the Cuban Link [sic] album don't bite our shit") and all that "player bullshit." Apparently no one mentioned to RZA the irony of chastising "All that player dressing up . . . acting like this some kind of fashion," when they launched Wu-Wear Clothing two years earlier.

However, it is tough to argue with RZA's points since the intro launches into the resounding "Triumph." With that, the second disc, which critics have cited as the stronger of the two, is off to a blistering start. After "Triumph" is the equally bombastic "Impossible." R&B singer and Razor Sharp Records signee Tekitha uses the opening melody of Beethoven's "Sonata Pathétique" (1799) to sing, "For you to defeat, the Gods . . . impossible!," with a desperate timbre throughout the 4th Disciple–produced, and RZA-coproduced, track. 4th Disciple adds dingy bass and rugged drums to Beethoven's chords to create a menacing instrumental for the rhymes of RZA, U-God, and Ghostface. It is Ghostface's verse, a film-script worthy and particularly vivid tale of a victim of street violence, that received the most attention, earning the honor "Hip-Hop Quotable" for the entire year of 1997 in the February 1998 issue of *The Source Magazine*. Raekwon closes the song with a speech about the perils of gun violence.[10]

Raekwon continues with the cautionary tales in "Little Ghetto Boys." RZA samples Donny Hathaway's "Little Ghetto Boy" (1972) for the hook and O. V. Wright's "Ghetto Child" (1973) for the somber keys buried beneath the shadowy bass and distorted drums. Raekwon's verse is a narrative about a young neophyte drug dealer who ends up in a casket. However, Cappadonna's verse is about rappers mimicking the Wu-Tang aesthetic. "Half the East coast sounding like Rae," spouts Cappadonna midway through his first verse. While the support of Cappadonna for his brethren is commendable, his verse is still off topic. "Deadly Melody" follows with drums that are so distorted with reverb that it must be intentional. The song serves as a showcase track with most of the Wu-Tang players appearing (Masta Killa, U-God, RZA, Method Man, GZA, Ghostface, and Method Man charge Streetlife).

No easy task considering they manage to fit nine verses inside a four minute and 20 second track.

Inspectah Deck may be missing from "Deadly Melody" but on the selection that follows, "The City," he is the only participant. Though Deck is responsible for many of Wu-Tang Clan's more popular verses (his turns on "Triumph" and "C.R.E.A.M." are examples), at this point he has yet to release a solo album. Deck takes the 4th Disciple beat, distorted horn samples slipped in amid waning synth tones, as his own solo song. While the tune is adequate in its role as an album cut, it doesn't spark interest for an Inspectah Deck solo as much as any of his select verses.

The next few songs—"The Projects," "Bells of War," "The M.G.M."— ground the middle of the album, mainly because its two dominant players, Ghostface and Raekwon, are two of Wu-Tang Clan's most fervent and charismatic voices. "The Projects" begins with a quick skit-like intro where Raekwon places a phone call where the receiver, Wu-Tang Clan affiliate Shyhiem, tells him he's busy studying the 120 Lessons and to call him back at the God hour.[11] The song's title leads listeners to believe it is about housing project living, where all the song's participants (Raekwon, Method Man, Ghostface) have resided at one time or another. However, the song's players deliver rhymes focused more on style. Ghostface drops a particularly X-rated verse but Method Man delivers the stand-out double entendre quip when he rhymes: "Double O-seven mark, the secret agent that Max/well and Get Smart, through entertainment."[12]

"Bells of War" also sports a deceptive title thanks to its smoothly efficient drums, courtesy of jazz saxophonists Tom Scott's "Sneakin' in the Back" from the *Tom Scott and the L.A. Express* (1974) album, and warm bell chimes that are more gentle than explosive. Literally the middle of the album, the eighth song on the 16-song second disc (domestic version), "Bells of War" is the soul of the album. The song begins with a cocksure verse from U-God, and Method Man follows with an equally confident verse. RZA follows, delivering his typically verbally dexterous and almanac-worthy prose, via his trademark, choppy flow. He begins, "It's common sense how I master my circum-fer-ence, you dense/I get locked the fuck up, released on my own recognizance," and eventually praises his production skills via rap simile: "My tracks remain unforgettable, like Ol' Nat Cole."

After RZA ends his verse, there comes an extended interlude. First Masta Killa delivers a short but potent rhyme: "The weight of the fam is on our back and we can't fall/Victim to this long hall of fame, meaning nothin'/We came to punish the glutton with a substance that can't be contained, Wu-Tang." Method Man then quickly barks at "punk motherfuckers" who are scared to speak to Wu-Tang Clan members in the club. Finally, Raekwon holds court with unnamed voices, the last sounds like Ghostface, discussing boxers including Pernell Whitaker and Mike Tyson.

When Raekwon finishes his fight-night commentary Ghostface begins the song's final verse, loaded with more of his abstract references. RZA closes out the song talking about the invincibility of the Wu-Tang Clan and it is in this particular rant where he famously says, "I was telling Shorty like, Yo Shorty, you don't even gotta go to summer school. Pick up the Wu-Tang double CD and you'll get all the education you need this year." Not necessarily the soundest of advice, but Wu-Tang Clan did have plenty of impressionable ears soaking in their teachings.

One of RZA's pupils in the sciences of hip-hop production is True Master, who produces "The M.G.M." Over steady drums, silky strings, and a clipped sample of a vocal hum, Ghostface and Raekwon trade rhymes two to three lines at a time, finishing each other's sentences and thoughts, like the old friends they are, about a fight-night adventure at Las Vegas' M.G.M. Grand Hotel for a little over two minutes. A short but endearing song due to the savvy rhyme duo within a group that is Raekwon and Ghostface, the song's brevity makes it sound like a sonic appetizer. The next song trades rhyme savoir-faire for Ol' Dirty Bastard's belligerent bombast on the microphone. On "Dog Shit" Ol' Dirty Bastard at times raps from the perspective of a canine. Over clashing piano chords and cavernous drums, he barks, "Ol Dirt Dog, but I'm not dogged out, here comes Rover sniffing at your ass, But pardon me bitch, as I shit on your grass, that means hoe, you been shit-ted on!" The song should be taken at its face value—the Wu-Tang Clan's court jester's contribution to the album. Lost in Ol' Dirty Bastard's boisterous delivery, and general misogyny, are fundamentally sound rhymes such as "She flew in like calm breeze, tall brown skin her weave like palm trees, I went coconuts, Dipped my Dunkin' between your Donut."

"Dog Shit" is Ol' Dirty Bastard's penultimate appearance on *Wu-Tang Forever*. In hindsight it is a telltale sign of the doomed Wu-Tang Clan member becoming less and less of a presence in the Wu-Tang Clan's realm. Ol' Dirty only managed to appear on GZA's *Liquid Swords* album during the first wave of Wu-Tang Clan releases, and would only release one more proper album of new material before his death in 2004. Despite a spotty recording career, Ol' Dirty was still one of Wu-Tang Clan's most popular artists so his inclusion in group efforts, no matter how limited, was essential.

"Duck Seazon" features verses from RZA and Method Man book-ended by two verses from Raekwon. Solemn tones are laid over a generic drum track leaving the listener no choice but to pay attention to the rhymes. The song is a weak point in the strong second half of *Wu-Tang Forever* for this reason. The last 30 seconds of the track feature sample sounds of a kung-fu film battle with weapons followed by dialogue about someone "daring to rebuild the Wu-Tang Clan." The same kung-fu fight audio is used throughout "Hellz Wind Staff," another standout Wu-Tang Clan marathon effort. Relatively frequent guest Streetlife delivers the first verse followed by Ghostface, Inspectah Deck, Method Man, RZA, and Raekwon. A swift drum track manages to help heighten the intensity of the humming bass line, which is sampled from The Doors' "The End" from the group's 1976, self-titled debut album.

More rappers continue to make space for themselves over the next instrumental, this time from True Master, on "Heaterz." The song features the MCs rhyming over a loop of 1964's "Giving Up," by Gladys Knight & the Pips, which has been slowed down and retrofitted with burlier drums. Pretty standard brash battle raps abound here, with the song's biggest curiosity being Ol' Dirty Bastard's contribution of a scant four lines. A pleasanter surprise is the seductive and sophisticated "Black Shampoo." Rap songs with romantic flare have been done by Wu-Tang Clan members before (Ghostface's "Camay" comes readily to mind), but this is a standout track that happens to be a solo effort (Method Man does speak at length at the song's epilogue) from U-God, the Wu-Tang Clan's least revered member. This is mostly due to a deficiency in appearances beginning all the way back with "Protect Ya Neck" when U-God contributed a scant four-bar rhyme to the seminal Wu-Tang Clan song. Suddenly the prospects of a U-God solo album seemed more feasible.

After "Black Shampoo" concludes, all the Wu-Tang Clan members are absent on "Second Coming," an R&B song sung by Tekitha. Considering lyrics such as, "False MC's are melting, in the dark, all the weak LP's are going down," are wailed by Tekitha over sobering chords with resolute intensity, the song is a soulfully sung ode to the Wu-Tang's continued reign. "Second Coming" immediately segues into "The Closing," the finale of the domestic version of *Wu-Tang Forever*, where Raekwon uses his soapbox to let rival MCs know he's aware of their copycat antics. The international version of *Wu-Tang Forever* includes "Sunshower," a RZA solo that he's attested to containing his favorite personal verse of all time, and an "International Remix" of "The Projects," whose only difference from the original is an alternate, string-laden beat.[13] RZA told *Rolling Stone Magazine* that he created "Sunshower" in a mere three minutes: "It's about five, six, seven different sounds up in there. . . . Throw thunder and lightning to it . . . then make a loop off that. Most rap uses two bar loops, one bar loops; I made an *eight*-bar loop. . . . When the shit all mixes together, it's going to sound crazy, man."[14]

With both aspiring and established producers keeping tabs on RZA's modus operandi, the overwhelming addition to his production arsenal on *Wu-Tang Forever* is his use of string samples. In a 1997 story, "Strains of Violin in Slick, Smooth Rap," the *New York Times* compared the album's production to a Pynchon novel thanks to its dense and complex collage of sounds while noting, "Violins are all over the album."[15] In his 1997 review of *Wu-Tang Forever* in the *Village Voice*, writer Greg Tate noted, "Not since Isaac Hayes—the RZA's number one influence, I'd wage—has any black pop artist used strings in a sexier or spookier manner."[16] RZA and Wu-Tang Clan would eventually go on to work with the late Isaac Hayes, who appears and performs on their next album, *The W* (1999).

Until then, Wu-Tang Clan would enjoy their relatively triumphant return. With *Wu-Tang Forever*—as certain members had now become bankable stars in their own right—RZA managed to temper everyone's growing egos into a united front with his production. It's a wonder the final product sounds so cohesive since RZA didn't have the control he wanted on the album. In hindsight, he told *Trace Magazine* in 1998 that the album was too slapdash and certain members were not coming to the studio to collaborate.[17] Even though it lacked radio accessible tracks, *Wu-Tang Forever* was still a huge hit. The album debuted at #1 on both the *Billboard* R&B/Hip-Hop Albums chart and the *Billboard* Hot 200 chart.

Despite the modest radio play, *Wu-Tang Forever* would eventually sell four times platinum. *Wu-Tang Forever* stayed on the *Billboard* charts for 41 weeks.[18] The CD version of the album was an enhanced compact disc, first introduced in 1994, and was the first release under an agreement with BMG and America Online that granted buyers who weren't already subscribers 50 free hours of AOL service.[19] Even without the added value of enhanced CDs, rap consumers were embracing rap double albums. "If there was any question whether rap fans would shell out for double CDs, it was answered by chart-topping sets from the Notorious B.I.G., Bone Thugs-N-Harmony, the Wu-Tang Clan, Rakim and 2Pac," reported *USA* Today in 1997.[20]

On its release the critical reception to *Wu-Tang Forever* was overwhelmingly positive. "Like their forebears in Public Enemy, Wu-Tang are musical revolutionaries, unafraid to bring the noise along with their trunk of funk," wrote *Entertainment Weekly* in 1997.[21] The *Village Voice* saw the album as more evidence of hip-hop's never-ending lifeblood: "This has been the history of Hip-Hop from the get-go: soon as you declare Hip-Hop dead, Hip-Hop reanimates," wrote Greg Tate in his positive review of the album.[22]

In time, perhaps after the excitement of Wu-mania had worn off, praise for the album would wane. Twenty-seven tracks of Wu-Tang's lyrically complex and cerebral material is hard to swallow in one sitting. Also, and perhaps most importantly, Wu-Tang Clan wasn't the only sizeable fish in the hip-hop pond at the time of their sophomore album's release. Said journalist Elliott Wilson in his 2000 *XXL Magazine* cover story on Wu-Tang Clan of *Wu-Tang Forever*'s indifferent reception, "The biggest reason the lengthy opus has been stained with the flop tag is simply that '97 was the year of Bad Boy."[23] Indeed, Bad Boy Records music was ruling the hip-hop charts, streets, and parties. The Sean "Diddy" Combs–led label's commercial dominance was irrefutable. The Notorious B.I.G.'s posthumous *Life After Death* (1997) album would eventually be certified 10 times platinum and Diddy's (then billed as Puff Daddy & The Family) *No Way Out* (1997) album would eventually be certified seven times platinum. Even rapper-turned-actor Will Smith's *Big Willie Style* (1997) album would end up selling nine times platinum.

Instead of pandering to the mainstream with easily remembered pop hooks and '80s samples, a la Bad Boy, Wu-Tang Clan made an impact on the mainstream while sticking to their musical script. "This group is probably the most important one in hip-hop today," opined the *New York Times* in 1997.[24] *Wu-Tang Forever* also marked the end of RZA's five-year plan where he executed complete creative control of Wu-Tang Clan's musical output, group-wise and individually. "For the first five albums, up through Wu-Tang Forever. Everything went exactly as planned," said RZA in Brian Coleman's book *Check the Technique: Liner Notes for Hip-Hop Junkies.*[25]

Considering the indelible success RZA achieved, it's a wonder more Wu-Tang Clan members didn't continue with the program. However, the subsequent years, and albums, would find Wu-Tang Clan members trying to prove that they were capable of solo success without RZA's heavy-handed influence. RZA would also release solo material, not including his 1994 released side project with the Gravediggaz titled *6 Feet Deep.* There were also still solo albums to be released from Inspectah Deck, U-God, and Masta Killa.

The new wave of Wu-Tang Clan solo releases—solo albums released after Wu-Tang Clan's second album *Wu-Tang Forever*, but before their third album, *The W*—would have fleeting moments of success. But the period would be marred by some musical and topical experimentation that, though noble, would alienate many of their longtime listeners. However, finding the musical gems in this period of Wu-Tang Clan music is well worth the hunt.

NOTES

1. Smith, R. J., "Phantoms of the Hip-Hopera," *Spin Magazine*, July 1997, 70 (68–74, 126).

2. DeCurtis, Anthony, "Wu Tang Family Values," *Rolling Stone Magazine*, July 10, 1997–July 24, 1997, 86.

3. Fernando, Jr., S. H. (add reporting by Selwyn Seyfu Hinds), "Lords of Chaos," *The Source Magazine*, June 1997, 104 (104–110, 132).

4. RZA and Chris Norris, *The Tao of Wu* (New York: Riverhead Books, 2009), 132.

5. "Hip-Hop Quotable: Inspectah Deck," *The Source Magazine*, June 1997, 41.

6. Diehl, Matt, "More Tang for the Buck," *Entertainment Weekly*, June 6, 1997, 65.

7. Morales, Riggs, "The Death of Sampling," *The Source*, December 2000, 55.

8. Pareles, Jon, "Pay Attention: Reinvention; No Prevention," *The New York Times*, November 5, 1998, Section E, 1.

9. "Whips" is hip-hop slang for cars; *18 Bronzemen* is a kung-fu film.

10. "Hip-Hop Quotable: Ghostface 'Impossible,' " *The Source Magazine*, February 1998, 71.

11. The "God Hour" is 7:00 PM, corresponding to the numeral seven (7), which stands for "God and perfection" in the Nation of Gods and Earths' "Supreme Numerals."

12. To max is hip-hop slang to relax or cool out while agent Maxwell Smart is the main character of the spy themed, late 1960s TV sitcom *Get Smart*.

13. Diehl, Matt, "Microphone Fiend," *XXL Magazine*, August 2001, 114 (114–17).

14. Smith, RJ, "Phantoms of the Hip-Hopera," *Spin Magazine*, July 1997, 72 (68–74, 126).

15. Strauss, Neil, "Strains of Violin in Slick, Smooth Rap," *The New York Times*, June 10, 1997, 13.

16. Tate, Greg, "Wu-Dunit," *Village Voice*, June 24, 1997, 63.

17. Ashon, Will, "RZA as Bobby Digital" *Trace Urban Magazine*, November 1998, 54 (48–56).

18. Bower, Amanda, Castronovo, Val, Minhua, Ling, Martens, Ellin, Rawe, Julie, Song, Sora, Stein, Joel, and Tyrangiel, Josh, "Theories of Relativity," *Time Magazine*, December 11, 2000, 39.

19. Bermant, Charles, "Using the World Wide Web to Enhance Music Compact Disks," *The New York Times*, May 5, 1997, 9.

20. Jones, Steve, "Led by Puff Daddy, Rap Rhythms Underscore All Urban Music," *USA Today*, December 29, 1997, 4.

21. Diehl, "More Tang for the Buck."

22. Tate, Greg, "Wu-Dunit," *Village Voice*, June 24, 1997, 63.

23. Wilson, Elliott, "Victory," *XXL Magazine*, October 2000, 106.

24. Strauss, Neil, "Strains of Violin in Slick, Smooth Rap," *The New York Times*, June 10, 1997, 13.

25. Coleman, Brian, *Check the Technique: Liner Notes for Hip-Hop Junkies* (New York: Villard, 2005, 2007), 452.

CHAPTER 7
The Re-up: The Second Wave
(More Wu-Tang Clan Solos)

1997 was fiscally a great year for hip-hop. "Urban music had a decidedly hip-hop flavor this year, as rappers dominated both commercially and critically. And most R&B was either rap-laced or had a hip-hop sensibility," said *USA Today* at the end of 1997.[1] Wu-Tang Clan was intrinsic to this success since their sophomore album *Wu-Tang Forever* sold 600,000 copies during its first week of release in June 1997, and was certified four times platinum by October 1997. RZA believes that during the recording of the album the administration of Wu-Tang Clan music was more of a democracy than the dictatorship it had previously been. *Wu-Tang Forever*'s #1 debut on the *Billboard* R&B/Hip-Hop Albums chart and *Billboard* Hot 200 chart marked the end of RZA's iron rule.[2] Thus, 1997 would mark the end of the uninterrupted rise and reign of the Wu-Tang Clan, sort of.

"The group's next step is to expand its grip and reach more white teenagers and students, making it the pre-eminent collective—period," wrote Neil Strauss in a 1997 *Rolling Stone Magazine* story on RZA.[3] A tour with the hip-hop friendly rock band Rage Against the Machine across the United States was a good way for Wu-Tang Clan to make further inroads into new listening demographics. The group's live shows were a powder keg of energy that their fans usually enjoyed, but the performances were mostly spot dates and smaller venues. RZA was keenly aware of the group's need to continue penetrating into mainstream America. With their radio and video play not commensurate with their popularity, they would bring their music to the people. However, other members of Wu-Tang Clan weren't thinking as long term as RZA. Instead of focusing on winning new fans by barnstorming to Rage's White, college crowd, Wu-Tang members wanted to perform for more familiar audiences. The prospect of making more money on their own tour, the matter of more solo records to be made, and individuals citing new priorities—family, financial, et al.—were surely a factor as well.

Nevertheless, RZA managed to talk Wu-Tang Clan into embarking on the Rage Against the Machine headlined tour, but never finished. RZA cites the tour (after instances of missing members and violence at shows, Wu-Tang Clan would be replaced in August 1997 by Philadelphia hip-hop group The Roots) as the moment Wu-Tang Clan unofficially disbanded.[4] It would not be the only time. Legal troubles, which were always around the corner with Wu-Tang Clan, began piling on as well.

In October 1997, Method Man was charged for allegedly knocking a bouncer unconscious at Manhattan nightclub the Palladium, though the charges were eventually dropped.[5] In November 1997, Ol' Dirty Bastard was arrested in Brooklyn over charges of not paying $35,000 in child support. In December 1997, Ghostface Killah was caught carrying a .357 Magnum handgun with hollow point bullets in Harlem, New York.[6] Late 1997's troubles would only continue into the following year.

It wasn't all bad, though not exactly good, for Wu-Tang Clan in the media's scope. In February 1998, Ol' Dirty Bastard and some friends saved a child (Maati Lovell) who was pinned under a car after being struck by the vehicle in Manhattan. About a day after news of the heroics was reported, on February 25, 1998, Ol' Dirty Bastard infamously interrupted Shawn Colvin's Song of the Year Award acceptance speech at the 40th Annual Grammy Awards. "Puffy is good . . . but Wu-Tang is the best," said the rapper in regard to *Wu-Tang Forever* having lost out in the Best Rap Album category to Diddy's *No Way Out*. The Grammy Awards stunt would be one of many examples of Ol' Dirty Bastard's extracurricular antics—in late June 1998 the rapper was shot, though not gravely injured, by thugs who robbed him of jewelry in his girlfriend's home—overshadowing his musical output.

RZA slowed his musical output during this period as well. He had already begun studying music theory during the recording of *Wu-Tang Forever*, and at the time of an interview with *Rolling Stone* that appeared in September 1997, it was reported that he was at work on

13 records by Wu-Tang Clan affiliates. These auxiliary groups included R&B singer Tekitha, rapper Killah Priest, as well as the group—put together by RZA—he was a member of—Killarmy (with 60 Second Assassin, Prodigal Sunn, and Hell Razah). These are just a few of Wu-Tang Clan's extended family of acts.

After *Wu-Tang Forever*, willfully or not, RZA gave up his duties of overseeing the entire Clan's direction. Thanks to the demand of individual members to share their talents, even the best laid of RZA's plans were constantly being altered on the fly. Shortly before the release of the *Bobby Digital in Stereo* album, in a 1997 interview with *Trace Magazine* RZA revealed just how difficult it was to follow any sort of plan or schedule with regards to Wu-Tang Clan's solo acts:

> [Cappadonna] wasn't originally planned. Deck was supposed to have came before Ghostface. Because Ghost came with Raekwon, *Cuban Linx* business caused Ghostface to come before Deck. . . . There shoulda been a second ODB album by now but his own way of doing business and doing work has prohibited that. There shoulda been a second Method Man album already also. But our own business and Meth's business from jumping on everybody else's goddamn records prevents some of those things.[7]

Moving forward, RZA maintained close ties with Ghostface, U-God, Masta Killa, and the many Wu-affiliates while Oli "Power" Grant was tasked with Raekwon and Inspectah Deck. RZA's brother, Mitchell "Divine" Diggs, was charged with Method Man and Cappadonna, and unsurprisingly Ol' Dirty Bastard was a loose cannon.[8] Speaking on the then upcoming release of *Wu-Tang Forever*, in mid-1997 RZA told *Rolling Stone*, "After this Wu-Tang album, I'm gonna pull back some from producing any album. I think I laid down a good pattern of hip-hop production for the whole world. . . . I brought strings into hip-hop. . . . I got everybody running back to snoop for piano loops. So, with that foundation laid down, I think Ghostface, Raekwon and Meth could produce their own albums. Then, on the next Wu-Tang album, we'll come back and put that into one big bowl of soup for you again."[9]

Of the albums released after *Wu-Tang Forever* and before Wu-Tang Clan's next group album, *The W*, in November 2000, as he predicted, RZA's participation was scattershot. For example, he would executive produce, provide production for, and perform on Ghostface Killah's *Supreme Clientele* but would be completely absent from Raekwon's *Immobilarity*. In most cases, especially for the latter, RZA's presence would be sorely missed.

It was not until November 1998, over a year since *Wu-Tang Forever*'s release, that Wu-Tang Clan members would release new albums; Method Man's sophomore effort *Tical 2000: Judgement Day*, and RZA's solo debut, *RZA as Bobby Digital in Stereo*, hit stores within a week of each other.[10] GZA/Genius would follow with *Beneath the Surface*, his third album, in June 1999. Inspectah Deck would finally release his debut album, *Uncontrolled Substance*, in September 1999, followed shortly by Ol' Dirty Bastard's sophomore re-up *Nigga Please*. It would be U-God's turn at a solo album with *Golden Arms Redemption* in October 1999, and Raekwon's sophomore album *Immobilarity* would arrive a month later. Finally, with Wu-Tang Clan's rep for consistently praised product starting to become shaky, Ghostface would deliver his triumphant album *Supreme Clientele* on January 25, 2000.

METHOD MAN, *TICAL 2000: JUDGEMENT DAY*

It would be more than a year before the arrival of the new millennium and whether the angst at Y2K's onset was real or feigned, Method Man named his album *Tical 2000: Judgement Day*. Holding true to the Wu-Tang Clan's intrinsic use of Five Percent Nation rhetoric and philosophy, the album's title had mathematical implications. Method Man told *Rolling Stone Magazine* prior to its release, "It's my second LP, right—that's T2,: Tical, Tical. It's called T 2000. Two thousand is two words; each starts with T. Method Man is two words that start with M. Year 2000 is the millennium. What does millennium start and end with? M! Two M's. M is also the Roman numeral for 1,000, two of them is 2,000. My second LP, 2,000. Ya know? I'm just perfect with this LP right now."[11]

Tical 2000 has its moments of moody, apocalyptic themes and sounds that syncs with the fear and paranoia, mostly of the unknown, that often come with new millenniums. *Tical* was a grungy work with bombed out, gloriously lo-fi sounds. "His new album is an exposition of the same order: diverse, moody and fluid. It showcases more of

Meth's vocal and rhythmic abilities than his platinum-selling debut *Tical*," said *Rolling Stone Magazine* of the new album in a profile of the rapper.[12] But unlike its predecessor, *Tical 2000*'s audio soundscapes would not be handled entirely by RZA, who contributes his production prowess to only three of the album's 17 proper songs. Critics pointed at *Tical 2000*'s copious use of skits as one of its weak points. While there are 17 songs on the album, once skits, intros, and outros are included, the number of tracks on the CD balloons to 28 with the album clocking in a shade over an hour and 14 minutes.

With RZA's presence dialed back, Method Man solicited beats from producers descended directly from the RZA family tree in True Master and 4th Disciple. The album also has beats from notable outsiders including Havoc (of Queens-based rap group Mobb Deep), Erick Sermon, and the Trackmasters. But the key component of any Method Man album is his baritone and dexterous flow, which *Newsweek* describes as "a rasp so abrasive you'd swear a scratchy turntable was welded to the back of his throat," in its review of *Tical 2000*.[13]

The album's official lead single was "Judgement Day." Produced by Method Man, with 4th Disciple receiving coproducer credit, the track's marauding mix of evil tones and spooky effects is worthy of its title. After a spoken-word intro where he mentions "The last hardcore MC's" are "working on a cure that would end the pestilence," Method Man storms the track with rhymes attesting to his readiness for the end of times, charismatically. "P.L.O. pack the slingshot flow, plant the seed, let the garden grow, And stick that rhyme where the sun don't shine, darts pierce your heart like a Valentine," he says in the second verse, referring to the "P.L.O. mentality" he's been referring to since the first *Tical* and "darts" again referring to Wu-Tang's rhymes. "Judgement Day" clocked in at six minutes and its length (after the first and second verse, the third is a repeat of the first) ultimately hindered its chances of mass radio play. "Judgement Day" managed to peak at #42 on the *Billboard* R&B/Hip-Hop Songs chart.

Even with the lead single's mediocre performance at radio, *Tical 2000: Judgement Day* debuted at #2 on *Billboard*'s 200 chart and at #1 on *Billboard*'s R&B/Hip-Hop Albums chart. The albums debut was no small feat since 10 major music acts (including Garth Brooks's *Double Live*, Whitney Houston's *My Love Is Your Love*, Ice Cube's *War & Peace 1—War Disc*, Jewel's *Spirit*, and Mariah Carey's *#1s*) would release albums on November 17, 1998, a day dubbed Super Tuesday.[14] "The album is both anarchic and appealing, hardcore and thoughtful," said writer dream hampton of the album in her review of the album in the *Village Voice*.[15] *Tical 2000* would be certified platinum by the end of 2008, helped on by its second single "Break Ups 2 Make Ups."

Four years since his solo debut, and five years since being introduced to the world with Wu-Tang Clan, Method Man had begun refining his ability to create songs that were accessible to listeners beyond his devoted fan base. "Break Ups 2 Make Ups" could be called a retread of the Grammy winning "All I Need." But instead of Mary J. Blige on the hook, and Sean Combs's remixing work, the featured singer is male R&B vocalist D'Angelo. Method Man would work with D'Angelo on his heavily anticipated *Voodoo* (2000) album, appearing with Redman on the song "Left Right." But until then, "Break Ups 2 Make Ups" would be their first collaboration.

The music for "Break Ups 2 Make Ups" was produced by Qu'Ran Goodman (of rap group Da Youngstas) and the Trackmasters (Jean-Claude "Poke" Olivier and Samuel "Tone" Barnes), the latter having found success making commercially friendly hip-hop music with artists including Jay-Z, L.L. Cool J, and female rapper Foxy Brown. Method Man, while working on what was likely Ghostface's *Supreme Clientele* album, ran into Barnes at New York City's Hit Factory Studios and the producer expressed interest in working with the rapper.[16] Method Man says he had to track Barnes down after their first meeting but eventually "Break Ups 2 Make Ups" was recorded, with D'Angelo's vocals—the singer coos "I'm still in love with you babe" for the chorus—added to the song later.

"Breaks Ups 2 Make Ups" features a pleasant acoustic guitar playing throughout the track and rather tepid drum programming. Method Man's lyrics deal with a cheating ex-girlfriend, women jealous of his new girlfriend, and a girl trying to make a boyfriend jealous with him in the first, second, and third verses, respectively. The song would barely crack the *Billboard* Hot 100 chart, entering and peaking at #98. The R&B flavored cut would fare better on the *Billboard* R&B/ Hip-Hop Songs chart, peaking at #29. In about four years the Trackmasters would work with Wu-Tang Clan on their fourth album *Iron Flag*.

RZA's contributions to *Tical 2000* are decent songs but not necessarily some of the album's strongest, as the producer's reputation would have us believe. "Perfect World" is the album's first proper song and features Method Man pounding his chest with cocksure rhymes over RZA's grim synth and rather unadorned drums. While it serves its purpose as an appetizer-type song, this is no musical masterpiece. RZA's next two productions are "Suspect Chin Music" and "Retro-Godfather." "Suspect Chin Music" utilizes a slumping bass line and what sounds like an electrified kazoo for Method Man and guest artist Streetlife to verbally reprimand fake thugs, as its chorus suggests.

"Perfect World" and "Suspect Chin Music" seem to be have been made without the use of samples.[17] With a year of music theory under his belt, RZA was trying his hand at actually playing music. In hindsight, RZA has admitted that learning music theory cost him some of the rawness that won him his production favor, with early beats in that period not being up to par. He told *The Source Magazine* in 1999, "I had confused myself. Because I tried to keep playing, and I was losing some of my rawness. So I had to go through a year of weak beats, of corny beats. Then, after I got those out of me, I started getting some good ones again."[18]

RZA had not completely abandoned samples when he created the instrumental for "Retro-Godfather," easily the best of his three contributions to *Tical 2000*, and one of the album's best songs. RZA samples the sweeping synth from Vince Montana's "Warp Factor II" (1978) that gives the song a regal vibe, or as Method Man says at the track's onset, "Take it back . . . 70's style." On the first chorus, Method Man interpolates Denroy Morgan's chorus from "I'll Do Anything for You" (1981) with his own gruff baritone and additionally cribs the lyrics, "There's not a problem that I can't fix, 'cause I can do it in the mix," from Indeep's "Last Night a DJ Save My Life" (1982) for the second chorus.

Tical 2000 generally gets a bad rap, but past the filler of excessive skits—"You Play Too Much" with comedian Chris Rock is the only redeeming and truly funny skit of the bunch—there is a core of gratifying cuts on the album. True Master handles the bulk of the music commendably, and since he is a student of RZA, the music overall retains the established Wu-Tang audio aesthetics, though there are no prominent kung-fu samples. True Master's best tracks are the brawny "Grid

Iron Rap" and the intoxicating "Torture." On "Grid Iron Rap," Method Man again teams up with his pet project Streetlife to launch braggadocious rhymes over jarring piano chords. "Torture" is a sonic 180-degree turn with winding tones that inspire Method Man to deliver his rhymes in a relaxed cadence that makes his threatening rhymes about the misuse of his "Johnny Blaze" nickname sound all the more sinister. RZA's apprentice True Master proved himself to be capable of continuing his teacher's legacy of consistently appealing production with his turn on *Tical 2000*.

The critical reception to *Tical 2000* was mixed. Method Man, at this point in his career, hadn't met much critique to his music, and a particular quote in a 1998 *Rolling Stone* profile of the rapper illuminates that fact: "I write a lot of what I call fly shit—it's subliminal, and it can fly right by you. It feels good when I'm appreciated for it. When I'm not, it's like people telling you your life isn't good enough."[19]

RZA, *BOBBY DIGITAL IN STEREO*

Intro/B.O.B.B.Y. /Unspoken Word/Slow Grind African/Airwaves/Love Jones/N.Y.C. Everything/Mantis/Slow Grind French/Holocaust (Silkworm) /Terrorist/Bobby Did It (Spanish Fly) /Handwriting on the Wall/Kiss of a Black Widow/Slow Grind Italian/My Lovin' Is Digi/Domestic Violence/Project Talk/Lab Drunk/Fuck What You Think/Daily Routine

---

Listeners who wanted to hear music from RZA, rather than his trainees, didn't have to wait too long since his debut solo album, *RZA as Bobby Digital in Stereo*, landed on store shelves exactly a week after *Tical 2000*. "Bobby Digital" is an alter-ego RZA created. Bobby Digital is an out-of-control teenager, the superego to RZA's more refined id. According to RZA, he had to go through being Bobby (his given name being Robert Diggs) to become RZA. This rationale was also part of a handy explanation as to why his debut album would not be called *The Cure* as he previously mentioned to various media outlets. In 1997, RZA told the *New York Times*, "Bobby tends more to his lower nature, whereas the RZA tends to his higher nature. But I couldn't do the RZA album until I got this Bobby Digital out of me."[20] As for the "digital" aspect, it also was convenient considering the coming of Y2K, and the exponentially increasing use of computers in society. "When you become digital, you become digits—pure Mathematics. So, to be digital means to see things clearly, for what they are and not what they appear to be," explains RZA in the *Wu-Tang Manual*.[21]

RZA took the alter-ego concept to the extreme, donning a mask, similar to the one worn by Bruce Lee while playing Kato in *The Green Hornet*, to denote being in "Bobby Digital" mode. He details in *The Tao of Wu* (2009) getting an actual sidekick and armoring a car for him to venture into the world as a real-life superhero, though he never actually did. Instead, RZA channeled his creativity into the concept album that is *RZA as Bobby Digital in Stereo*. The album plays out like a soundtrack to the still-unreleased film of the same name that was planned to accompany its release. The album cover art, created by renowned comic book artist Bill Sienkiewicz, with inspiration from the movie poster of Blaxploitation film *Coffy*, alluded to the album's duality as a soundtrack.

While the album's lyrics are analogous to RZA's baser instincts in lieu of the righteous and scholarly rhymes he is known for in Wu-Tang Clan albums and solo projects, the beats on *Bobby Digital in Stereo* were to follow in RZA's progression as a producer, fully utilizing the music theory he began learning and implementing with the previous year's *Wu-Tang Forever*. In 1999, RZA told *The Source Magazine*, "I learned how to play chord progressions. That shit is taking me to another level, son. My shit is still crazy. Before I would sample something . . . now I can just play that."[22]

RZA's use of keyboard based samplers, beginning with the Ensoniq EPS, made this advancement all the more natural. And like all things RZA, he took the use of keyboards to the extreme, using a total of 17 keyboards to create the album's "digital orchestra."[23] The album sets the tone of RZA's newfound musicality with its first two tracks. The "Intro" features a pulsing organ that hosts the ramblings of an excited voice whose only immediately discernable words are "Bobby." "B.O.B.B.Y." immediately follows; RZA is heard sarcastically saying, "Ultimate Breakbeats and shit right? Niggas still, makin money off of those shits. Looping the same shits for a thousand years and shit right?" The statement is full of irony since RZA himself had sampled material that was featured in the *Ultimate Breaks & Beats* albums he was referring to for songs in his own production discography. No matter the loose hypocrisy, RZA was clearly marking his disdain for "obvious" loops, as he would continue to do in the future. Also, RZA uses samples, though none too obvious, for music heard on the album.

"B.O.B.B.Y." may be a RZA solo song but is typical of Wu-Tang Clan bravado. "Yo, you know us to be robust, the greatest crew since Cold Crush, this poisonous slang keep MC's avoiding us," raps RZA—ahem, Bobby Digital—in its first verse. The song's track features short, synth-heavy chord progressions with marching drums. Despite being *Bobby Digital in Stereo*'s lead single, overall the song lacked any real lasting appeal, managing to only peak at #92 on *Billboard*'s R&B/Hip-Hop Songs chart. The next song, "Unspoken Word," is easily more interesting of a track mainly because RZA uses a high-pitched voice as a key component of the track. The voice's squealing tone, matched to a humming bass line and sprinting drums, and RZA rapping in a hurried pace, gives the song a frenetic atmosphere. "Unspoken Word" is the first real look into the Bobby Digital persona as he announces his arrival with the song's opening line: "Word's on the street dun dun Bobby's going digital, hovering the city inside the Wonder Woman's invisible . . . jet."

A longtime film buff, RZA wanted to make his own superhero movie. But he met resistance in Hollywood when he told them he had ideas but lacked a script. Not the best way to land a million-dollar movie deal. Naturally, RZA decided to create the film, whose plot revolves around a rapper who derives his powers from smoking marijuana blunts dipped in a special additive called "honey," by funding it himself. But since the accompanying film—described as a "self-financed direct-to-video sci-fi/kung-fu adventure fantasy" in 1998 by *USA Today* and other media outlets—*Bobby Digital in Stereo* was never packaged with the album as originally planned, the plot of the film was relayed by RZA in press, usually when he was recounting Bobby Digital's inception, and via song.[24]

Before listeners can get too deep into the Bobby Digital tales they are given an intermission of sorts with "Slow Grind African" and "Airwaves." "Slow Grind African" is one of several "Slow Grind" tracks spread throughout the album ("Slow Grind French," "Slow Grind Italian") that feature a woman delivering a message in a sexy voice in the denoted language.[25] "Slow Grind African" features soft, conga-like drumming that segues smoothly into the King Tech produced

"Airwaves." RZA's delivery on the song places him more in his cocky Wu-Tang Clan stance than that of the hyper-egotistical Bobby Digital. The track's thickly filtered bass line and chants of "Wu-Tang, Wu-Tang," countered with RZA saying "Wake up, wake up," give it a decidedly trance-like feel. Also, added sound effects of searching for and landing on a new radio station shore up its intermission-like effect.

Bobby Digital then returns to, dare we say, share his sensitive side on "Love Jones." Starting with a conversation between RZA and a female, the track liberally interpolates 1972's "Love Jones" by 1970s R&B group Brighter Side of Darkness for its chorus while the groove is lifted from the Mighty Ryeders' "Star Children" (1978). RZA may be well regarded for his deft use of samples, but his knack for romantic lyrics is suspect. His opening line—"Yo girl you shining like a brand new spankin black glock or a thousand hundred dollar bills inside a shoebox"—is about as smooth as RZA gets.

RZA's flow when rapping has always been choppy, and as a point of contention surrounding his merits as an MC, has been heavily debated. Writer dream hampton, who also made sure to point out his wanton misogyny, is not particularly a fan of RZA's rhyming, noting in a *Village Voice* review of *Bobby Digital in Stereo*, "RZA is not a good MC. Period. His aggressive delivery may be crammed with knowledge and mathematics . . . but his rhyme style grates the nerves."[26] To RZA's credit, the uniqueness of his delivery has also been cited as a positive since individuality has always been a cause for celebration in hip-hop music.

After the sedate "Love Jones," listeners are brought back to attention with the beguiling "NYC Everything." RZA coordinates bells, whistles, shimmering synth, and vocal runs into a head-nod-inducing track with plenty of swing. RZA handles the first verse while Method Man takes care of the second with numerous clever one-liners. "They busting bullets over Broadway, deep cover; I'm like Larry, when the fish burn, I burn rubber cause I'm not an easy lover," rhymes Method Man, slyly referencing Woody Allen's film *Bullets Over Broadway* and actor Laurence Fishburne's starring role in the film *Deep Cover*. Method Man received another "Hip-Hop Quotable" in *The Source Magazine*'s January 1999 issue for his verse on "NYC Everything."[27]

RZA recruits another of his Wu-Tang Clan acolytes, Masta Killa, for the next song, "Mantis." Featuring high-pitched tones played over a base of steady drum kicks and piano keys, the track is suitable for the rapper's deliberate but sedate vocal delivery. Its use of sampled kung-fu dialogue gives the song the feel of a Wu-Tang Clan album cut with a Bobby Digital accent. After "Mantis," a quick detour is heard with "Slow Grind French," which uses the same organ heard on the album's intro, and is quickly followed by "Holocaust (Silkworm)." The song opens with the voice of a singer mournfully singing "Digital . . . Bobby Digital" (utilized again for the chorus) as its drums kick in and rattle at a steady pace with vibrato synth throughout the track. A couple of new artists are heard on the track, Holocaust and Dr. Doom, who bookend RZA's second verse. Ghostface closes out the song with a stylistically sound verse full of his usual ad hoc references: "Who shot JJ, it was Mudbone," quips Ghostface, revealing he watches TV sitcom *Good Times* (JJ Evans) and cartoon *Fat Albert & The Junkyard Gang* (Mudbone).

"Terrorist" follows, sporting rote drum programming and serving as a showcase for more MCs. The limp beat does little to boost the lyrically decent, at best, performers. "Bobby Did It" suffers similarly from a lack of top-notch rappers. RZA's and Ghostface's verses easily outmaneuver those of Timbo King and Islord who would have been best better left off the song. Female rapper Jamie Sommers, last heard mocking Ghostface at the start of "Wildflower" (*Ironman*), holds her own with the Wu-Tang Clan elder statesmen as her verse closes the song.

"Handwriting on the Wall" features heralded California rapper Rass Kass and RZA delivering pointed verses over the same organ motif heard on "Intro" and "Slow Grind French." Rass Kass is known for using esoteric rhetoric in his lyrics, thus shares good chemistry with RZA on the too short (1:47) song. On "Kiss of a Black Widow" RZA recruits a rarely heard Ol' Dirty Bastard to deliver a raunchy, though apropos, verse on the song. The final interlude track, "Slow Grind Italian," follows and marks the start of the album's concluding tracks.

On "My Lovin is Digi" RZA again uses the violin sounds he favored on *Wu-Tang Forever*. On the second verse he mentions Inspectah Deck's *Uncontrolled Substance*, which would not be released until 1999. The song's somber instrumentation is executed well enough but is no standout in RZA's extensive body of work. The sharp drums and low-key pianos on "Domestic Violence" don't snap listeners back to attention as much as its vocals. Two seconds in Jamie Sommers is heard incessantly repeating, "You ain't shit, your daddy ain't shit, your brother ain't shit, your money ain't shit," and so on and so forth. Meanwhile, a woman's voice is heard accenting the same commentary in song. "Domestic Violence" carries the same lover-scorned sentiment as Ghostface's "Wildflower" in that RZA uses the entire song to chastise a female who isn't holding up her end of the relationship. The difference with RZA's is that the female's side of the story is better represented, albeit via her constant "You ain't shit" banter.

To RZA's credit he doesn't condone hitting a woman, as the song's title may allude to, though verbal abuse is nothing to be made light of. The song ends with the two sides quarreling (RZA accepts a call from U-God, only to be disturbed by Sommers's ranting) like little schoolchildren. The novelty of the back and forth verbal bashing makes "Domestic Violence" a pretty entertaining song. One particular line where RZA brashly rhymes, "You wish you could fuck/Bitch, all you can do is dick suck," finds Sommers retorting with "Your ass can't fuck, that's why your wife left your monkey ass," turns out to be strikingly personal. Years later, in *The Tao of Wu* (2009) RZA reveals that his wife had cheated on him.

After "Domestic Violence," the album limps to a close with four songs that just aren't memorable. On "Project Talk," RZA trades lines with Kinetic 9 (a member of Killarmy) about familiar scenarios seen in any projects (police violence, crime, gossip, etc.). The concept has been done before, and better with Capone-N-Noreaga's "Phone Time" and The Firm's "Phone Tap" being a couple of examples. "Lab Drunk" is the better of the four thanks to its marching drum pattern and pulsing bass line. "Fuck What You Think" is another string-infused groove cradled by fleet drums but it is also a posse cut and the rappers heard, Islord and 9th Prince of Killarmy (the latter is RZA's younger brother), are mediocre at best. Similarly, RZA nobly shares the microphone on the album's closer, "Daily Routine," but again, the guest rapper, Kinetic 9, doesn't contribute a particularly impressive performance.

Critics and fans are generally split in a hate it or love it standoff surrounding *Bobby Digital in Stereo*'s merits. RZA produced all of the *Bobby Digital in Stereo* tracks, except for the Inspectah Deck–produced "Kiss of a Black Widow" and the King Tech–produced "Airwaves." While the quality of RZA's production on the album is often debated, what can't be argued is that the album's method was a distinct turn from the sample-infused sound he established himself with in the past. "Instead of the sweeping, cinematic assemblages of samples that made the Wu-Tang Clan unstoppable, most of Bobby Digital's backup seems to come from a single computerized keyboard that's unchanging and shallow, even tinny," said the *New York Times* in its 1999 review of *Bobby Digital in Stereo*.[28] Even *The Source Magazine*, early, longtime Wu-Tang Clan supporters, noted that all the instruments played didn't necessarily improve RZA's beats in its three and a half mic review of the album.[29]

Despite the mixed reaction, *Bobby Digital in Stereo* managed to debut at #16 on the *Billboard* Hot 200 Album chart and at #3 on the *Billboard* R&B/Hip-Hop Albums chart. RZA was able to mix all his eclectic personal interests—kung-fu movies, comic books, women, science fiction, marijuana, et al.—in one place under his own terms without having to consider the needs of Wu-Tang Clan. RZA was still aware of the soapbox his artistry afforded him but managed to sneak in lessons amid the wanton extravagance. He told *USA Today* in 1998, "Women, money and cars—we talked about that (on Raekwon's influential *Only Built 4 Cuban Linx*); now the whole industry is stuck on that. But that is only one side of our coin. There are too many people out here starving for us to be acting like it's all about money and being players without coming with any knowledge."[30]

But without the personality and bravado of the Wu-Tang Clan, and beats that just don't take off, the album is plagued by lulls in energy. Nevertheless, RZA manages to create enough moments of musical nirvana to eke out a successful debut solo album (it was certified gold in February 1999). The following year, 1999, would see more releases from Wu-Tang Clan members, but unlike their previous efforts, praise was not as easy to come by, if deserved at all.

GZA/GENIUS, *BENEATH THE SURFACE*

The previous year only saw two proper releases from Wu-Tang Clan— Method Man's *Tical 2000* followed by RZA's *Bobby Digital in Stereo*. The year 1999 would be more prolific with a total of five releases: GZA/Genius's *Beneath the Surface*, Ol' Dirty Bastard's *Nigga Please*, Inspectah Deck's *Uncontrolled Substance*, U-God's *Golden Arms*

Redemption, and Raekwon's *Immobilarity*). Method Man would also release *Blackout!*, a collaborative project with New Jersey rapper Redman.

RZA's participation in the aforementioned could be considered scant at best. The most beats he contributes to any one project is four on Ol' Dirty Bastard's *Nigga Please*, and he doesn't appear at all on Raekwon's *Immobilarity*. GZA's and Raekwon's albums would be follow-ups to previous albums that are considered hip-hop classics— Ol' Dirty Bastard's is acclaimed as well, though not on the scale of the others. Inspectah Deck and U-God would finally release their debut albums with the former being highly anticipated, particularly among Wu-Tang Clan fans, thanks to his ear-catching verses on group albums and guest appearances on solo projects.

GZA was the first to release an album, *Beneath the Surface*, on June 29, 1999. RZA performs the chorus on "Hip Hop Fury" and speaks fleetingly at the beginning of the song "Crash Your Crew," which features Ol' Dirty Bastard's lone appearance singing its hook. But while all the beats on GZA's previous standout effort, *Liquid Swords*, were produced by RZA (both are credited as executive producer on *Beneath the Surface*), he only contributes one track, "1112," to *Beneath the Surface*. The title "1112" references the Supreme Mathematic's designation of males (and "Knowledge") as the numeral one (1) and females (and "Wisdom") as the numeral (2). In order of appearance on the song, there are three males (GZA, Masta Killa, Killah Priest) followed by female artist Njeri Earth. The track is an assemblage of cascading strings, typical of RZA during this period, supported by an up tempo drum pattern. GZA dedicates his verse to extended metaphors about production, opening his verse with, "Bobby said, 'Fuck spending 50 on a whip, buy equip/Mental flip, got a thousand tracks stored on a chip." With the song being a posse cut, the rest of the track's participant's verses are more about bravado than a particular topic.

As for the rest of the album's sound, producers Arabian Knight and Allah Mathematics—both can be considered students of RZA—handle the majority of the tracks. "I can't really say what he does with his music, but whatever it is . . . I love it," is what GZA told *The Source Magazine* in 1999 about working with Arabian Knight who at the time was signed to his Liquid Swords Entertainment and is credited as a co-executive producer on the album.[31] Genius has also said that

Beneath the Surface's beats are "bouncier" and "more colorful" than those of *Liquid Swords*.[32]

The pair of RZA protégés—RZA introduced Mathematics, who at the time was and still is the Wu-Tang Clan's DJ, to the Ensoniq ASR-10 in 1995—do a commendable job orchestrating some of the album's best tracks.[33] Mathematics produces "Publicity," which loops and compresses a jarring string sample from Terry Knight and the Pack's "I (Who Have Nothing)" (1966). In "Publicity," GZA incorporates the names of various hip-hop publications into his lyrics in the same manner as *Liquid Swords*'s "Labels" did with record labels. Of the song's inception, in 1999 GZA told *The Source Magazine*, "One day I was in the studio [and] Timbo King from Royal Fam had a line written down that had two magazines in it. And I was like, 'That's something I would like to touch.' So I asked him and then rebuilt it and made it a masterpiece."[34]

Arabian Knight helms "Breaker, Breaker," which uses more strings but it seems that he plays the sounds rather than looping a sample. The creeping strings are matched to a solid set of drums, and GZA's rhymes are as fluidly poetic as ever: "To check fault in oneself is pure loveliness/ You break the mirror that reminds you of your ugliness," he rhymes. For his second verse, GZA received a Hip-Hop Quotable in the August 1999 issue of *Source Magazine*.[35] The chorus to "Breaker, Breaker"—GZA says, "Breaker, breaker, one nine, clear the line/Can you read me? Extorted your rhymes, MC's should expect the worst/I stay alert and shoot first"—is fitted with a CB microphone effect. It serves as a dedication to his father who at one point drove trucks for a living.[36]

"Breaker, Breaker" only managed to peak at #80 on *Billboard*'s R&B/ Hip-Hop Songs chart. Nevertheless, the album debuted at #1 on the *Billboard* R&B/Hip-Hop Albums chart and #9 on the *Billboard* 200 chart. Despite the critical praise given to *Beneath the Surface*, on its release and solid sales, it would be certified gold in August 1999, the album failed to become as highly regarded as its direct predecessor.

INSPECTAH DECK, *UNCONTROLLED SUBSTANCE*

Inspectah Deck didn't have to worry about outdoing a previous album since *Uncontrolled Substance*, released September 7, 1999, was his debut. But expectations were high for Deck's album off the strength of his compelling verses littering Wu-Tang Clan albums and solo projects. A number of his cameos outside of traditional Wu-Tang circles—Big Pun's "Tres Leches (Triboro Trilogy)," Gang Starr's "Above the Clouds," and Pete Rock's "Tru Master"—also spurred interest in the unsung Clansman's debut. But the album was purportedly delayed because of the flood that destroyed RZA's basement studio in 1995—the same year of its original intended release.

Despite being a founding Wu-Tang Clan member who joined up in 1993, shortly after being released from Elmira Stare Correction Center for drug dealing, even ancillary affiliate Cappadonna managed to release his debut album, *The Pillage* (1998), over a year earlier.[37] Inspectah Deck sees *Uncontrolled Substance*'s delay as beneficial, telling *The Source Magazine*, "From the standpoint of coming from a group, all the albums we put out, all the tours, all the shows and everything, it gave me the confidence right now to come out as an individual. I'm taking everything I learned through the last six years of this fucking rap shit and applying it to me."

Though RZA is still noted as the album's executive producer, he only contributes a couple of beats to *Uncontrolled Substance* that incredulously are relatively some of the album's weakest. "Movers & Shakers" employs a horn riff that isn't particularly exciting, and "Friction," which features a pair of verses from Masta Killa, fares a bit better thanks to a spooky sample of 1974's "One Way Street" by Memphis Soul singer/songwriter Ann Peebles. Of the 16 tracks, not including the "Intro," Inspectah Deck produces five songs. Of those songs, the spry crime tale "Word on the Street," which lifts its piano chords from Ernie Hines's "What Would I Do" (1972), and the mesmerizing "Elevation," which utilizes a moving sample of David Axelrod's "Terri's Tune" (1975), are two of the album's best numbers.

Uncontrolled Substance's overall production is marked by a profuse use of samples from its producers that include in-house Wu-Tang Clan producers Allah Mathematics, 4th Disciple, and True Master as well as outsiders such as the renowned Pete Rock, formerly of early 1990s, Mt. Vernon, New York–based hip-hop group Pete Rock & CL Smooth. Pete Rock's contribution was likely a tradeoff for Inspectah Deck's appearance on the prior year's "Tru Master" single from the producer/rapper's solo debut, *Soul Survivor* (1998)—both artists were also label mates on Loud Records.

Finally given his chance at individual glory, Inspectah Deck delivers a commendable effort that received overwhelmingly favorable reviews. Inspectah Deck held his own on solo songs and recruits a number of Wu-Tang Clan guest appearances, though the majority of them are lesser heralded members, such as Masta Killa and U-God, and close affiliates including Streetlife and La the Darkman. Time would not see *Uncontrolled Substance* held in the same regard as previous Wu-Tang Clan solo debuts because it falls just a bit short of the superior threshold those albums set. Though none of the singles serviced to radio ("R.E.C. Room," "Show N Prove," "Word on the Street") would chart, *Uncontrolled Substance* managed to peak at #19 on the *Billboard* Top 200 Albums chart and peak at #3 on *Billboard* R&B/Hip-Hop Albums chart. Its sales numbers, below gold but past 350,000 albums sold, are modest.

OL' DIRTY BASTARD, *NIGGA PLEASE*

Recognize/I Can't Wait/Cold Blooded/Got Your Money/Rollin' Wit You/Gettin' High/You Don't Want to Fuck With Me/Nigga Please/Dirt Dog/I Want Pussy/Good Morning Heartache/All in Together Now/Cracker Jack

---

Inspectah Deck's time in the spotlight would be overshadowed by his friend and fellow Wu-Tang Clan founding member Ol' Dirty Bastard. The perniciously titled *Nigga Please* would be released on September 14, 1999, one week after Inspectah Deck's *Uncontrolled Substance*. "Uncontrolled" could easily be tagged to Ol' Dirty Bastard whose antics were becoming increasingly bizarre, even by his standards. Ol' Dirty Bastard told anyone who listened that he changed his name to Osirus during September 1996's Day of Atonement in the wake of Tupac's death because he didn't feel comfortable with kids calling him Ol' Dirty.[38] But by the time *Nigga Please* was released, he was going by Big Baby Jesus. In a cover story for *XXL Magazine* writer Larry "Blackspot" Hester detailed Ol' Dirty demanding $50,000 from the publication to take photographs for the respective story. Also noteworthy is that at the time of publication, the album was to be called *The Black Man Is God, the White Man Is the Devil* but was then changed to *God Made Dirt and Dirt Don't Hurt*.[39]

But more imperative than the album's proposed titles or trivial rap monikers were Ol' Dirty Bastard's run-ins with law enforcement, which were quickly going from head scratching to disturbing. His conduct within a couple of weeks of March 1998—saving a girl trapped under a car, crashing the Grammy Awards stage—were such that *Time Magazine* named him, albeit irreverently, the Citizen of the Week.[40] In November 1998, the rapper was arrested for allegedly threatening to kill his girlfriend. On January 15, 1999, he was arrested for attempted murder after an alleged shootout with NYPD street crime unit officers. To his credit, a Grand Jury refused to indict the rapper because while police said he had a gun, ODB maintained that it was a cell phone.

Despite all of these shenanigans, by February 1999 Ol' Dirty Bastard decided to focus on completing his second album, *Nigga Please*. Nevertheless, in July 1999, police pulled over ODB in Brooklyn and found crack cocaine in the car he was driving.

All of his legal fees, and a substance abuse problem, meant Ol' Dirty Bastard's bills were certainly piling up. According to RZA, who serves as one of the album's executive producers and contributes four beats to the project—ODB wanted $20 million from his Elektra record label to make the album.[41] In 1999, RZA explained to *Rolling Stone Magazine* the issues surrounding the creation of the album:

> It took a while for "Nigga Please" to happen. The main struggle was having Dirty focus on his shit. Dirt was going through so many trials and tribulations: He got arrested; he had personal problems, court dates; he's got a lot of children, a lot of women, a lot of people against him; and he's got a conspiracy in his head. Keeping him pinned down is a struggle.[42]

Considering Ol' Dirty Bastard's aforementioned attempted shake down of *XXL Magazine*, RZA was not kidding. Ol' Dirty Bastard's constant flux ended up fueling the album. Dante Ross, the Elektra Records A&R that signed him to the label, told *Vibe Magazine* in 1999 that "He's utterly dysfunctional and lives on the edge. My man's living it. There's no line between art and life with him."[43] Whether it was a respect for his talents or the chance to witness his, at times, oddball behavior, *Nigga Please* featured production from some of the hottest hip-hop producers of the time, including the Neptunes (Pharrell Williams and Chad Hugo) and Irv Gotti. The former actually contributed three of the album's best tracks including the opener, "Recognize," that features comedian Chris Rock poking fun at ODB's penchant for trouble when he quips, "I'm Chris Rock, I'm chillin' with the O.D.B., so I'm in the wrong place, at the wrong motherfuckin' time with the wrong motherfuckin' man," over rumbling drums and guitar plucks.

The Irv Gotti–produced "Can't Wait," which gloriously samples the theme from 1980s cop show *TJ Hooker*, follows with Ol' Dirty Bastard using a speedy, double-time rap flow. The two final Neptunes productions follow: "Cold Blooded" and the album's lead single "Got Your Money." *Nigga Please*'s album cover—a stoned-looking Ol' Dirty Bastard is in a Sly Stone worthy, body-hugging outfit and wearing a long, curly black wig—pays homage to Rick James. It figures Ol' Dirty Bastard would remake one of the late funk musician's biggest hits, 1983's "Cold Blooded." Ol' Dirty Bastard's version plays like a straight remake until, instead of a bridge, the rapper adds an explicitly rhymed verse. Never the best of singers, though it never stopped him from trying, the rapper carries the tune efficiently enough so as to not ruin its novelty as the Neptunes provide a busy track of shimmery synth and crisp drums. "As off-beat as Dirty always is, the raw self-exposure in his voice proves the rapper to be one of the more compelling singers of his generation," noted *Vibe Magazine* in its review of *Nigga Please*.[44]

After, comes the dance-party-friendly "Got Your Money," Ol' Dirty Bastard's biggest hit. Dirty's lyrics and delivery are lucid compared to other songs in this collection. The song's enticing hook—"Hey Dirty, baby I got your money"—is sung by Kelis, the female R&B/Pop singer who, at the time, was still a relative unknown. The beat is driven by powerful percussion that, though un-credited, sounds like the drums from Michael Jackson's 1982 hit "Billie Jean." The playful tune would hit #26 on the *Billboard* Hot 100 chart, #19 on the *Billboard* R&B/Hip-Hop Songs chart, and #4 on the *Billboard* Rhythmic Top 40 chart.

After "Got Your Money" perks up listeners' ears, Ol' Dirty Bastard returns to battle rap form with the Irv Gotti and Mr. Fingers–produced "Rollin' Wit You." The song is infamous for the rapper's rants of "I'm tellin you bitch ass niggas ... If y'all colored bitch ass faggot punk ass motherfuckers don't see that these white people are trying to take over your shit . . . Don't worry, your baby's happy the Ol' Dirty Bastard is here." Besides rapping, "I shut whole fuckin' world down, you white motherfuckers could never, y'all can't ever take over," is the last of his anti-White ravings on the song. The rest of the song's rhymes are stream-of-consciousness boasts, mostly about his love/hate relationship with women and rapper bravado, over tumbling piano chords set to a stiff drum track. If the song sounds like Ol' Dirty Bastard put together line after line in different takes until a full song was completed, it's because he did. Irv Gotti told *The Source Magazine* so in 1995: "He would do the ad-libs first and then he would do the rhymes one line at a time. . . . If there were some girls in the studio, he would throw them in the booth and have them say something about him."[45]

The next two songs are forgettable. Ol' Dirty Bastard doesn't even appear on the Buddha Monk–produced posse cut "Getting' High," which features guest rappers 12 O'Clock, La The Darkman, and Shorty Shit Stain. "You Don't Want to Fuck With Me" features Ol' Dirty Bastard's nonsensical boasting over rote horn swells from producers Irv Gotti and DL. "Nigga Please," "Dirt Dog," and "I Want Pussy" are produced by RZA and provide a steadying effect to an album whose focus has begun to waver. The title track uses a funk horn sample with plenty of swing before going into breezy organ riffs for Ol' Dirty Bastard to rhyme over. The opening lines reveal Ol' Dirty Bastard could be a witty wordsmith whenever he wanted to be: "All music must obey me, all pain must obey me/I cripple my enemies/Got that careful vocabulary."

But by the second verse, Ol' Dirty Bastard's increasing paranoia is heard when he raps, "Kill all the government microchips in my body, I'm the paranoid nigga at your party." "Dirt Dog," also coproduced by Buddha Monk, features more rambling verses that are only salvaged by a murky but beguiling groove and its call-and-response hook. On "I Want Pussy" RZA samples creepy synths from 1968's "You've Made Me So Very Happy" by Blood, Sweat & Tears and outfits it with stringent drums. The beat is necessary since the song is little more than a four-bar verse preceded by Ol' Dirty Bastard extolling he wants "Pussy for free," and followed by "Yeah my momma cannot protect y'all." The song only makes sense when considering Ol' Dirty Bastard was reported to have anywhere from two to 14 children by multiple women.

After the crass "I Want Pussy," Ol' Dirty Bastard shows his tender side by incredulously singing a Jazz standard, Billie Holiday's "Good

Morning Heartache." Again, Dirty's singing is barely passable but mercifully R&B singer Lil Mo is featured on the song and her vocals tend to dominate the mix with the track's live instrumentation giving it a sophisticated feel. After the intimate mood is set, "All In Together Now" follows with a rather spastic track of crackly drums and deep bass.[46] At first the song could be taken as amends to the anti-White rhetoric he spewed on "Rollin' Wit' You" when at the track's onset he proclaims, "I'm a Dalmation . . . Motherfucker I'm white *and* I'm black, what?" But when the song finally starts, which also is heavy on the Five Percent Nation rhetoric, it's pretty clear that it's anything but the hip-hop version of Stevie Wonder and Paul McCartney's "Ebony and Ivory." The album closes with "Cracker Jack," a song filled with copious amounts of misogyny but worth listening to for RZA's lush instrumental that uses a breathy vocal clip as an integral part of the groove.

Nigga Please received a mostly positive reception from critics, who usually pointed to Ol' Dirty Bastard's ad hoc ravings on the mic as more genius than, say, drunkenness. *Vibe Magazine* called the album "a biblical storm set to funk beats."[47] *Nigga Please* would debut at #10 on the *Billboard* 200 chart and #2 on *Billboard* R&B/Hip-Hop Albums chart. Somehow Ol' Dirty Bastard manages to deliver a work of musical art despite the tumult around him. RZA unwittingly foretold ODB's future when discussing *Nigga Please*'s creation with *Rolling Stone Magazine* in 1999, saying, "Rick James got into a lot of trouble. He kept a lot of bitches up in his crib, he had a problem with drugs, but he was a funky motherfucker. Just like ODB. You hear about the great brothers that we lost in the hip-hop industry like Tupac and Biggie, but Dirty's still here with that pain."[48]

Unfortunately, only five years after the release of *Nigga Please*, Dirty would join Tupac and the Notorious B.I.G. in death, not at the hands of an unknown assassin but by a combination of cocaine and Tramadol (a prescription painkiller) in his system.

U-GOD, *GOLDEN ARMS REDEMPTION*

There would be plenty more Wu-Tang Clan music before Ol' Dirty Bastard's death. First up after Dirty's sophomore triumph was U-God's *Golden Arms Redemption*. U-God, who also went by the moniker Golden

Arms, was the last original Wu-Tang Clan member to release a solo album.[49] Demand for a solo album from the Staten Island native just wasn't comparable to his peers. According to RZA, since there were no record labels seeking to sign U-God to a solo deal, the producer signed him to his own Razor Sharp Records, which released *Golden Arms Redemption* on October 5, 1999.[50]

U-God has had a particularly contentious relationship with RZA—usually over royalty payments and likely personal differences as well. When asked about their dispute in a 2008 AllHipHop interview, RZA noted: "Even if I did owe you [that], U-God, after all these years of millions you made, motherf**ka, you gonna come back and b***h about a $170,000? I'm the one who gave you, when nobody would sign U-God, I gave him a million dollar f**king deal! And of that million dollars, I put seven hundred thousand that's in his pocket. And the rest went to making the record [U-God's debut, Golden Arms Redemption], and I still spent hundreds of thousands on videos for 'That's Gangsta' and 'Bizarre,' and all that."[51]

"Bizarre" is *Golden Arms Redemption*'s lead single. The song is most notable for being produced by Bink! [sic], who extensively uses a Marvin Gaye vocal sample ("So bizarre . . .") from his tune "Far Cry" (1981), throughout the song. The follow-up single, the True Master–produced "Dat's Gangsta," with its turgid guitar sounds, did not chart at all. Participation from U-God's Clan mates is at a minimum on *Golden Arms Redemption*. Inspectah Deck and Method Man, appear on the plodding, True Master–produced posse cut "Rumble" and Raekwon, as well as Hell Razah, appear on the ominous "Shell Shock." U-God's artist Leathaface participated in both of the aforementioned tracks but does little to justify his participation thanks to rote rhymes.

U-God's powerful baritone voice has made him a punchy addition to many a Wu-Tang Clan song going back to "Protect Ya Neck" and including solo album favorites such as "Wu-Gambinos" and "Knuckleheadz" from *Cuban Linx*. "Black Shampoo," his solo turn on *Wu-Tang Forever*, also revealed the viability of a solo project from the rapper. However, the *Golden Arms Redemption*'s overall production failed to properly back U-God's authoritative voice with any sort of musical accompaniment that would inspire repeated listening. Even RZA's contributions, the synth flushed "Stay In Your Lane" and the faux organ filled "Turbo Charge," were marred by the tinny, ineffectual keyboard sounds that also faltered in parts of *Bobby Digital in Stereo*. *Golden Arms Redemption* managed to muster only an entry at #58 on the *Billboard* 200 chart but did more respectably on the *Billboard* R&B/Hip-Hop Albums chart, entering at #15.

RAEKWON, *IMMOBILARITY*

While U-God's debut was met with general indifference, the next album in the Wu-Tang Clan compendium was one of 1999's most highly anticipated hip-hop albums. Raekwon the Chef's *Immobilarity* was the follow-up to his classic debut album *Only Built 4 Cuban Linx* . . . , which was held in such a high regard by the hip-hop press and fans. *Immobilarity* inherited a world of pressure to meet its predecessor's benchmark for quality and adoration.

Perhaps because he was keenly aware of this, in the run up to the album's release, Raekwon went out of his way to inform fans that *Immobilarity* was not going to be a rehash of *Cuban Linx*'s urban Mafioso tales. The Chef was now a successful rap artist, so drug dealing was a thing of the past.[52] In a 2000 *XXL Magazine* feature story on Wu-Tang Clan, Raekwon says, "I don't sell drugs no more so I can't keep talkin about it every five minutes. I realized so many of my fans are of all nationalities, colors and creeds, and race; kids, adults, youngsters, everybody, mothers, grandmothers! So I said I gotta give everybody a piece of the pie."[53]

Raekwon's reasoning for leaving the gratuitous drug raps of *Only Built 4 Cuban Linx* . . . was noble. But fans are fickle and were accustomed to Raekwon's tales of criminal enterprise and balked at his attempts to rap more about righteousness and redemption for past wrongs. Fans would eventually get a proper sequel to *Only Built 4 Cuban Linx* . . . However, *Only Built 4 Cuban Linx* . . . *Pt. II* wouldn't be released until 14 years, and one more Raekwon album (*The Lex Diamond Story* [2003]), later.

"We have no interest nor investments in anything illegitimate," says Raekwon on *Immobilarity*'s intro track. After more dialogue about moving on from his past life, the intro closes with Raekwon uttering,

"Just when I thought I was out, they pulled me back" a la fictional character Michael Corleone in *The Godfather III*. The *Immobilarity* album is inspired by the film whose plot includes Michael Corleone investing in the real-life Società Generale Immobiliare, a powerful Italian real estate company, as a means to make his family's illicit business legitimate. However, Raekwon backslides into more narcotic-fueled rhymes stories on the aptly titled, drug-reference-dogged "Yae Yo," the first proper song of the album.

But on the majority of *Immobilarity* Raekwon is lyrically trying to move beyond the Mafioso tales in earnest. On "Real Life," tales of cars, chains, and cocaine are traded in for stories of extended jail stays and the realities of street violence. It is not that Raekwon never touched on the latter themes, it is just that on *Immobilarity* he focuses more on the consequences of the fast life. "Jury" is a stern warning about the perils of street life over a beautiful piano loop of Chris Spheeris's "Andalu" (1994) over which Raekwon purposely raps, "Yo, the block is draining and scary/A nigga might die out here or be in some jail law library." And perhaps as a way of showing he is capable of waxing philosophic on topics beyond street tales, Raekwon raps about his affection for choice footwear on "Sneakers"—a lively, piano-drenched number produced by Pete Rock—and musters a tepid sequel to Ghostface's hit "All That I Got Is You" with his own, "All I Got Is You Pt. 2," an ode to his mother that liberally samples Lionel Richie's "Penny Lover" (1983).

Immobilarity's greatest downfall isn't merely an audience unwilling to accept Raekwon asserting his topical versatility. Raekwon's rhyme flow is still top notch and his wordplay and slang had not lost a step, as listeners hear on a song like the lyrically harried "100 Rounds." What *Immobilarity* is missing, in the way of crucial ingredients last heard on *Only Built 4 Cuban Linx . . .* , is apparent when looking at the production credits. While RZA had managed to leave his mark on his old All In Together group member Ol' Dirty Bastard's *Nigga Please*, and at least contributed to U-God's *Golden Arms* album, he is completely absent from *Immobilarity*. Even RZA's usual executive producer credit was not to be. The executive producers of *Immobilarity* are Raekwon and Oli "Power" Grant, the longtime business manager of Wu-Tang Clan. Grant taking a more prominent role in seeing the release of Raekwon's *Immobilary* was planned, but a total lack of participation from RZA was unprecedented for a Wu-Tang Clan project.[54]

In place of RZA, upcoming producers such as Triflyn ("100 Rounds," "Power") and The Infinite Archatechz ("Casablanca," "Jury") deliver production that sounds uninspired and generic, making RZA's absence all the more apparent. Compounding the problem of average-at-best beats is the absence of Ghostface. With the two artists essentially partnering up on both of their previous releases, a lack of any Ghostface rhymes is initially perplexing. But after taking time out to let other Wu-Tang soloists release their debuts (it had been over four years between Raekwon albums), the rapper felt it necessary to prove he could deliver an album without the assistance of his trusted partner.[55] The only other Wu-Tang Clan members to appear on the album are Method Man and Masta Killa. Raekwon also makes sure to showcase his own crew of rappers he was mentoring called American Cream Team. Its most notable member was Lord Superb, who goes on to appear on Ghostface's forthcoming *Supreme Clientele*.

In spite of Raekwon's capability as a solo artist in the truer sense of the word, not a single song from *Immobilarity* managed to chart or gain significant radio play. This shouldn't have been too much cause for concern considering Wu-Tang Clan and its individual projects never received significant amounts of airplay compared to their mainstream contemporaries. But it had to sting Raekwon because in 2000 he told *Vibe Magazine* that making forays into radio rotations was one of his goals with the album.[56] Nevertheless, and likely since the Wu-Tang Clan brand was still strong in 1999, *Immobilarity* entered the *Billboard* 200 chart at #9 and entered the *Billboard* R&B/Hip-Hop Albums chart at #2.

But the fan, and critical, consensus was and still is that *Immobilarity* is not on par with its predecessor, *Only Built 4 Cuban Linx . . .* Most reviews of the album pointed to the album's weak production, and particularly its total absence of RZA-produced tracks. RZA and Raekwon's relationship is one of Wu-Tang Clan's most enigmatic. On occasions their chemistry as beat supplier and rapper are exquisite; as heard on *Cuban Linx . . .* and just about any RZA-produced track Raekwon chooses to rap over. Then there are cases like RZA's AWOL status on *Immobilarity* and Raekwon's public bashing of Wu-Tang Clan's fifth album, *8 Diagrams*, in 2007 that point to a rift.

GHOSTFACE KILLAH, *SUPREME CLIENTELE*

Intro/Nutmeg/One/Saturday Nite/Ghost Deini/Apollo Kids/The Grain/Buck 50/Mighty Healthy/Woodrow the Basehead (skit) / Stay True/We Made It/Stroke of Death/Iron's Theme (Intermission) /Malcolm/Who Would You Fuck/Child's Play /Cherchez LaGhost /Wu Banga 101 /Clyde Smith (skit) /Iron's Theme (Conclusion)

The same, though to a lesser extent, sort of quizzical relationship RZA has with U-God and Raekwon is seen with Ghostface later on in their careers. Ghostface sued RZA in 2009 after alleging royalties the rapper was due hadn't been paid to him by the producer.[57] But in late 1998 and 1999, while recording *Supreme Clientele,* all was well with the old friends and former apartment mates. A good energy and commitment to making the best album possible was crucial because for the first time, the Wu-Tang Clan's once stainless record of success was spotty. Raekwon's album, for all intents and purposes, was a dud while albums from Inspectah Deck, Method Man, and RZA had its advocates but were apathetically received. GZA's and Ol' Dirty Bastard's albums were relative successes but didn't match the indelible impression their previous releases made on hip-hop music.

Perhaps the greatest evidence of Wu-Tang Clan's fall from grace was when Freddie Foxx aka Bumpy Knuckles released his album *Industry Shakedown* in June 2000 and audaciously rapped on "R.N.S.," "I'm bout to save Hip-Hop like Ghost did the Wu." Foxx was referring to Ghostface's album, *Supreme Clientele,* released on January 25, 2000. But let's not get ahead of ourselves. The journey to *Supreme Clientele,* one of Wu-Tang Clan's greatest records ever, begins in 1999 when Ghostface began recording his triumphant sophomore album.

Parts of *Supreme Clientele* were written in Africa, where Ghostface had traveled with RZA to seek alternative treatment to the diabetes he had been recently diagnosed with. Though nowhere near as frequent as his friend and group member Ol' Dirty Bastard, Ghostface too had legal troubles. In February1999, Ghostface plead guilty to charges stemming from a 1995 robbery case where the parking valet of a Manhattan nightclub called the Palladium (now a New York University dorm) claimed the rapper and his entourage assaulted him and stole $3,000. Instead of taking the case to trial, Ghostface settled for a six-month incarceration (he served four months) at Rikers Island Correctional Facility and five years of probation.

A couple of months before Ghostface's incarceration, Epic Records serviced radio with the song "Mighty Healthy." Produced by Allah Mathematics, the eerie keys heard on the track are sampled from 1972's "Wish That I Could Talk to You" by the Sylvers and supported with the familiar drums of Melvin Bliss's "Synthetic Substitution." Ghostface delivers one long extended verse, full of stream-of-consciousness references and also manages to interpolate a rare hip-hop record by Divine Force called "Holy War" (1987). Another song, "Cobra Clutch," which is also produced by Mathematics and uses a sped-up sample of R&B singer Lyn Collins's cover of "Ain't No Sunshine"—and appears on *RZA presents Wu-Tang Killa Bees: The Swarm* (1998)—was also in consideration to be a single as well. But with Ghostface in jail, promotion of a single and upcoming album halted. *Supreme Clientele* was originally scheduled for a February 1999 release, then moved to May 1999 before finally being released in January 2000.

On his release from jail in May 1999, Ghostface got back to work to regain lost momentum with a friend in tow. "In the early 90's stages it was me and him that was buildin' it up," Ghostface told *The Source Magazine* in 2000 about his and RZA's friendship, continuing, "So the first nigga that was my main motherfucka was him."[58] It's ironic that the previous Wu-Tang release, *Immobilarity* by Raekwon, did not include participation from Ghostface and RZA at all. Now the two exiles were responsible for the next album in line, both sharing executive producer credit along with Michelle "Divine" Diggs.

The years after 1997's *Wu-Tang Forever* saw RZA's continual influence on the Wu-Tang sound wane. Other Wu-Tang Clan producers such as 4th Disciple, Mathematicsm and True Master, though RZA's disciples, assumed more of the production work and were even known as the Wu-Elements.[59] But on *Supreme Clientele*, RZA is involved—the album's back cover notes "All songs arranged by The RZA & Ghostface Killah"—and the Abbot (the RZA) is back where he belongs, in the driver's seat as lead producer. RZA was not the sole beatsmith on *Supreme Clientele* but after producers including JuJu of The Beatnuts, Carlos Broady, and Phantom of the Beats submitted their beats, their job was essentially finished. Using the mixing techniques he picked up while creating *36 Chambers* and *Wu-Tang Forever*, as well as the first wave of Wu-Tang Clan solo albums in between those releases, after the beats were submitted, RZA "needle and threaded it together" into the Wu mold.[60]

Supreme Clientele begins with an "Intro" composed of an audio sample from the *Marvel Super Heroes* syndicated cartoon, with the dialogue taken from the introduction of the *Iron Man* episodes. With the tone of a rap superhero set forth, Ghostface launches into the album's first track, the majestically orchestrated "Nutmeg." Produced by Black Moes-Art aka Mo The Barber (he was Ghostface's barber), the track reworks sampled elements from Soul singer Eddie Holman's rather melancholy "It's Over" (1977) into the blast of energy that is "Nutmeg." Ghostface delivers two lively verses, taking time to gloat about his return after the second stanza, telling would-be rappers they "should be studying their arts instead of studying me," before RZA, in Bobby Digital mode, wraps up the song with a lurid but sharp third verse.[61]

A glorious instrumental theme continues with "One." A vocal run and chord progressions from The Sweet Inspirations's "You Roam When You Don't Get It at Home" (1973) are sped up to create the song's intense instrumental, credited to JuJu of The Beatnuts. With the word "one" being heard at the end of every second bar, the song features Ghostface's off-kilter rhymes in full effect. "Ayo, crash through, break the glass, Tony with the goalie mask/That's the pass, heavy ice Rollie laying on the dash [One . . .]/Love the grass, cauliflower hurting when I dumped the trash," raps Ghostface at the beginning of the two-verse song's last verse.

Ghostface's distinctive rhyme style of putting words together that sound good, regardless of if they make sense to the listener or not, was used on the previously mentioned "Cobra Clutch." It would be heard in varying doses in all of Ghostface's future projects. Ghostface explained its emergence in an interview with AllHipHop.com in

2007: " 'Cobra Clutch' was abstract, an abstract joint. . . . See I created a style when I did 'Nutmeg' and 'One' and all the other sh*t. I was in Africa and I was like, 'Yo I'ma make a rhyme not meaning nothing.' . . . People started getting me confused. Like, 'Damn I don't know what he's talking about.' But it wasn't meant for you to know what I was talking about cause it was just a style that I created."[62] Or more simply put, he told *The Source Magazine*, "We just say fly shit, that sound fly to our ear."[63]

On the next song, "Saturday Nite," Ghostface delivers rhymes that are more easily followed. The rapper is in storytelling mode and over producer Carlos Broady's swelling strings, sampled from Lamont Dozier's "Black Bach" (1974), he drops a quick tale of being harassed by police. Ghostface mentions his own issues with the authorities when he raps, "You mind popping your trunk, slow your pace/Starks fixed your face, copped out to six, five years probation," detailing the events that landed him in jail months before. "Saturday Nite" is only a quick one minute and 39 seconds long and abruptly stops, but is quickly followed by "Ghost Deini."

It should be noted that at this point the album's track listing on the back cover no longer coincides with the track listing in the credits inside the album packaging. It likely stems from a song called "In the Rain" being removed from the album due to sample clearance issues shortly before its release.[64] "In the Rain" is Ghostface's dedication to a murdered friend named Wise Allah where the rapper is emotionally rhymes over 1972's "In the Rain" by the Delfonics.

As for "Ghost Deini," it begins with more dialogue from the *Iron Man* cartoon heard on the "Intro" track. Ghostface does the usual rapper boasting and bragging over the Blaquesmiths-produced track's rugged beat of crackly percussion, swelling synth, and spry chords, courtesy of a diced sample of the Michael Masser crafted instrumental "My Hero Is a Gun" from the *Mahogany Original Soundtrack* (1975). Rapper Superb, last heard on Raekwon's *Immobilarity*, tacks on the concluding third verse. At the time, Ghostface told *The Source Magazine* that Superb "put the icing on it." Ghostface's thoughts on Superb likely changed for the worse when in 2004 the guest rapper, who had been incarcerated for a numbers of years, claimed that he in fact wrote most of *Supreme Clientele*. Ghostface disputed this claim, saying that Superb might have written a few lines in the studio but that the album was all his own creation. The Wu-Tang Clan member's previous work on Wu-Tang Clan albums and solo work since *Supreme Clientele* make Superb's claims a tough pill to swallow.

Back to *Supreme Clientele*, Ghostface keeps the pedal on the gas with "Apollo Kids." Produced by Hassan (aka Hass G of early Staten Island hip-hop group The UMC's) the beat maintains the heavily orchestrated feel of the previous song by using stately brass horn and string samples from the title track of Solomon Burke's *Cool Breeze Original Soundtrack* (1972) that are led by a snare-filled drum pattern. Ghostface's rhymes are heavy on the slang but nevertheless gleamed from real life. When Ghostface rhymes, "F.B.I. try and want word with this, Kid who pulled out bust a shot up in the Beacon," he is alluding to an infamous show at New York City's Beacon Theater where the Notorious B.I.G. and Wu-Tang Clan, at the time intense rivals, performed on the same night, which ended with gunfire. Another oft-quoted line from the single "Apollo Kids" is Ghostface's chorus where he raps "these rhymes are like Ziti." In 2000 *XXL Magazine* asked him specifically about the reference and Ghostface's answer can be applied to any of the lines, and song titles, even the most slang savvy of listeners are unable to decipher: "Niggas love lasagna, and ziti and all that shit. . . . Ziti is good, ziti is hot. My raps is good, the ultimate. . . . Whatever comes to my mind at that time, even if it's a word that you'll be like, 'Ghost, what the fuck do this mean?' I knew what it meant when I wrote it! It's like forgetting a thought sometimes."[65]

"Apollo Kids" was *Supreme Clientele*'s lead single and managed to peak at #32 on the *Billboard* Hot Rap Singles chart. Also notable about the song is its inclusion of a punchy verse by Raekwon. After "Apollo Kids," listeners are given a break from the elaborate productions thanks to the bare-bones breakbeat feel of "The Grain." RZA is on the beat (and also raps) and uses vocal and drum samples off of Rufus Thomas's "Breakdown (Part 2)" (1971) and a piano run heard on 1971's "Do the Funky Penguin" (also by Thomas) as well, that will sound familiar to longtime fans of 1980s hip-hop. For the song's third verse RZA and Ghostface rehash a part of ODB's "Don't U Know" from *Return to the 36 Chambers*, which in itself is an interpolation of the Delfonics's "In the Rain." This could be a consolation of sorts since "The Grain" was added to *Supreme Clientele* after Ghostface's version of "In the Rain" (at times titled "Wise (In the Rain)") was unable to be used.

RZA was honored with a "Hip-Hop Quotable" for his verse in *The Source Magazine*.[66] Speaking on "The Grain," in 2000 Ghostface told *The Source Magazine*, "Breakbeats is the essence to all this hip-hop shit. I'd rather rhyme to a breakbeat more than what I rhyme to anybody's beat."[67]

"Buck 50" continues the breakbeat theme; this time it is Funk singer Baby Huey's "Hard Times" (1971) that gets looped for Ghostface and guest rappers, in order of appearance, Method Man, Cappadonna, and Redman, to bludgeon. The MCs are in rap battle mode but "Buck 50" still retains the feel of a thoughtfully constructed song. Ghostface supplies a two bar verse that acts as a bridge after Method Man's verse as well as after the choruses. Following "Buck 50," "Might Healthy" completes *Supreme Clientele*'s core trio of breakbeat-based tracks.

The "Woodrow the Basehead Skit" gets its own track before the album continues on with the hypnotizing, though too short (1:42), "Stay True." On *Supreme Clientele*'s back cover the song is called "Deck's Beat" because not only is it produced by fellow Wu-Tang Clan member Inspectah Deck, the beat was previously used on "Elevation" from his *Uncontrolled Substance* album. Ghostface couldn't resist having a turn at the beat that loops a particularly haunting piano passage from David Axelrod's "Terri's Tune."[68] After the rather subdued groove that dominates "Stay True" is finished, and after some more *Iron Man* cartoon dialogue about Tony Stark's perseverance, the listener is brought to attention by the celebratory strings of the Carlos Broady produced "We Made It," which features guest verses from Superb, Chip Banks, and Hell Razah. While it is a typical example of an established rapper giving his lesser comrades a chance to rap alongside him, "We Made It" differs in that it is not inferior in quality to the rest of the album's songs. Thanks to the track's melody, snatched from Syl Johnson's "I Hate I Walked Away" (1973), it is easily one of *Supreme Clientele*'s most compelling songs.

After the feel-good rhythms of "We Made It" come to a close, listeners are thrown off tilt with the abrasive, RZA-produced "Stroke of Death." The song sounds disconcerting initially because the beat is composed of what sounds like a vinyl record being violently spun backwards, allowed to play, then violently spun backwards again, over and over. RZA adds a drum track sampled from the Harlem Underground's cover of Bill Withers's "Ain't No Sunshine" (1976). Add confidently delivered rhymes from rappers Solomon Childs, Ghostface, and RZA, and "Stroke of Death" is a surprisingly appealing tune. It is an example of RZA's knack for finding seemingly infeasible sounds and turning them into practical music. "Stroke of Death" is only a clipped two minutes long and leads into "Iron's Theme," which has an unknown vocalist capably, at best, singing, "Wu-Tang Clan and Iron Man, lead us to the promised land," to the melody of Jazz pianist Gap Mangione's "Free Again" (1968).

"Iron's Theme" serves as an intermission and is followed by "Malcolm," which appropriately commences with a sample of Malcolm X's "After the Bombing" speech conducted on February 14, 1965. According to Ghostface, he wrote the song before his four-month prison stint the previous year to a different track but he felt the rhyme was appropriate when he heard Malcolm X's voice.[69] The rhyme on "Malcolm" is an extensive story rap where Ghostface describes a would-be thug on the first verse and a robbery gone wrong, maybe committed by the individual described in the first verse, at a nightclub in the second verse, all with fly-on-the-wall detail. As the song nears its close, Malcolm X's voice is heard saying, "they try and project the image to the public that this is being done by thieves, and thieves alone. And they ignore the fact that no, it is not thicvery alone. It's a corrupt, vicious, hypocritical system that has castrated the Black man; and the only way the Black man can get back at it is to strike it in the only way he knows how." The poignant quote serves to give perspective into the malicious actions Ghostface describes in the song.

After "Malcolm," the crass skit "Who Would You Fuck" follows where Ghostface and his buddies loudly discuss which female rappers they would sleep with if given the opportunity while 1968's "Rain, Rain, Go Away" by Bob Azzam is heard playing in the background. "Childs Play" follows and continues the sexual innuendo as Ghostface describing prepubescent crushes. Produced by RZA, the track's drums and guitar samples are from rock band Mountain's "Long Red" (1972) yet another popular hip-hop breakbeat, while the sultry organ melody heard throughout the song is from George Jackson's "Aretha, Sing One for Me" (1972)

After Ghostface gets the puppy love musings out of his system, "Cherchez LaGhost" erupts through the speakers. A female vocalist is heard singing, "Tommy Mottola lives on the road, he lost his lady two months ago, maybe he'll find her, maybe he won't, oh wonder." The lyrics are cribbed directly from the Dr. Buzzard's Original Savannah Band 1976 disco hit "Cherchez Le Femme," just in case you couldn't figure it out from the song's title. Produced by Carlos Bess, whose wife (Madam Majestic) is the female vocalist on the song, the longtime Wu-Tang Clan engineer replaces the original's disco rhythms with hip-hop flavored drums sampled from "Greedy G" by funk band the Brentford All-Stars. The creeping bass line and the song's built-in danceability has made it one of Ghostface's most recognizable hits. Though it only reached #98 on the *Billboard* Hot 100 chart, it made it to #42 on the *Billboard* R&B/Hip-Hop Songs chart and #3 on the *Billboard* Hot Rap Singles chart. Wu-Tang Clan's U-God contributes a notable second verse to the song. "Cherchez LaGhost" was *Supreme Clientele*'s second single and the label wanted Ghostface to add another verse since he only had one on the song, but a version with additional lyrics from the rapper was never released.[70]

After the up-tempo "Cherchez LaGhost" comes the decidedly down-tempo "Wu-Banga 101." Allah Mathematics produces the song and uses a sludge thick bass line and a vocal clip swiped from 1963's "Queen of Tears" by Gladys Knight & The Pips. All the guest rappers on the track—GZA, Cappadonna, Raekwon, and Masta Killa—deliver solid verses with Ghostface managing to include two. The album should have concluded here but Ghostface decides to include a "Clyde Smith" skit, which features a disguised voice—although the cadence and style of speech clearly gives away that it is Raekwon—chastising individuals not giving him his proper respect, specifically rapper 50 Cent. After this detour, the album comes to a close with another turn of "Iron's Theme," which concludes with the same *Iron Man* cartoon introduction music heard at the start of the album. "With *Ironman*, I was going through a lot of trials and tribulations. But with this joint I'm trying to be a little bit more reflective and introspective," Ghostface told *The Source Magazine* in 1999.[71] Mission accomplished.

Acclaim for *Supreme Clientele* on its release was universal, and affection for the album has only grown with time. *The Source Magazine* rated the album four and half out of five mics and called it "the mother of all Wu-affiliated sophomore albums," with the only fault of note being Ghostface's dense slang.[72] *XXL Magazine* gave the album an XL rating and *Vibe Magazine* gave it an enthusiastically positive review, noting its "luscious linguistics and potent production that support its claim of supremacy."[73] *Supreme Clientele* was so critically lauded that many said that it literally saved the Wu-Tang Clan.[74] *Supreme Clientele*, which *The Source Magazine* astutely observed, "is a Wu album in the Wu-est sense," was a return to form and reestablishment of faith in the Wu-Tang Clan. "*Supreme Clientele* is the first Clan-stamped album (not counting Method Man's 1999 collaboration with Redman, *Blackout!*) since *Ironman*, really, to move the pencil-chewing music-critic crowd and hoodied-down hard rocks alike," wrote journalist Dave Bry in 2000 in *Vibe Magazine*.[75]

NOTES

1. Jones, Steve, "Led by Puff Daddy, Rap Rhythms Underscore All Urban Music," *USA Today*, December 29, 1997, 4.

2. RZA and Chris Norris, *The Tao of Wu* (New York: Riverhead Books, 2009), 133.

3. Strauss, Neil, "What Do You Do When You're One of Hip-Hop's Most Creative Producers?," *Rolling Stone*, September 4, 1997, 38.

4. RZA and Chris Norris, *The Tao of Wu* (New York: Riverhead Books, 2009), 133.

5. Owen, Frank, "Wu-Tang Clan Is Sumthing Ta Fuck Wit," *The Village Voice*, May 30, 2000, 43.

6. Owen, *The Village Voice*.

7. Ashon, Will, "RZA As Bobby Digital" *Trace Urban Magazine*, November 1998, 56 (48–56).

8. Bonnano, Jonathan, "Return of the Dragon" *The Source Magazine*, March 2000, 207–208.

9. DeCurtis, Anthony, "Wu-Tang Family Values," *Rolling Stone*, July 10, 1997–July 24, 1997, 86.

10. Method Man's *Tical 2000: Judgement Day* was released on November 17, 1998, and RZA's *Bobby Digital in Stereo* was released on November 24, 1998.

11. Bozza, Anthony, "Method Man Is Ready for his Close-Up," *Rolling Stone Magazine*, December 1, 1998, 59.

12. Ibid.

13. Croal, N'Gai, "Method to the Madness," Newsweek, November 16, 1998, 86.

14. Farley, Christopher John, and Thigpen, David E., "Super Tuesday! Big Stars With Big Albums Make for Pop Music's Biggest Day Ever," *Time Magazine*, November 23, 1998, 104.

15. Hampton, Dream, "Oh Gods," *Village Voice*, December 15, 1998, 128.

16. Gill, John, "Rhyme & Reason: Method Man Tical 2000: Judgement Day," *The Source Magazine*, March 1999, 45–46.

17. Samples not being credited does not mean they were not used, as there are many examples of these types of occurrences in RZA's production discography.

18. Croal, N'Gai, "Who Is Bobby Digital?," *The Source Magazine*, January 1999, 146.

19. Bozza, Anthony, "Method Man Is Ready for his Close-Up," *Rolling Stone Magazine*, December 1, 1998, 59.

20. Pareles, Jon, "Pay Attention: Reinvention; No Prevention," *The New York Times*, November 5, 1998, 1.

21. RZA and Chris Norris, *The Wu-Tang Manual* (New York: Riverhead Books, 2005), 91.

22. Croal, N'Gai, "Who Is Bobby Digital?," *The Source Magazine*, January 1999, 144 (142–46).

23. Jones, Steve, "Wu-Tang Clan's RZA Fits Pieces Into 'Digital' World," *USA Today*, December 8, 1998, 4D.

24. Ibid.

25. The "African" being spoken in "Slow Grind African" is anyone's guess.

26. Hampton, Dream, "Oh Gods," *Village Voice*, December 15, 1998, 128.

27. "Hip-Hop Quotable: Method Man 'N.Y.C. Everything,' " *The Source Magazine*, January 1999, 182.

28. Pareles, Jon, "Hip-Hop Stretches a Common Deadline," *The New York Times*, December 31, 1998, 6.

29. Marcus Reeves, "Record Report: Bobby Digital in Stereo," *The Source Magazine*, January 1999, 177–178.

30. Jones, Steve, "Wu-Tang Clan's RZA Fits Pieces Into 'Digital' World," *USA Today*, December 8, 1998, 4D.

31. Gonzales, Michael A., "Back to the Lab: In the Studio with GZA," *The Source Magazine*, July 1999, 54.

32. Kwak, Donnie, "The Great Book of GZA," *Stress Magazine*, Issue 21, 36 (34–36).

33. Barone, Matt, "Numerology," *Scratch Magazine*, September/October 2005, 59 (58–59).

34. Alvarez, Gabriel, "True Mathematics," *The Source Magazine*, August 1999, 196 (192–96).

35. "Hip-Hop Quotable: GZA/Genius "Breaker, Breaker," *The Source Magazine*, August 1999, 226.

36. Alvarez, "True Mathematics."

37. Cockfield, Jr., Errol A., "Catching Red," *The Source Magazine*, March 1999, 121 (120–24).

38. Valdes, Mimi, "Right and Exact," *Vibe Magazine*, September 1997, 118.

39. The Blackspot, "Shaolin Shadowboxing," *XXL Magazine*, August 1999, 108.

40. Stein, Joel, "People: Citizen of the Week." *Time Magazine*, March 9, 1998, 53.

41. Diehl, Matt, "Dirty Stories," *Rolling Stone*, November 11, 1999, 36.

42. Ibid.

43. Jenkins, Sacha, "Looking For Jesus," *Vibe Magazine*, December 1999/January 2000, 172.

44. Bry, Dave, "Revolutions: Ol' Dirty Bastard," *Vibe Magazine*, November 1999, 186.

45. Byers, R K, "Get Dirty," *The Source Magazine*, December 1999, 224 (176–182, 224).

46. This wouldn't be the last song from a Wu-Tang Clan artist called "All In Together Now, or some variance, with All In Together being the original group consisting of RZA, GZA and Ol' Dirty Bastard.

47. Bry, *Vibe Magazine*, 185–86.

48. Diehl, Matt, "Dirty Stories," *Rolling Stone*, November 11, 1999, 36.

49. Masta Killa, who wasn't a formal Wu-Tang Clan member until *Wu-Tang Forever*, would not release a solo debut album, *No Said Date,* until June 2004.

50. http://allhiphop.com/stories/news/archive/2008/07/02/20247797.aspx

51. Ibid.

52. Raekwon relays the sentiment in multiple interviews, including: Wilson, Elliott, "Victory," *XXL Magazine*, October 2000, 158; Alvarez, Gabriel, "Spit Darts," *The Source Magazine*, December 1999, 167–174; *Vibe Magazine*, March 2000.

53. Wilson, Elliott, "Victory," *XXL Magazine*, October 2000, 158.

54. Bonnano, Jonathan, "Return of the Dragon" *The Source Magazine*, March 2000, 207–208.

55. Alvarez, Gabriel, "Spit Darts," *The Source Magazine*, December 1999, 168 (167–74).

56. The Consigliere™, "The Mobfather," *Vibe Magazine*, March 2000, 144.

57. AbduSalaam, Ismael, "RZA: Breaks Down the Ghostface Killah Lawsuit," September 29, 2009; http://admin.allhiphop.com/stories/features/archive/2009/09/29/21956222.aspx.

58. Bonanno, Jonathan "Gotti," "Last Man Standing," *The Source Magazine*, March 2000, 216 (210–17).

59. Croal, N'Gai, "Who Is Bobby Digital?," *The Source Magazine*, January 1999, 146 (142–146).

60. Bonanno, Jonathan "Gotti," "Return of the Dragon," *The Source Magazine*, March 2000, 208 (206–9).

61. Ghostface's rant at the end of the third verse actually is an interpolation of quotes used by the characters "Dragonfly Jones" and "Jerome" in the sitcom *Martin*.

62. Blanco, Alvin, "Ghostface Killah: Iron Manual," December 4, 2007; http://allhiphop.com/stories/features/archive/2007/12/04/18959440.aspx.

63. Bonanno, *The Source Magazine*, 215.

64. Inside the album, the songs in order of appearance are: 1. "Nutmeg" 2. "One" 3. "Saturday Nite" 4. "In the Rain" 5. "Mighty Healthy" 6. "Apollo Kids" 7. "Buck 50" 8. "Deck's Beat" 9. "G-Dini" 10. "Malcolm" 11. "We Made It" 12. "Child's Play" 13. "Cherchez La Ghost" 14. "Wu-Banga". The song in order of appearance, and unnumbered, on the back cover are: "Nutmeg," "One," "Saturday Nite," "G-Deini," "Apollo Kids," "The Grain," "Buck 50," "Mighty Healthy," "Stay True" "We Made It," "Malcolm" "Child's Play" "Cherchez La Ghost" "Wu-Banga."Neither version included the album's skits and intro/outros, which were their own tracks.

65. Dee Tee One, "Slang Teacher," *XXL Magazine*, April 2000, 90 (88–92).

66. "Hip-Hop Quotable: RZA 'The Grain,' " *The Source Magazine*, March 2000, 250.

67. Bonanno, Jonathan "Gotti," as told to, "Rhyme & Reason: Ghostface Killah," *The Source Magazine*, April 2000, 49.

68. Ibid.

69. Ibid.

70. Bry, Dave, "Emotional Rescue," *Vibe Magazine*, June/July 2000, 136 (136–39).

71. Gonzales, Michael A., "Back to the Lab: In the Studio With Ghostface Killah," *The Source Magazine*, March 1999, 46.

72. Morales, Riggs, "Record Report: Ghostface Killah: Supreme Clientele," *The Source Magazine*, March 2000, 239–40.

73. The Blackspot, "Revolutions: Ghostface Killah Supreme Clientele," *Vibe Magazine*, April 2000, 176.

74. Alvarez, Gabriel, "Never Change," *XXL Magazine*, December 2001, 81 (80–86).

75. Bry, "Emotional Rescue," 138.

CHAPTER 8
Wu-Tang as a Brand, Music and Beyond

Beginning before the hit-or-miss second wave of Wu-Tang Clan music, strides were made to expand the group's marketability as a brand. Star rappers have always simultaneously, and often inadvertently, held positions as taste-making trendsetters due to their popularity and influence. An obvious example is the Run-DMC song "My Adidas," which, when combined with the rap group's donning of Adidas attire, opened the door to the possibilities, and benefits, of hip-hop's sway in the marketing of products. Adidas now counts Missy Elliott and Snoop Dogg as a couple of their celebrity endorsers.

A Wu specific example is the popularization of the Clarks Wallabee shoe. While the shoe from the originally British-based shoemaker was long a staple of fashionable West Indians in New York City, the footwear had fallen out of favor in hip-hop circles. Hip-hop fans tended to gravitate toward Timberland boots or sneakers for their footwear. But Wu members, particularly Raekwon and Ghostface Killah, wore Wallabees because not only did they find them aesthetically pleasing and comfortable, since no one else was really wearing them, they also weren't succumbing to trends. Thanks to their name checking of the shoe in songs—and the famed Ghostface skit in *Only Built 4 Cuban Linx ...* —in the mid to late 1990s Wallabees suddenly became a hip-hop staple. Ghostface justified calling himself the Wally Champ when *Ironman*'s album cover was littered with dozens of custom-dyed Wallabee shoes. But alas, purported overtures to Clarks about teaming up with Wu-Tang did not materialize. If anything, not only was it a clear-cut example of the Clan's marketing power, it begged the question, why not go into the business of Wu-Tang?

Naturally, Wu-Wear Clothing Inc. was established in 1995, with a brick-and-mortar store opened in Staten Island, New York, that sold all things Wu-Tang Clan. With bootleggers selling T-shirts with the Wu-Tang logo making money, they figured they should sell officially endorsed clothing themselves. The synergy between the music and brand was sheepishly exploited. For example, the women seen in Raekwon's "Ice Cream" video were wearing Wu-Wear branded T-shirts that were available for sale at the store. Another example is the RZA song "Wu-Wear: Garment Renaissance" from the *High School High Soundtrack* (1996) that featured the producer and Capadonna extolling the virtues of Wu-Wear Clothing in rhyme. The song served as a commercial for Wu-Wear and its performance on the charts—it reached #6 on the *Billboard* Hot Rap Single chart—amounted to plenty of free advertising.

Traditional media entities such as the *New York Times* and *Time Magazine* wrote glowing profiles about the Wu's expanding empire, marveling at the business acumen of RZA and the behind-the-scenes players Mitchell Diggs and Oli Grant. Indeed, Wu-Tang Clan's endeavors, for a group of men from the New York City ghettos, were nothing short of phenomenal. In 2000, *Time Magazine* would note, "During a three-year hiatus after their 1997 record-setting double album *Wu-Tang Forever*, the group's Wu-Wear clothing line hit $15 million in annual sales, a new Wu comic-book line briefly nudged out X-Men for the top spot in the country, and its first kung fu video game sold 600,000 units for Sony PlayStation."[1] In 1999, *The Source Magazine* also noted about RZA that, "His business blueprints for the Wu-Tang Clan make him one of rap's four most influential moguls of the decade (Dre, Puffy, and P are the others)."[2]

Besides their business ventures—the *Wu-Tang: Shaolin Style* video game released October 31, 1999, and *The Nine Rings of Wu-Tang* comic book series ran for a year (five issues, briefly outselling Marvel's *X-Men* series) starting in late 1999—various members of Wu-Tang Clan had begun pursuing acting, which further increased their visibility. Most of Wu-Tang Clan, with Oli Grant playing a prominent role, appeared in James Toback's 1999 film *Black & White*. Method Man has gone on to enjoy a successful acting career, appearing in a short-lived Fox TV show called *Method & Red* with Redman, as well as celebrated roles in HBO's *The Wire*. RZA would jump in front of the camera, too, appearing in numerous films including Jim Jarmusch's *Coffee and Cigarettes* (along with GZA), *Derailed*, and *American Gangster*. RZA's acting work was an extension of the soundtrack and scoring work he found himself increasingly conducting, beginning in 1999 with Jarmusch's *Ghostdog: Way of the Samurai*. More recently, RZA is set to direct *The Man with the Iron Fist*, which is set to star Oscar-winning actor Russell Crowe.

RZA, and therefore Wu-Tang Clan, was becoming one of the most powerful and influential artists in hip-hop and popular culture in general. Wu-Tang was running like a well-oiled machine by placing their imprint in various entities that naturally made sense. "It resembles a concept called the virtual corporation, in which a company maintains just a small core and outsources everything else," said *Time Magazine* of Wu-Tang Clan's growing conglomerate in 2000.[3] Amazingly, Wu-Tang Clan was still pumping out music while all these extracurricular endeavors were being pursued.

RZA's production prowess is what landed him all these opportunities. Naturally, rappers outside of the Wu-Tang circle increasingly began seeking his services, too. Notable productions from RZA include "Long Kiss Goodnight" from the Notorious B.I.G.'s *Life After Death* (1997); "Tres Leches (Triboro Trilogy)," featuring Inspectah Deck, from Big Pun's *Capital Punishment* (1998); and "Stand Up," featuring Ghostface, from Charli Baltimore's *Cold as Ice* (1999). Wu-Tang wasn't overly prolific when it came to appearing on the recordings of artists outside of their traditional Shaolin circle. When they did appear, they would often end up stealing the show as in the case of SWV's "Anything Remix" that featured Wu-Tang Clan, or Mariah Carey's "Fantasy Remix" with Ol' Dirty Bastard. By choosing quality over quantity with their cameos, Wu-Tang Clan only cemented their reputation for superior work. But as Wu-Tang Clan began to expand its reach with affiliate groups that used the group's hard-earned reputation as a proverbial foot in the door, oversight and quality control proved to be impossible.

After the first wave of solo releases, there were a number of ancillary acts that claimed the Wu-Tang Clan banner with the release of their own material. Even a diehard Wu-Tang Clan fan had a hard time keeping up with all of these satellite groups and soloists. A 1998 *Source Magazine* story dubbed the "second cycle" of Wu-Tang Clan music as Killarmy's *Silent Weapons for Quiet Wars* and *Dirty Weaponry*, Killah Priest's

Heavy Mental, Cappadonna's *The Pillage*, and Wu-Tang Killa Bees' *The Swarm*, all released in 1998.[4] Similarly to individual Clan members signing solo deals with various labels, RZA applied the concept to his own boutique labels. Razor Sharp Records was distributed by Sony/Epic and Wu-Tang Records was distributed by Priority Records. Most of the auxiliary Wu-Tang acts were signed to one of these labels at one point.

The most notable of these acts were fairly regular contributors on previous Wu-Tang Clan solo albums. Killarmy—originally consisting of rappers 9th Prince (RZA's younger brother), Dom Pachino, Islord, Killa Sin, and producer 4th Disciple, before adding rappers Beretta 9 and ShoGun Assasson—released a few warmly received albums including *Silent Weapons for Quiet Wars* (1997), *Dirty Weaponry* and *Fear* (1998), and *Love & War* (2001).[5] Killarmy was originally on Wu-Tang/Priority Records but none of their albums were released via the label—this would become the norm for Wu-Tang Records. Sunz of Man, the first group signed to Wu-Tang Records, was handpicked and put together by RZA and included rappers 60 Second Assassin, Hell Razah, Killah Priest, and Prodigal Sunn. The group released the well-received *The Last Shall Be the First* in 1998, which includes beats from RZA as well as True Master and 4th Disciple (together with RZA known as "Wu-Elements") and featured cameo appearances from Masta Killa, Method Man, Ol' Dirty Bastard, Raekwon, and U-God.[6] Sunz of Man would release albums after *The Last Shall Be the First* but no longer with any direct contributions from Wu-Tang Clan.[7]

Killah Priest only appeared on a handful of songs on *The Last Shall Be the First* because he had already begun his solo career in earnest, releasing his debut, *Heavy Mental*, in 1998. Killah Priest first came to prominence after cameo appearances on RZA's side project—the Gravediggaz's *6 Feet Deep* (1994)—and GZA's *Liquid Swords* and Ol' Dirty Bastard's *Return to the 36 Chambers*. *Heavy Mental*'s production was handled mostly by True Master and 4th Disciple. The album is a cult favorite that earned favorable reviews when it was released, with many publications pointing out his heavy use of religious symbolism in his rhymes. But after reportedly clashing with RZA, as well as no longer being managed by GZA's Liquid Swords Entertainment, Killah Priest severed his Wu-Tang Clan ties. Nevertheless, Killah Priest still enjoys a devoted following, having released at least eight solo albums as of 2010.

Cappadonna is the most popular of these Wu-Tang affiliates since at times he has been considered a proper Wu-Tang Clan member. The Staten Island rapper came up with original members of Wu-Tang Clan but he was incarcerated for selling crack cocaine when RZA began forming the collective and during the recording of *Enter the Wu-Tang (36 Chambers)*. Nonetheless, Cappadonna still managed to release his debut album, *The Pillage*, in March 1998, before original Wu-Tang Clan members Inspectah Deck, U-God, and Masta Killa released their own debut solo albums. Cappadonna leapt to prominence after a pair of scene-stealing verses on Raekwon's *Only Built 4 Cuban Linx...* ("Ice Cream") as well as his blistering verse on "Winter Warz," which first appeared on the *Don't Be a Menace to South Central While Drinking Your Juice in the Hood Soundtrack* (1996) before appearing on Ghostface Killah's *Ironman*, where he was noted as a "co-star" on the album's cover.

Cappadonna's copious use of slang made him a fitting addition when partnering with Raekwon and Ghostface. The verse on "Winter Warz," where while taking poetic license he brags about seeing his face on the $20 bill, is a perfect example of Cappadonna's reputation for extra-long verses that show little regard for the established 16 bars and chorus norm of rap songs. Cappadonna likened his songs to being akin to psalms as an explanation for this.[8] On its release, *The Pillage* earned a favorable three and a half out of five mic review in *The Source Magazine*.[9] However, *Vibe Magazine* was not as impressed, saying, "While slang fiends like Raekwon and Ghostface have an ultimate destination, Donna's are not as focused."[10] Cappadonna was signed to RZA's Razor Sharp Records, and the Wu's Zen master, along with the rest of the Wu-Elements contributed beats to *The Pillage*. The *Los Angeles Times* said in its review of the album, "RZA, who normally assumes all production duties on all Wu-related records, shares the music-making chores with a host of Wu's beat maker protégés, who supply enough tensile grooves and off-kilter rhythms to make Cappadonna's cackling battle raps resonate with a unique urgency."[11]

RZA and the Wu-Elements produced the compilation album *Wu-Tang Killa Bees: The Swarm, Vol. 1* (billed as *RZA Presents...*), which was released in July 1998. The album has a few bright spots including Cappadonna's previously released " '97 Mentality" (another song that helped build his buzz), and Ghostface's "Cobra Clutch." The aforementioned records and albums were legitimate rap offerings that probably would have been considered closer to superior efforts if not for the tremendous expectations the Wu-Tang logo by now intrinsically demanded.

Unfortunately, the Wu-Tang Clan–related releases that follow, with a few exceptions, were inherently inferior in terms of quality. A look at *The Swarm*'s roster reveals some of the dysfunction that infiltrated the ranks of Wu-Tang Clan's offshoots. The duo A.I.G. (rappers Allah Wise and Darkim Be Allah) and the group Royal Fam (which had a rotating roster of members, with Timbo King being the most consistent) never released an album on Wu-Tang Records. Black Knights Of The North Star was composed of two groups (Black Knights and North Star), both hailing from California.[12] Black Knights, consisting of rappers Crisis, Doc Doom (now deceased), The Rugged Monk, and Holocaust, would release their debut album, *Every Knight Is a Black Knight*, in 2004. The group is still working with RZA, most recently appearing on his 2008 solo album *Digi Snacks*. Northstar would release their debut, *Bobby Digital Presents Northstar*, in 2003 via Wu-Tang/Koch Records. Wu-Syndicate, rappers Joe Mafia, Napolean, and Myalansky, were from Virginia and originally known as The Syndicate but changed their names after signing to Wu-Tang Records. They would leave the label after the release of their debut album, *Wu-Syndicate*, in 1999. Rapper/producer Remedy is one of the most successful artists hanging from this Wu-Tang family tree of rappers. Caucasian and Jewish, Remedy executive produced Inspectah Deck's 2010 album *Manifesto* and runs his own independent Code Red Entertainment record label out of Staten Island.

The above-mentioned artists are just the start of an extensive list of performers RZA brought into the Wu-Tang fold with the intent of seeing them through as successful acts, though it rarely occurred. Female vocalist Tekitha, heard on *Wu-Tang Forever*, was signed to Razor Sharp Records and was going to help RZA make his mark in the R&B world, but her album never manifested. RZA also planned to release an album with Blue Raspberry, who was the Wu-Tang's primary female vocalist before Tekitha, called *Blunted Soul*, which did not come to fruition.[13] The same goes for female MC Jamie Sommers, heard on various Bobby Digital projects, with no album release to date. Besides RZA, other Wu-Tang Clan members had their own mentees such as Streetlife (associated with Method Man) who wouldn't release his debut *Street Education* until 2005, while La the Darkman (associated with Raekwon) would release *Heist of the Century* in 1998. Even overseas talent was sought, with rapper/producer Cilvaringz out of the Netherlands being signed to Wu-Tang International.[14]

RZA may have executive produced a number of these albums, but his actual contributions were haphazard. For example, RZA produced six of *The Swarm*'s 15 songs. But, on *Wu-Syndicate*, although he is credited as an executive producer he didn't produce a single song. No matter the Abbot's presence on the albums, even from a casual listen it was clear that the music on these projects is inferior to the rap status quo, and more so when compared to previous Wu-Tang releases from 1993 to 1997. Albums from groups like Wu-Syndicate and GP Wu failed to resonate with fans. Flooding the market with all these Wu-Tang stamped releases—in 1998 alone there were six Wu-Tang Clan–associated albums that hit store shelves, not including the solo albums of Method Man and RZA—was a case of quantity over quality.

RZA giving up the reigns of the core Wu-Tang Clan thoroughbred meant the neophyte acts could get some of his guiding attention, but these acts suffered the misfortune of catching RZA's production prowess in a transitional period. Whether it was a means to avoid sampling fees or to stay ahead of producers mimicking his techniques, RZA started learning music theory. RZA has often pointed the blame in the quality of music when it came to his beats to learning music theory and playing music, dulling the rawness he was known for. But even RZA himself has said that he had to make a number of corny beats before he started creating beats on par with his seminal work.[15]

A better excuse would be that RZA was stretched too thin. Wu-Element producers True Master, 4th Disciple, and Mathematics catch a bad rap by being lumped into the numerous amounts of lackluster music being produced. Some of the music these producers were responsible for during this Wu-Tang era was some of the better efforts. In actuality, it was a number of RZA's contributions that were lackluster. Adding to their plight was the impossible task of living up to the precedent of quality music the first wave of Wu-Tang Clan albums and solo projects left in their wake.

The inevitable crapshoot of musical quality found on the records of this period was beginning to adversely affect the Wu-Tang Clan brand. By 1998 even the *New York Times* had grown wary, writing, "The

Tang trademark, which from 1994 to 1997 guaranteed that a hip-hop album would zoom into the Top 10 the moment it was released, lost some of its cachet through dilution."[16] The once adamantine Wu-Tang brand no longer had a freshness guarantee. In 1997, RZA was #6 in *The Source Magazine*'s inaugural "Power 30" issue that celebrated hip-hop's most influential executives and moved down a notch to #7 the following year.[17] By 1999, RZA and Oli Grant had dipped to #29 in *The Source Magazine*'s Power 30 listing; cited for new albums from U-God, Inspectah Deck, Method Man and Raekwon, and RZA too along with the *Ghost Dog Soundtrack*. Beyond music, members acting in the film *Black & White* and the *Shaolin Style* video game were mentioned, too.[18] The Wu-Tang's fall from grace was tough for fans to handle considering the monumental albums the group delivered not too long ago. Thankfully, *Supreme Clientele* and *The W* restored faith in the Clan's abilities. Unfortunately, both albums arrived after two years of too many uninspiring offerings.

NOTES

1. Eskenazi, Mike, "Remaking Wu," *Time Magazine*, December 11, 2000, 82.

2. Croal, N'Gai, "Who's Bobby?," *The Source Magazine*, January 1999, 144 (142–46).

3. Eskenazi, "Remaking Wu."

4. Croal, N'Gai, "Who Is Bobby Digital?," *The Source Magazine*, January 1999, 146 (142–46).

5. Cook, Dara, "Record Report: Killarmy 'Fear, Love & War,' " *The Source Magazine*, September 2001, 290, 327. [3 ½ out of 5 mic album review]

6. Pollack, Scott, "Record Report: Sunz of Man 'Last Shall Be the First,' " *The Source Magazine*, August 1998, 170–71. [3 ½ out of 5 mic review]

7. *The Last Shall Be the First* was released via Red Ant Entertainment while a previous released titled *Nothing New Under the Sun*, originally due in 1996, was never released.

8. Alvarez, Gabriel, "The Dapper Don," *The Source Magazine*, April 1998, 63.

9. Chow, Durwin, "Record Report: Cappadonna 'The Pillage,' " *The Source Magazine*, May 1998, 146.

10. Mao, Chairman, "Revolutions: Cappadonna," *Vibe Magazine*, May 1998, 135–36.

11. Johnson, Brett, "Cappadonna Shows Range Away from Wu-Tang Clan," *Los Angeles Times*, April 11, 1998, 16.

12. The two groups were signed to Wu-Tang Records as Black Knights of the North Star.

13. Fernando, Jr., S. H. (add reporting by Selwyn Seyfu Hinds), "Lords of Chaos," *The Source Magazine*, June 1997, 108 (104–10, 132).

14. Bonanno, Jonathan, "Return of the Dragon," *The Source Magazine*, March 2000, 208.

15. Croal, N'Gai, "Who Is Bobby Digital?," *The Source Magazine*, January 1999, 146.

16. Pareles, Jon, "Pay Attention: Reinvention; No Prevention," *The New York Times*, November 5, 1998, Section E, 1.

17. "The Power 30," *The Source Magazine*, January 1997, 82.

18. Williams, Frank, "The Source's Hip-Hop Power 30," *The Source Magazine*, February 2000, 166.

CHAPTER 9
A New Millennium, Even More Wu

WU-TANG CLAN, *THE W*

Intro (Shaolin Finger Jab)/Chamber Music/Careful (Click, Click)/
Hollow Bones/Redbull/One Blood Under W/Conditioner/Protect
Ya Neck (The Jump Off)/Let My Niggas Live/I Can't Go to Sleep/
Do You Really? (Thang, Thang)/The Monument/Gravel Pit/Jah
World

Ghostface Killah delivered a classic album with his sophomore effort *Supreme Clientele*. Thanks in part to hip-hop's what-have-you-done-for-me-lately attitude when it comes to its artists, in 2000 Wu-Tang Clan regained some the clout it lost in the wake of mediocre albums. *Supreme Clientele* would be certified gold in March 2000, meaning the time was ripe for Wu-Tang Clan to reform and deliver another group album. *The W*, released November 21, 2000, would be Wu-Tang Clan's third album and it found the Shaolin rap heroes in a rather precarious situation. Hip-hop music was fast becoming the music industry's highest selling music genre thanks to its immense, global popularity. While Wu-Tang Clan had a hand in the genre's growth, the group as a unit and individually had not gained the mainstream notoriety of hip-hop peers such as Master P, Sean "Diddy" Combs, or Dr. Dre. Noted *Time Magazine*, "With its latest album, The W, RZA hopes to harness the brand's market power to better management in order to restage the Wu brand and set the Clan on a new growth phase."[1]

It had been three years since the last proper Wu-Tang Clan album, *Wu-Tang Forever*, which was a financial success thanks to its four-times platinum status. But with the passage of time the album was not considered the home run hit RZA and company were hoping for by critics and fans. Perhaps, as a way to affirm their position in the exponentially growing hip-hop/rap landscape, the Wu-Tang Clan announced their plans for a new album in June 2000. The album was tentatively to be called *The Worms in the Big Apple*.[2] Citing the distractions of New York City, the group decided to move out to California to better focus on recording the album. Recording was done at Track Record Studios in North Hollywood while the finishing touches on the album were made back in New York City at 36 Chambers Recording Studios. For three months the entire Clan, except for Ol' Dirty Bastard, lived together at a mansion on Los Angeles' Mulholland Drive, supposedly formerly owned by Warren Beatty.[3] As for Ol' Dirty Bastard, his legal troubles had culminated with being ordered by authorities to enter a drug rehabilitation center or face jail time. Ol' Dirty Bastard did manage to record verses for the album while on weekend furlough from a halfway house in LA, but only one song made the project.

One less rapper to consider integrating into the mix was actually a blessing (though fans wouldn't have minded more of Ol' Dirty Bastard's antics, on the microphone). Critics pointed out that *Wu-Tang Forever*'s 27 tracks over two discs made for a bloated affair that dulled the album's impact to listeners. With this in mind, RZA saw that *The W* on release only contained a relatively succinct 14 tracks. " 'The W' is a model of efficiency in comparison with the previous album, the overstuffed double-disc set 'Wu-Tang Forever,' " said *The San Francisco Chronicle* in 2000 in its review of the album.[4] Not only did RZA include fewer songs, he also needed to cut lines from verses for the purposes of space, which often meant hurt feelings among Wu-Tang Clan members.[5] Contention between RZA's executive decisions and the desires of individual Clan members would only continue to grow over the years.

Besides fewer songs, *The W* is also stripped down in its production aesthetics and in the density of its lyrics. Both of these particulars were done purposefully. As for the lyrics, simple rhymes and simple hooks made for palatable radio hits, and maybe gaining more fans once intimidated by the group's labyrinth of rhymes. Critics took note of the levity in some of the rhymes. *Rolling Stone* in its review of the album wrote, "The W has less of the Five Percent polemics, insider slang and rhythmic jabberwocky that have made Wu-Tang cult favorites."[6] In 2000, U-God assured *The Source Magazine* that for the Clan it was just a matter of switching the use of excessive jargon off and on when recording *The W*: "We know what we doing. But the time calls for simplex. . . . We can go there easy."[7] Similarly RZA, whose lyrics were traditionally some of Wu-Tang Clan's most intellectually heavy-handed rhymes, told *XXL Magazine* in 2001 that his own Clan members asked him to dial back on the deeply esoteric lyrics on *The W*.[8] Similar sentiments were relayed to *The Source Magazine* in a January 2001 feature story on the group.[9] RZA concedes that he took the advice, considering the group over himself.

As for *The W*'s production, RZA was back at the helm producing all of the tracks. In an interview with *Rolling Stone* conducted while he was in the midst of recording *The W*, he told the magazine, "This is like how we used to do it in the basement, ya know what I mean? We had 200 square feet to work with. I didn't know half of this shit back then."[10] RZA was getting back to basics, but doing so with the wealth of production knowledge he attained after being the principal producer in seven critically acclaimed albums since Wu-Tang Clan's *Enter the Wu-Tang (36 Chambers)* a distant seven years ago. In the same *Rolling Stone* story, Inspectah Deck asserted, "Everyone in hip-hop is going platinum with recycled beats. We're getting back to the gritty, witty unpredictable, and I think that's what fans want to hear."[11]

Fans finally got to hear new Wu-Tang Clan music with the fall release of *The W*'s lead single, "Protect Ya Neck (The Jump Off)," which manages to include verses from every member minus Ol' Dirty Bastard and including Cappadonna who, at the time, was considered an official member. RZA used a number of samples for the song, the most prominent being the drums from Lowell Fulsom's "Tramp" (1966). RZA seems to have assembled the drum track using kicks and snares from Sly & The Family Stones' "Sing a Simple Song" (1968) and The J.B.s' "The Grunt" (1970). The blues guitar lick heard throughout the song is sampled from Albert King's "Pretty Woman" (1969) while the bass line is from King's "Cold Feet" (1968). The result of this hodgepodge of musical sources is an instrumental every Clan member took turns rhyming over with finesse. The video and radio versions of the song feature the jittery beat throughout the song.

The album version switches beats at the start of U-God's verse as Cappadonna and GZA finish the song rhyming over the same drums minus the guitars that were replaced by throbbing synth.

"Protect Ya Neck (The Jump Off)" peaked at #52 on the *Billboard* R&B/Hip-Hop Songs chart and #9 on the *Billboard* Hot Rap Singles chart in early October 2000, a decent set up for the release of *The W* on November 21, 2000. Appropriately, *The W* commences with a sample of dialogue from a kung-fu film, *The 5 Deadly Venoms*. This precursor of an intro, titled "Intro (Shaolin Finger Jab)" on the credits, leads right into the first proper track, "Chamber Music." Method Man is heard saying "We're back!," just as Raekwon starts rhyming, followed by GZA, Method Man, and Masta Killa. The beat features a rapidly firing snare drum between crushing kick drums with keyboard accents. Apparently sample free, the beat lacks any of the "tininess" RZA's production was plagued with starting with 1998's *Bobby Digital in Stereo*. There are no nursery rhymes here—"It be the lost tribe, seven days locked in the dungeon/Foaming at the mouth, mad dog in this production," raps Method Man—and the mood for the album is set, raw and uncut Wu-Tang Clan.

"Careful (Click, Click)" is full of more cocksure rhymes, with a theme of warning, from a full roster of MCs (RZA, Masta Killa, Cappadonna, U-God, Ghostface, Inspectah Deck) over a minimalist beat of razor-sharp percussion, gunshot sounds, and forbidding sound effects. With so many rappers on the near five minute track, "Careful" was a good choice for a third single, though it did not manage to chart. Its video was essentially banned from video shows due to excessive guns on camera, which didn't help matters.

"Hollow Bones" follows with Raekwon, Inspectah Deck, and Ghostface making their typical street tales sound interesting via their slang-heavy prose. "We seen the eyes, laying up playing the cut/What, stay in the truck, something told me duck/Folding me up, my shoulders struck," is how Raekwon describes getting shot. The track features a pained vocal moan and has a melody, sampled from Syl Johnson's "Is It Because I'm Black" (1970), that gives it the feel of mourning perfect for the trio's passion-fueled bars.

"Redbull" is an aggressive number (thanks to rumbling drum kicks and a cascading synthesizer) that kicks off with a verse from Redman followed by Method Man and Inspectah Deck. Raekwon handles the hook (he repeatedly chants, "It's just a hobby that I picked up in the lobby"). Though Redman and Method Man teamed up the previous year to release the highly successful *Blackout!* collaboration album, it marked the first time an outside artist with no direct ties to the Staten Island collective appeared on a Wu-Tang Clan group album. Besides Redman, Nas (who had appeared on Raekwon's *Only Built 4 Cuban Linx . . .*), Snoop Dogg, and Busta Rhymes also make appearances on *The W*. These contributions are an attempt for Wu-Tang Clan to diversify their audience but the results of this particular move are mixed. While all the guest MCs contribute admirably to the songs, there is no standout performance that justifies those verses not being handled by a Wu-Tang Clan member instead. In 2000, *Time Magazine* saw it as more evidence of RZA's talents in its review of the album, noting, "Guest-star-heavy albums sometimes burst apart like overstuffed grocery bags. RZA's solid guidance keeps everything together."[12]

One Wu-Tang Clan member who certainly wouldn't have minded more mic time in general was Masta Killa, the only rapper in the collective who had yet to release a solo album. Masta Killa made a strong case to have his solo project moved to the front of the assembly line with "One Blood Under W." Masta Killa performs the song's only two verses as Reggae legend Junior Reid interpolates his own "One Blood" (1990) for the hook. Masta Killa abuses the chopped and rearranged horn blast samples RZA lifts from the John Barry & Orchestra's version of the "James Bond Theme" (1962). Despite Masta Killa's solid individual effort in "One Blood Under W," his solo album, *No Said Date*, would not be released for another four years.

Ol' Dirty Bastard had managed to release a couple of albums but his only appearance on *The W* would be on "Conditioner." It was reported that Ol' Dirty Bastard provided vocals for up to five tracks on the album before checking himself in for a court ordered psychological evaluation in January 2000 in Los Angeles.[13] Convenient, since Wu-Tang Clan was recording in LA, but "Conditioner" is easily *The W*'s most lackluster song. The beat is a boring piano run laid over nondescript drums with Ol' Dirty Bastard's bland hook ("MC Conditioner, you could never say this boy's a amateur" repeated over and over) just as uninspired as his rhymes. Snoop Dogg's performance is a tad bit more energetic but mired by the boring mood the track elicits. Perhaps to make amends for "Conditioner's" blandness, a GZA performance is tagged on to the last minute and a half of the track. Over reverb-heavy drums, GZA drops what sounds like an ably delivered freestyle rhyme. The previously discussed "Protect Ya Neck (The Jump Off)" follows and combined with the GZA freestyle tagged onto the end of the previous song helps to further recapture the listener's attention. Oddly, after these two contributions GZA only appears on one more song on *The W.*

While Snoop Dogg's contribution, though no fault of his own, ended up being superfluous, rapper Nas fairs better as a guest on "Let My Niggas Live." The track opens with sampled movie dialogue of an inmate musing about his destiny to be killed by a crooked police officer taken from the film *Short Eyes* (1977). Over a distorted but gripping bass line Raekwon, Nas, and Inspectah Deck show great chemistry while reciting lyrics filled with references to being raised in the tough streets of New York City. The rock solid album cut is quickly followed by "I Can't Go To Sleep," which sequesters listeners for a highly emotional three and a half minutes.

"I Can't Go To Sleep" features the rhymes of just Ghostface and RZA. Ghostface opens the song by name checking deceased rappers: "Technique is ill son, watch how I spill one/peace to Biggie, Tupac, Big L and Big Pun." Ghostface delivers his rhymes, which deal with not sleeping well with the thoughts of starving babies and Black on Black crime, in a highly emotive cadence that finds the rapper sounding like he's on the verge of tears. His rap pleas are bolstered by the song's liberal sampling of the masterfully orchestrated string intro of Isaac Hayes's version of "Walk On By" from the late Soul icon's *Hot Buttered Soul* (1969) album. Hayes himself appears on the song, coolly part singing, part talking on the chorus: "Don't kill your brother, learn to love each other/Don't get mad 'cause it ain't that bad/Look at who you are, you've come so far/It's in your hands, just be a man." RZA then follows, exponentially increasing the song's political stance by rhyming about the murders of Malcolm X, Martin Luther King Jr., and John F. Kennedy Jr. and speaking on institutionalized racism as a whole. Despite Wu-Tang Clan's propensity for misogyny and condoning negativity, "I Can't Go To Sleep" is a good example of the group's ability to deliver conscious lyricism, and well. Though no real answers are provided, besides the usual Wu-Tang Clan ethos of gaining knowledge of self, the song is a welcome reprieve from their usual shtick.

Wu-Tang returns to their usual bluster with "Do You Really (Thang, Thang)." DJ Kay Slay, a former graffiti artist who at this point was gaining increased notoriety for his mix tapes, opens the track as a hypeman, proclaiming the song to be a "Wu-Banger." The song fits the criteria of a Wu-Tang posse cut since it features self-aggrandizing rhymes from Streetlife, Method Man, Masta Killa, and Inspectah Deck over cavernous drum kicks, snares, and lilting strings. The song is produced by Allah Mathematics, who sneaks in a short, subtle sample of piano chords from David Porter's "Hang On Sloopy" (1971) for the breakdown portion of the beat, which also marks the start of the song. "Do You Really (Thang, Thang)" is another solid album cut and one of only two songs RZA didn't produce himself (he does mix both).

The last minute and 10 seconds of the "Do You Really" track has RZA and an unidentified Clan member chanting, "Got to check out the W" before the producer starts to rhyme. The song is "The W" and would appear (minus RZA's verse) on import versions of Wu-Tang Clan's fourth album, *Iron Flag*, to be released a year later. Before RZA gets too far into his rhyme, Ghostface is heard saying turn that down, and suddenly realizes that the individuals he has been observing and contemplating assaulting—play acting, of course—are actually Raekwon and Busta Rhymes.[14] The two rappers, along with GZA, aggressively tag team the cacophony of door beating drums and thundering bass of "The Monument." A shade over two and half minutes, the song plays like a quick pit stop before the album segues into "Gravel Pit."

For "Gravel Pit," RZA opens with a tweaked sample of the opening horn riff from James Brown's "It's a Man's Man's Man's World" (1966), but the dominant melody heard throughout the song is a brightly tuned sample of Antoine Duhamel's "Belphegor Theme" (1965). RZA dug seriously deep to find the latter sample considering it is the opening theme music to a French miniseries from 1965. Retro-fitted with commanding drums, the rappers appearing on the track, after a quick RZA intro (now going by the alias "Bobby Boulders"), are Method Man, Ghostface, and U-God. Raekwon contributes a bridge (spent hyping the song between Ghostface's and U-God's verses) while a female vocalist named Paulissa Morgan (sometimes spelled Paulisa), aka Madam Majestic, sings, "Check out my gravel pit," and variations thereof, throughout the song. "Gravel Pit" is *The W*'s second single but despite all of its musical machinations, it didn't fare much better than "Protect Ya Neck (The Jump Off)" on the charts. "Gravel Pit" peaked at #70 on the *Billboard* R&B/Hip-Hop Songs chart and #20 on the *Billboard* Hot Rap Singles chart.

The subdued and roots Reggae spirited "Jah World" closes the album with Ghostface and RZA again delivering an emo-fueled song. Ghostface's verse touches on the theme of the African slave trade ("Sweat from the white man's head/Fell on our daughters as she cried, giving white man head, almighty," croaks Ghostface) while Junior Reid provides the song's chorus. RZA closes with a verse steeped in disdain for the world's literal whitewashing of history; "Curse to the wicked snakes who try to snatch the truth away/Cursed be the ones who try to take our youth away," he raps. Rather than closing with the downcast "Jah World," Wu-Tang Clan sneaks in a bouncy, Allah Mathematics song called "Clap" at the end of the track as a bonus.[15]

On its release, *The W* was subjected to mostly positive reviews though there were cases of middling opinions about the album. *The Source Magazine* gave the album a rather average three and half out of five mics rating, going as far as to say that the Clan was stronger as individuals than a group.[16] Interestingly, the considerably more highbrow *New Yorker* gave *The W* high praise, noting in a roundup of their favorite albums of 2000, "Staten Island's hip-hop royals rebound from their dropsically sophomore release, 'Wu-Tang Forever,' with a lean master-piece."[17] *Time Magazine* was also enthused with the album, noting, "RZA is in top form as a producer, laying down beats for each number that are spare but never simplistic and that reverberate with menace, like footsteps following you down an alleyway late at night."[18]

The W came in at #5 on the *Billboard Hot 200* chart and debuted at #1 on *Billboard* R&B/Hip-Hop Albums chart. By December 2000 the album was already certified platinum. Seven years since their debut, the Wu-Tang Clan was inarguably still one of hip-hop's premier rap groups. However, they were no longer the new kids—actually, grown men—on the hip-hop block. The *Village Voice* pointed to the group's size as one of its liabilities: "With nine voices, nine styles competing for your ear, even the most carefully crafted Wu-Tang album flirts with chaos, and the listener is left to separate milestones from mistakes. The W bursts with inspiration, but what does it all mean? You can't help wishing there was someone in charge."[19]

If the leader is to blame, all fault for the album's possible shortcomings lands squarely on the shoulders of RZA. But to his credit, RZA was hampered by a couple of circumstances beyond his control. Ol' Dirty Bastard, even with his off the (music) record antics, was nevertheless still one of Wu-Tang Clan's most unique and enthusiastic voices. Going back to *Wu-Tang Forever* where he only appeared on six songs (across a 27-track double album), ODB was becoming less and less of a presence on Wu-Tang Clan albums. This was ultimately due to his trouble with authorities and his own helter-skelter attention span leaving him unable to fully participate with the Clan's recording schedule. The sheer number, or lack thereof, of appearances isn't the only factor when keeping in mind that ODB only appeared on less than half of Wu-Tang's *Enter the Wu-Tang* debut but still managed to be one of its more memorable performers. Ol' Dirty Bastard's lone contribution to *The W*, the slipshod "Conditioner," was lacking. GZA, too, one of Wu-Tang Clan's most efficiently searing lyricists, played a limited role on *The W*, though his performances were more memorable than Ol' Dirty Bastard's.

Since the Wu-Tang Clan was no longer being run like a dictatorship, a democratic approach was being taken when it came to creating music. The higher profile—thus bigger ego possessing—soloists certainly were not ceding to RZA's every whim. And RZA had formally relinquished complete control of Wu-Tang Clan's musical direction after the completion of *Wu-Tang Forever*. Aware that their lyrics were sometimes considered almost impenetrable, some members began mentioning the need to spoon feed the masses to their sounds and words.[20] In 2000 Ghostface told *Trace Magazine*, "We learned that sometimes you gotta stoop down to they level. That's how come Puffy can sell ten to 15 million records, Puffy make 'em dance. We make 'em think, but there's more dumb niggas than smart niggas."[21]

RZA didn't start blazing the dance charts, but he finally regained his production footing when he started striking a balance between his keyboard playing and use of samples. This development was heard in the run up to *Supreme Clientele*, and should also include RZA's work on the *Ghost Dog: Way of the Samurai Soundtrack*, which the film's director, Jim Jarmusch, personally handpicked the producer to score. It also includes Method Man's and Redman's *Blackout!* album in which he produced two notable tracks, "Cereal Killer" and "Run 4 Cover." But as for *The W, Rolling Stone Magazine* said it "completes a comeback that began when Ghost dropped his second solo effort, Supreme Clientele, at the top of this year. Coming after non-orgasmic releases by Method Man, Ol' Dirty Bastard, Raekwon, Inspectah Deck and U-God, Clientele hit the spot by going back to the Wu-Tang: vocal samples from cult-y culture figures, furious rhymes and, perhaps most important, the wicked ear of the RZA overseeing the entire project."[22]

In the near future, RZA would gain more acclaim for his soundtrack and scoring work and follow in Method Man's footsteps as an actor in his own right. Until then, RZA was back in a production groove.

There were only two albums released from the core Wu-Tang Clan camp after *The W*: the RZA as Bobby Digital's *Digital Bullet* and Ghostface Killah's *Bulletproof Wallets*. With Wu-Tang Clan back on track, these two albums were fast-tracked for a release. Ghostface's *Bulletproof Wallets* would lead fans and critics to deem him Wu-Tang Clan's most consistent member, and RZA's *Digital Bullet* album would prove to be just as enigmatic as his Bobby Digital persona.

RZA, *DIGITAL BULLET*

Intro/Show You Love/Can't Lose/Glocko Pop/Must Be Bobby/ Brooklyn Babies/Domestic Violence Pt. 2/Do U/Fools/La Rhumba/ Black Widow Pt. 2/Shady/Break Bread/Bong Bong/Throw Your Flag Up/Be a Man/Righteous Way/Build Strong/Sickness

---

Bobby Digital in Stereo was released via Gee Street Recording but *Digital Bullet* was released via the independent Koch Records. The album loosely follows a narrative of Bobby Digital going through his usual lurid motions before eventually deciding between continuing on as the crude character he dutifully describes or seeking redemption for his lascivious ways and leaving his vulgar lifestyle behind. For fans paying close attention, *Digital Bullet* is yet another album from RZA *not* called *The Cure*. In 2000, the producer explained the reason behind *The Cure*'s increasingly mythic nature to *The Source Magazine*: "The Cure is so intimate in writing that you gotta live that *Cure* shit. I was living like Bobby Digital in '98, '99, na'mean?" Apparently RZA still had more Bobby Digital to unleash a couple of years later.[23]

Released August 28, 2001, the beats on *Digital Bullet* are more animated and crystalline than its predecessor. Even with his refined production, RZA still manages to experiment with sounds and rhythms. The album's first single was "Brooklyn Babies," which appropriately starts with a woman yelling at Bobby Digital for being a deadbeat (by the end of the song she says she still loves him, though) and features an electro beat that slows and speeds up intermittently like traffic with electric guitar accents and the singing of the Force MD's on the chorus. On "Black Widow Pt. 2," an Ol' Dirty Bastard solo song, RZA dices up a sample of a woman's wail into a passionate moan that permeates the entire track. True Master produced *Digital Bullet*'s second single, "La Rhumba," and continues RZA's tendency to use nonconventional hip-hop beats by matching stuttering Latin strings and horns with even-keeled drums and stalwart chord notes. RZA and his guest rappers (Method Man, Killa Sin, and Beretta 9) stay on course by each focusing their verses on the topic of wooing ladies. "La Rhumba" only crept into #98 on the *Billboard* R&B/Hip-Hop Songs chart.

This topical focus unfortunately comes and goes throughout *Digital Bullet*. But the biggest problem is the project's extensive guest list of official Wu-Tang bandmates (Masta Killa, GZA, Ol' Dirty Bastard, et al.) and extended family (Beretta 9, Streetlife Jamic Sommers) that limit RZA's time on the microphone. Of the album's 18 songs, RZA performs by himself (not counting choruses) on only five songs. This is unfortunate because these true solo songs such as the bouncy, Mathematics produced "Must Be Bobby" or the soulful "Be a Man" are some of the album's best. Starting with "Be a Man," *Digital Bullet*'s final songs ("Righteous Way," "Build Strong," "Sickness") all showcase Bobby Digital rapping by himself. Possibly because he is no longer exposed to the ill-advised influence of his peers, he is also more reflective and introspective. "Got a closet full of kung-fu flicks and nasty pictures, a library to decipher anything religious/He beg for mercy, we pray for Allah forgiveness," he raps over supple horns and warm drums on "Righteous Way," which includes extensive and soulful vocals from Junior Reid.

But the battle between RZA and Bobby Digital, good and evil, is most profound on "Build Strong." When RZA ultimately starts rapping he repeats a verse twice save for the last few lines. Beginning with "problems surround me," the first run through ends with "cause from me springs the divine Prince Rakeem/With the ability to set myself free/But B.O.B.B.Y he don't want to die/He don't want to die he don't want to try/So I'm forced to cry and get trapped up for living my life inside a lie." The verse is then repeated except on the second round, after saying "Prince Rakeem," RZA ends with, "Give myself the opportunity/and set free and be all I can be/Be all I can be and not a nigga just trapped up in luxury."

Bobby Digital may have finally decided to become righteous but critics were at odds about the quality of his musical testimonial. There were positive reviews of *Digital Bullet*; *The Source Magazine* gave the album a highly respectable three and a half out of five mics rating but believed that the production was "flat" and AllMusic.com noted that, "RZA's rhymes are often as evocative and opaque as the kung-fu flicks he loves," while giving the album a four out five star review.[24] The *Village Voice* was less forgiving with Robert Christgau listing the album under the heading "Dud of the Month" in his "Consumer Guide" column.[25] *Rolling Stone Magazine* insightfully assessed that "lacking the original RZA's sense of purpose and ability to evoke top performances from his supporting crew, *Digital* comes off as a lark" in its two and half out of five star review of the album.[26] *Digital Bullet* performed decently on its initial release, peaking at #24 on *Billboard* 200 chart, #9 on the *Billboard* R&B/Hip-Hop Albums chart, and #1 on the *Billboard* Independent Albums chart.

GHOSTFACE KILLAH, *BULLETPROOF WALLETS*

Intro/Maxine/Flowers/Never Be the Same Again/Teddy (Skit)/Theodore/Ghost Showers/Strawberry/The Forest/The Juks/Walking Through the Darkness/Jealousy (Skit)/The Hilton/Ice (Interlude)/Love Session/Street Chemistry

---

Critics and fans may have been conflicted by RZA's maddening mix of alter egos and unpredictable production tactics, but they were universally enamored with the musical output of Ghostface. After waiting almost four years after his *Ironman* debut to release his second album, *Supreme Clientele*, his third album, *Bulletproof Wallets*, arrived in stores less than two years later on November 13, 2001. *Supreme Clientele* was considered a landmark album and still fresh in the minds of listeners who were eager to see if Ghostface could produce another work of similar acclaim. Never lacking in confidence, Ghostface was primed for the task, recording the majority of *Bulletproof Wallets* during the summer of 2001 in Miami, where he always enjoys the vibe and takes up residence as well.[27]

Originally the Wu-Tang duo of Raekwon and Ghostface were to record the sequel to *Only Built 4 Cuban Linx . . .* in Miami. But while recording tracks for the project, it was decided since they felt they needed to release some radio-friendly material—something a proper *Cuban Linx* follow-up would lack by default—they would release solo albums first. Raekwon's album at the time was planned to be called *RAGU* (an acronym for Rae And Ghost United) while Ghostface's was *Bulletproof Wallets*.[28] "Everything I do is straight up and down bulletproof. . . . There are a lot of rappers out there, but a lot of brothers can't touch what I do. My wallet is bulletproof," Ghostface explained to *Billboard Magazine*.[29]

Everything Ghostface did was getting special attention from fans. At the 2001 Source Awards Wu-Tang Clan showed up with Ghostface wearing a bracelet that had a golden eagle protruding from it that was nearly a foot high. Couple that with Ghostface's penchant for dinner plate–sized medallions and wearing colorful bathrobes while on stage, and the result is one of Wu-Tang Clan's most popular members.

Bulletproof Wallet's lead single was a made-for-radio rap ditty called "Never Be the Same Again" that featured R&B singer and Bad Boy Records artist Carl Thomas's cool falsetto on the chorus. Ghostface has always praised his love for 1960s and 1970s soul music but "Never Be the Same Again" has a distinctly vanilla R&B vibe—thanks to the production team Lilz & PLX—with its breezy keys and somber chords. Nevertheless, "Never Be the Same Again" did not do exceptionally well on the charts, hitting #65 on the *Billboard* Hot R&B/Hip-Hop Singles & Tracks chart and #21 on the *Billboard* Hot Rap Singles chart.

"Never Be the Same Again" is a blatant play for radio spins but maintains the spirit of a Ghostface track and doesn't sound like a sellout record because of his self-deprecating rhymes. The song's narrative is about a wayward girlfriend that cheats on Ghostface. The rapper's raw honesty is simultaneously endearing—"It's alright though, maybe he came up with the right dough/Bigger dick, I don't know, must have been the best flow," he raps after finding out another man has slept with his girlfriend.

Bulletproof Wallets was released on November 13, 2001, and like its immediate predecessor features Ghostface rhyming over a dizzying array of soul sampling beats along with vivid and creative storytelling throughout the album's songs. Also, on *Bulletproof Wallets* Ghostface and RZA are back at the helm co-handling A&R and album sequencing duties as on *Supreme Clientele*. Raekwon, seen on the album's cover with Ghostface, also reclaims his guest billing status, last held on the *Ironman* album, with "featuring Raekwon" written underneath the album title artwork. At the album's start the two rappers are heard lamenting the fact that radio isn't playing their records, rappers are biting (mimicking) their music, and people are failing to recognize the trends they started (wearing Clarks Wallabee shoes, drinking Cristal champagne, etc.). Regardless, the duo presses on with Ghostface yelling at the track's conclusion, "Niggas gonnna fuck around and get their balloon popped, straight up!"

After Ghostface's exhortation on the first proper track, "Maxine" kicks in; the RZA-produced beat is driven by gritty synth keys and snappy drums kicks and hi-hats. Originally the track utilized an undisclosed sample but the label was unable, or unwilling, to clear it. Instead the sample was replayed using live musicians.[30] "Maxine" is an intricate tale about two drug-addicted women, Pam and Maxine, who steal drugs from a dealer named Moonie. The scorned dealer breaks into Pat's home seeking retribution but by song's end has the tables turned on him by Maxine and her kids. The song closes with a chant of "All in together now," which will be familiar to Wu-Tang Clan fans since the phrase and its variations turn up in various Wu-Tang Clan albums.

"Flowers" is another variation of a previous version in its own right as rappers Raekwon, Method Man, Superb, and Ghostface take turns rhyming over a sample of Bob James's "Take Me to the Mardi Gras" (1975), as classic a hip-hop breakbeat as any ever made. Unfortunately, the "Flowers" heard on the album, and a number of other songs, would be victims of sample clearance issues. Prior to the release official first single "Never Be the Same Again," mix show DJs were serviced with a 12″ vinyl single that had a song called "The Watch" on the A-side and "Flowers" on the B-side.

"The Watch" is a concept song in which Ghostface is literally chastising the watch he is wearing on his wrist after it points out (yes, the watch supposedly talks) that despite his accolades, the rapper has yet to blow up; "Come on, watch, I'm the star of the show," says Ghostface mid-rhyme, quickly followed by "so blow then," this latter part of the sentence being the watch mocking its wearer. Ghostface returns to rapping from his own perspective—calling the watch "a son of a bitch"—but the watch isn't going to just accept the tongue lashing. Raekwon, rhyming from the watch's perspective, handles a second verse where he goes so far as to say Ghostface is sore about not getting any airplay. "All you hear is X and Jigga, ha ha you vexed nigga," raps Raekwon referring to the success rappers DMX and Jay-Z, respectively, had at getting radio spins. The song is only bolstered by its beat, a sample of 1973's "I'm Gonna Love You Just a Little Bit More Baby" by Barry White.

"The Watch" didn't make it onto *Bulletproof Wallets*. Clearing the Barry White sample was just going to be too expensive.[31] "Flowers" remained on the album but the energy and spirit of the original was vastly diminished on the album version, which consisted of replayed elements rather than the sample. Scrubbed of its samples "Flowers" follows "Maxine" on the album, which makes it clear to listeners that once again the track listing seen on a Ghostface album's back cover does not match the true song sequence due to last-minute song removals and changes in the song order. While the track listing notes that "The Sun" was the album's first song, it never made the album. "The Sun," which features guest verses from RZA, Raekwon, and Slick Rick, cleverly rhyming about the importance of the center of the solar system, was supposed to open the album but RZA was unable to find the records he sampled.[32] This is another shame since "The Sun" is an impeccable song that was only heard on subsequent mix tapes and bootlegs.

These last-minute alterations effected critical reception of the album. *The Source Magazine* gave *Bulletproof Wallets* a superior four and a half out of five mics rating.[33] However, the album reviewed featured the original "Flowers," "The Watch," and "The Sun" as well as "Good Times," a popular mix-tape song sniped from the album because of its beat's rampant uses of a sample of the theme from 1970s TV sitcom *Good Times*. In 2007 Ghostface told AllHipHop.com he believes that "if I would have kept 'The Sun' on it and I would have kept

'The Watch' . . . and a few other joints on there it would have been a classic . . . up there with *Supreme [Clientele]* and *Ironman*."[34]

Despite the void left by so many missing songs, *Bulletproof Wallets* still manages to be an above average Wu-Tang release. After "Flowers" and "Never Be the Same Again" is the one minute interlude "Teddy Skit" where Superb introduces Ghostface crooning an XXX-rated interpolation of Harold Melvin & the Blue Notes's 1975 hit "Hope That We Can Be Together Soon" over a sped-up sample of its instrumental. The seductive tones heard in Ghostface's singing are jilted loose by "Theodore." The up-tempo track produced by Allah Mathematics features what sounds like sweet notes from a harp getting propelled by aggressive drums. Ghostface leads off with the first verse but the track is a showcase for his new crew of rapping protégés called Theodore Unit. Trife Diesel and Twiz appear on and ably handle the infectious groove. Ghostface would go on to release compilation albums with Theodore Unit as well as have various members appear on his future albums.

"Ghost Showers" also served as *Bulletproof Wallets*' second single. Ghostface wanted Jennifer Lopez to be the guest vocalist on "Ghost Showers" but was unable to secure the actress/singer. Instead Madam Majestic, the same female vocalist heard on "Cherchez LaGhost" and Wu-Tang Clan's "Gravel Pit," sings on the song. "Ghost Showers" is in direct lineage to *Supreme Clientele*'s relative hit "Cherchez LaGhost." While "Cherchez LaGhost" is a near facsimile of the Dr. Buzzard's Original Savannah Band's "Cherchez Le Femme" from their self-titled 1976 debut, "Ghost Showers" liberally cribs elements of the song "Sunshower" from the same album. Produced by Chad Liggio and Tally Galbreth, "Ghost Showers" is a contrived attempt at a club hit and has the proper ingredients thanks to the song's party-ready rhythm, straightforward lyrics, and a sample of Biz Markie's "This Is Something for the Radio" (1988) that underlies Ghostface's verses. However, "Ghost Showers" did not resonate with audiences as much as its predecessor, peaking only at #77 on the *Billboard* R&B/Hip-Hop Songs chart compared to "Cherchez LaGhost" at #42 on the same chart.

"Ghost Showers" is followed by "Strawberry," a stout album cut. Producer Allah Mathematics raises the BPMs of a string and vocal section of legendary Stax artist/songwriter David Porter's "Storm in the Summertime" from his *Victim of a Joke? An Opera* (1971) album. Killa Sin cocks and aims sound rhymes at would-be foes in the first verse, which has absolutely nothing to do with the second verse wherein Ghostface gives intimate details of coitus with a woman while his friends listen from behind a door.

"The Forest" follows and further showcases Ghostface's expert and imaginative storytelling ability. Across two verses Ghostface weaves a loosely plotted tale of drug dealers, shootings, and criminal plots. This is nothing novel considering Ghostface's discography except, instead of detailing the actions of typical housing project and ghetto mayhem, the rapper utilizes famous cartoon characters for his stories. The rapper manages to name check everyone from Scrooge McDuck and the Smurfs to The Jetsons's dog Astro and Disney's Goofy. For good measure, he also manages to throw in his own version of the Three Little Pigs. Ghostface's rhymes are coddled by the sweeping horns producer Alchemist samples from "Ballad of Matheia" (1974) from the self-titled debut of short lived 1970s R&B band The Imaginations.

Fond childhood memories of cartoons end with "The Juks," another Alchemist-produced track where Ghostface, Superb, and Trife relay rhymes that occasionally touch on the topics of neighborhood dice games and keeping cash in their pockets. "Walking Through the Darkness" is familiar to anyone that purchased 1999's *Ghostdog: The Way of the Samurai*. It is Ghostface rapping over Tekitha's "Walking Through the Darkness" from the aforementioned album. The song uses a sample of the melodic organ opening of Bobby Womack's "Across 110th Street" (1972). After another quick interlude titled "Jealousy"— "What made you buy the same shoe as me," laments Ghostface over the sounds of a woman somberly and repeatedly saying "jealousy"— Raekwon reunites with his rhyme partner for "The Hilton."

Serving as a loose sequel to "The MGM" from *Wu-Tang Forever*, on "The Hilton" Ghostface and Raekwon this time are at a Hilton Hotel, where they get ambushed by an assassin wielding a pair of guns. Nevertheless, the duo still manages to escape and get word to have the individual who hired the would-be murderer receive his proper comeuppance. Carlos "6 July" Broady provides the instrumental, which delectably dissects a slice of vocals from Michael Jackson's "Maria (You Were the Only One)" (1971). After the crime noir tales of "The Hilton," another one-minute song, "Ice," follows. Rsonist (né Gregory Green) of production team the Heatmakerz samples a revved portion of strings from Donny Hathaway's "She Is My Lady" (1971) for a short but potent punch of a song at *Bulletproof Wallets'* tail end. "Love Session," produced by the Underdawgs, follows and is a rather blasé R&B track that features singing duo Ruff Endz on its chorus, though with none of the panache of "Never Be the Same Again." The album closes on a higher note with "Street Chemistry." Alchemist is again at the helm using what is an unknown soul vocal sample and warm chords for Prodigal Sunn and Trife, book-ended by a pair of Ghostface verses, to enthusiastically, and in Wu-Tang parlance, hurl darts at the track.

On its release, *Bulletproof Wallets* reached #34 on the *Billboard* 200 chart and #2 on the *Billboard* R&B/Hip-Hop Albums chart. The *Village Voice*'s esteemed critic Robert Christgau gave the album an A- rating.[35] Bulletproof *Wallets* was Ghostface's third successful solo album in a row and enough for *Vibe Magazine* to dub him "an MC superhero" in its enthusiastic review of the album.[36] Few tracking the Wu-Tang Clan's ascension could have seen Ghostface's climb to the top of the group's dog pile. In *Rolling Stone Magazine*'s three and half out of five stars review of the album, writer Pat Blashill noted, "Ghostface Killah has often seemed a little like a rhythm guitarist: underappreciated but totally essential."[37] In the group's salad days, Ghostface was a mid-level talent when compared to the immediate star power of members such as the wily Ol' Dirty Bastard or the reluctant sex symbol Method Man. But by consistently delivering quality music, Ghostface became a fan favorite and a dependable resource for the Wu-Tang Clan's brand of hip-hop music.

Despite its praise, *Bulletproof Wallets* underwhelmed at retail. The album only sold a tad over 60,000 units its first week and has never been certified gold. In the meantime, other members of Wu-Tang Clan were eager to release more music to prove Ghostface's critical success didn't come at the cost of the talented crew that spawned him falling off. But any more solo albums were going to have to wait a bit longer; Wu-Tang Clan had another album to release.

NOTES

1. Eskenazi, Mike, "Remaking Wu," *Time Magazine*, December 11, 2000, 82.

2. "Wu-Tang Clan Worm Their Way Back With New Album and Tour," *New Musical Express*, June 20, 2000.

3. Wilson, Elliott, "Victory," *XXL Magazine*, October 2000, 106.

4. Sullivan, James, " 'W' Is Child's Play for Wu-Tang," *The San Francisco Chronicle*, December 10, 2000, 48.

5. Wilson, "Victory."

6. Ex, Kris, "RECORDINGS: Wu-Tang Clan 'The W,' " *Rolling Stone Magazine*, December 14, 2001–December 21, 2001, 169.

7. Johnson, Jr., Billy, "Back to the Lab: Wu-Tang Clan," *The Source Magazine*, October 2000, 66.

8. Diehl, Matt, "Microphone Fiend," *XXL Magazine*, August 2001, 114.

9. Osorio, Kim, "Operation W: Back at the Front," *The Source Magazine*, January 2001, 167 (162–69).

10. Weingarten, Marc, "Wu-Tang Take L.A.," *Rolling Stone Magazine*, August 31, 2000, 27.

11. Ibid.

12. Farley, Christopher John, "Searching for the Perfect Beat," *Time Magazine*, December 11, 2000, 83.

13. "Wu-Tang Clan," New Musical Express.

14. In the following years Raekwon and Busta Rhymes would form a business relationship that was set to culminate in the release of *Only Built 4 Cuban Linx . . . Pt. II*. However, it did not come to fruition with Busta Rhymes not having an executive producer credit on the album when it was finally released.

15. The song's principle players (Ghostface, Raekwon, and Method Man) would go on two release a collaborative album, *The Wu-Massacre*, 10 years later.

16. King, Aliya S., "Record Report: Wu-Tang Clan: The W," *The Source Magazine*, January 2001, 192, 194.

17. "Twelve Favorites from Our 2000 CD Rotation," *The New Yorker*, January 8, 2001, 12.

18. Farley, "Searching for the Perfect Beat."

19. Sanneh, Kelefah, "Sobs, Static, and Sweat," *Village Voice*, December 26, 2000, 131.

20. Bonanno, Jonathan "Gotti," "Last Man Standing," *The Source Magazine*, 216. Wilson, Elliott, "Victory," *XXL Magazine*, October 2000, 106. Brannan, Eddie, "Phantom of the Opera," *Trace Urban Magazine*, Issue 22 ~2000, 53.

21. Brannan, Eddie, "Phantom of the Opera," *Trace Urban Magazine*, Issue 22 ~2000, 53 (50–55).

22. Ex, *Rolling Stone Magazine*.

23. Bonnano, Jonathan, "Return of the Dragon," *The Source Magazine*, March 2000, 208.

24. Cook, Dara, "Record Report: RZA 'Digital Bullet,' " *The Source Magazine*, October 2001, 200. LeRoy, Dan, "Review: Digital Bullet," All Music.com, http://allmusic.com/cg/amg.dll?p=amg&sql=10:axftxqr0ldfe.

25. Christgau, Robert, "Consumer Guide," *The Village Voice*, February 5, 2002, 43.

26. Ex, Kris, "Reviews: RZA as Bobby Digital 'Digital Bullet,' " *Rolling Stone Magazine*, September 13, 2001, 112.

27. Johnson, Elon, "See-Through Soul," *The Source Magazine*, February 2002, 88.

28. Alvarez, Gabriel, "Never Change," *XXL Magazine*, December 2001, 83 (80–86).

29. Baraka, Rhonda, "Words & Deeds," *Billboard Magazine*, October 6, 2001, 42.

30. Golianopoulos, Thomas, "Chain Reaction," *Scratch Magazine*, March/April 2006, 82 (76–82).

31. Wang, Oliver, "Phantom Tracks," *Scratch Magazine*, July/August 2006, 32.

32. Ibid.

33. Osorio, Kim, "Record Report: Ghostface Killah: Bulletproof Wallets," *The Source Magazine*, January 2002, 142–43.

34. Blanco, Alvin, "Ghostface Killah: Iron Manual," December 4, 2007; http://allhiphop.com/stories/features/archive/2007/12/04/18959440.aspx.

35. Christgau, Robert, "Ghostface Killah: Bulletproof Wallets," *The Village Voice*, February 5, 2002, 63.

36. Patel, Joseph, "Ghostface Killah: Bulletproof Wallets," *Vibe Magazine*, December 2001, 187–88.

37. Blashill, Pat, "Ghostface Killah: Bulletproof Wallets," *Rolling Stone Magazine*, December 6, 2001–December 13, 2001, 147.

CHAPTER 10
Chinks in the Clan's Armor

WU-TANG CLAN, *IRON FLAG*

In the Hood/Rules/Chrome Wheels/Soul Power (Black Jungle)/Uzi (Pinky Ring)/One of These Days/Y'All Been Warned/Babies/ Radioactive (Four Assassins)/Back in the Game/Iron Flag/Dashing (Reasons)

Mostly due to Ghostface Killah's consistency and a solid group effort (*The W*), Wu-Tang Clan regained some of the traction it lost in the few years after *Wu-Tang Forever*'s 1997 release. In any genre it is understood that an artist is only as good as his or her last hit, and Wu-Tang Clan wasn't immune to this axiom. Rather than settle into another wave of solo albums from its individual members, Wu-Tang Clan chose to move forward with another group effort, in little more than a year after their previous release. Wu-Tang Clan's fourth album, *Iron Flag*, was released on December 18, 2001, only a couple of months after Ghostface Killah's *Bulletproof Wallets* was released to a lukewarm commercial reception but critical acclaim.

As early as June 2001, de facto leader RZA had plans to record another Wu-Tang Clan album, telling *NME Magazine* the working title of the project was *WW2*, and at the time consisted of tracks recorded while working on *The W*. Method Man, however, was not convinced, also telling *NME*, "Right now we're going through a little internal shit, bullshit. . . . Right now we're all working together to build a family structure back again. Fuck an album. Let's be a family again."[1]

While the majority of the previous two Wu-Tang Clan albums were recorded in California, *Iron Flag* was recorded in New York City at Sony Studios. A good amount of the album was recorded in a New York City that was numb after suffering the September 11, 2001, terrorist attacks that leveled the World Trade Center and murdered thousands. Wu-Tang Clan, too, though certainly not on the level of New York City as a whole, was going through its own trials and tribulations. Ol' Dirty Bastard's legal troubles only continued since the recording of *The W*. Shortly after appearing on stage, while on the lam from the police, with Wu-Tang Clan at the album release party for *The W* in New York City's Hammerstein Ballroom, Ol' Dirty Bastard was recaptured. The rapper had been imprisoned since and would not appear on *Iron Flag*. Meanwhile, GZA, one third of the All In Together crew that was the precursor to Wu-Tang Clan, was not around much during the recording of *Iron Flag*. GZA ultimately recorded his tracks (he appears on five songs) at his own home studio, and submitted his verses via Pro-Tools files.

During the recording of *Iron Flag*, Ghostface was also busy recording his *Bulletproof Wallets* album but still managed to come through and participate. As for Cappadonna, who seemed to be a full-time member on the previous album, he was totally absent from *Iron Flag*. The reason could be because of a *Village Voice* story that ran in May 2000 that named his then manager Mike Caruso as a federal informant. This was probably only part of the reason—Cappadonna had expressed dissatisfaction with his perception as a member of the Clan to the press—since Ghostface continues to have a business relationship with Caruso to this day that does not seem to have impacted his position in the Wu-Tang hierarchy.

Despite these hiccups, *Iron Flag* was released to a public full of fans clamoring for a new Wu-Tang Clan album no matter what the extenuating circumstances. The album's lead single is the resounding "Uzi (Pinky Ring)." Produced by RZA, who again handles the majority of the album's production and musical direction, the track has a marching rhythm courtesy of a blistering keyboard vamp and trombone sample lifted from jazz musician and composer J. J. Johnson's "Parade Strut" from the original soundtrack of Blaxploitation film *Willie Dynamite* (1974). Like all proper Wu-Tang Clan lead singles, the song features participation from every member, save for Ol' Dirty Bastard. "Uzi (Pinky Ring)" didn't fare on the charts as Wu-Tang Clan would have hoped, reaching only #93 on the *Billboard* R&B/Hip-Hop Songs chart and #16 on the *Billboard* Hot Rap Singles chart. Going off history, a lack of radio penetration should have been little cause for concern but Wu-Tang Clan was faced with the added challenge of turmoil at longtime label home Loud Records. By March 2002, the Sony Music Group's Columbia Records absorbed and shuttered the label.[2] Fortunately, according to some, *Iron Flag* was already in record stores by then.

Iron Flag carries on tradition and the first song, "In the Hood" (1972), opens with sampled dialogue from a kung-fu flick that, when paraphrased, simply says, "You're about to hear a story," before an exasperated RZA is heard informing listeners that Wu-Tang Clan is still here. As RZA's rant comes to an end, the track's horns, sampled from Billy Paul's "Brown Baby," blast into auditory view. Masta Killa, Inspectah Deck, and Streetlife each take a turn rhyming while Reggae artist Suga Bang Bang handles the chorus with chants of "Murder" through a thick West Indian accent. The rugged song's pile-driving instrumental and rugged rhymes set the album's tone: back to basics Wu-Tang Clan.

"Rules" follows with Wu-Tang Clan getting decidedly political. As the first to rhyme on the song, Ghostface makes his feelings about 9/11 clearly heard from the onset. "Who the fuck knocked our buildings down?/Who the man behind the World Trade massacres, step up now," barks Ghostface, eventually closing with, "America, together we stand, divided we fall/Mr. Bush sit down, I'm in charge of the war!" The Allah Mathematic–produced track utilizes a miniscule portion of a horn section from Ann Peebles "You've Got the Papers (I've Got the Man)" (1979). When hearing the original compared to "Rules," the added dimensions Mathematics added (what sounds like a James Brown vocal clip and a quick guitar riff) reveals that the RZA protégé has come into his own as a high-caliber producer. The rest of the song's participants—Inspectah Deck, Masta Killa, Streetlife, Raekwon, and Method Man—focus their rhymes on unity. The concept of togetherness against all odds is surely one of the keys, or rules, to Wu-Tang Clan's success.

On "Chrome Wheels," only two of the nine formal Wu-Tang Clan members are actually heard. RZA utters "Bob Digi" at the songs beginning (his name is also dropped on the hook, wrenchingly sung by Madam D) revealing that it is likely a track held over from his Bobby Digital recording sessions. This possibility is further evidenced by RZA telling *XXL Magazine* that he had to convince Wu-Tang Clan to even record the song. "Wu-Tang Clan" in this case is only Raekwon since the other artists on the song are Wu-affiliates 12 O'Clock and Prodigal Sunn.[3]

More of the official Wu-Tang roster returned for the RZA-produced "Soul Power (Black Jungle) as Raekwon, Masta Killa, Ghostface, and U-God get on the sparse but guttural hi-hat and drum filled track. With Ol' Dirty Bastard confined, Wu-Tang recruits hip-hop's original court jester Flavor Flav of seminal rap group Public Enemy to add on to "Soul Power." Flav does an admirable job on the song, teaming with U-God on the hook and reminiscing with Method Man about their mutual Long Island, New York, roots on the outro. Though Ol' Dirty's contributions were becoming rare in general, longtime fans and listeners couldn't help but notice and miss his absence.

After the terse but funky "Soul Power" comes to an end the previously discussed "Uzi (Pinky Ring)" follows, which is then trailed by "One of These Days." The total opposite in speed and content to "Uzi (Pinky Ring)," on "One of These Days" rappers Inspectah Deck, Raekwon, and U-God drop hustling tales over thick drum kicks and a soulful vocal sample of Donny Hathaway's "I Believe to My Soul" (1970). The beat on "One of These Days" merely seems adequate making for a song that begins to sound tedious. The track is produced by Nick "Fury" Loftin— at the time allegedly one of Wu-Tang Clan's marijuana suppliers—one of two non-Wu-Tang producers who provide tracks for *Iron Flag*.[4] On *The W* long-term fans took exception to the addition of "outsider" performers such as Busta Rhymes and Redman on a Wu-Tang Clan album. While there are no such specially invited interlopers on *Iron Flag*—not including Flavor Flav's hypeman role on "Soul Power" or Ronald Isley Jr.'s singing on "Back in the Game"—a new precedent was the inclusion of outside producers—the aforementioned Nick Fury and the Trackmasters—on a proper Wu-Tang Clan album.

If a listener hadn't bothered to skip ahead, "Ya'll Been Warned" brings *Iron Flag*'s musical direction back from the doldrums of "One of These Days." Producer True Master snatches a guitar riff from 1964's "In My Heart" by Stax group Barbara & The Browns and adds a grim bass line and rhythmic drums. A searing, Wu-Tang worthy battle rap track, Method Man, RZA, Inspectah Deck, and Raekwon (who starts his verse with a bit of back and forth with Masta Killa) take turns verbally posturing over the pulsing rhythms. After the high of "Ya'll

Been Warned," the Wu-Tang Clan roller coaster dips low again with "Babies."

A somber, atmospheric track that opens with a despondent horn and features a hollow, melancholy vocal snippet, "Babies" is the latest in a long line of Wu-Tang songs that feature a narrative detailing crooked cops on the take, violence, and ghetto anomie. Appropriately, master storytellers Ghostface, Raekwon, and GZA deliver poignant verses that breathe life into their words over RZA's stirring instrumental that also features Ol' Dirty Bastard's older brother Ramsey Jones's live drumming. "Babies," like "Uzi (Pinky Ring)," was recorded with live instruments replaying samples that could not be cleared otherwise. GZA presents the most cinematic verse in his typical verbally concise yet ultra-detailed method. He raps, "The money was the root and it's the instinct to make it/With they pockets and fridge naked, many aim to take it," explaining hood ethics in two lines.

GZA quickly returns for his next performance with the lead-off verse on "Radioactive (Four Assassins)" followed by Raekwon, Method Man, and Masta Killa. The song was originally recorded in 2000 and was supposed to appear on Masta Killa's then forthcoming debut. But with the group in need of another grimy cut, he selflessly volunteered it to appear on *Iron Flag*.[5] There would be no solo songs on *Iron Flag*; all tracks feature at least three rapping participants, so it was more difficult for individual members to outshine others. In that regard, *Iron Flag* could be considered Wu-Tang Clan's most complete group album.

"Back in the Game" finds Wu-Tang Clan asserting their influence on the hip-hop game over a shuffling, Spanish guitar rhythm, and Ronald Isley Jr.'s soulful crooning on the chorus. Producers by Poke and Tone aka The Trackmasters, kung-fu dialogue opens the song ("If what you say is true, the Shaolin and the Wu-Tang can be dangerous"), but the slickly produced track is nothing like any previous Wu-Tang Clan song. Nonetheless, all of the track's rappers—Inspectah, Method Man, GZA, Raekwon, and Ghostface—sound comfortable relaying the worth and influence of the Wu-Tang Clan. "Vet status, y'all went a week with the belt/Few chicks felt your style, now you feelin yourself," raps Inspectah Deck. "Back in the Game" does prove—to whatever doubters there are incredulously left—that Wu-Tang Clan have the ability to adapt to a style of production that differs from their typical modus operandi. The song was released as *Iron Flag*'s third single in April 2002 and despite RZA's enthusiasm at the prospects of a radio hit, with Loud Records having shuttered the month before, "Back in the Game" never charted.

Iron Flag's title track follows and brings longtime Wu-Tang Clan devotees back to their comfort zone. RZA uses sublime strings and a high-pitched vocal from Ann Peebles's "The Handwriting Is on the Wall" (1978). RZA told *XXL Magazine* in 2002 that the beat that Raekwon, Masta Killa, and Inspectah Deck quickly fill with lyrical bluster was originally from a Cappadonna recording session.[6] The track is actually two songs. After Deck's final verse, near the three-minute mark, minimal, hollowed drums kick in, signaling the start of a new track. Rappers U-God, Ghostface, RZA, Masta Killa, and Raekwon drop lines that are followed by a refrain of multiple voices yelling "Good thing we brought the glock!" This call-and-response refrain is repeated throughout the song. The bombed out timbre of the song is reminiscent of the no-frills production aesthetics of *Enter the Wu-Tang*.

Thanks to the repetitive, over-synthesized production of "Dashing," which features rhymes from Inspectah Deck and GZA, *Iron Flag* closes on an unfulfilled note, with more kung-fu dialogue—"You have learned your style well . . . Wu-Tang style!"—at the song's end officially drawing the album to a conclusion. Import versions of *Iron Flag* have a 13th track titled "The W." The song is a leftover from *The W* album sessions—RZA can be heard singing the song's hook on *The W*—but is nevertheless an enjoyable song that has made the Internet file-sharing rounds.

In the eight years between the release of *Enter the Wu-Tang* and *Iron Flag*, the hip-hop landscape had changed drastically. Even though the Wu-Tang Clan had its own lexicon, the themes in their music kept them on common ground with their audience. But by the early 2000s that common thread was beginning to unravel, at least partially. In 2002, Inspectah Deck told *XXL Magazine*, "It's that point where the music is changing, the people are changing. They got a whole different language."[7] *Iron Flag*, with its blatant attempts at appeasing radio ("Back in the Game") and its proliferation of attempts at memorable hooks, was Wu-Tang Clan's attempt at competing with a hip-hop world that was increasingly obsessed with excess. Rappers such as New York's Jay-Z or New Orleans–based Cash Money Records' rappers Juvenile and Lil' Wayne were finding commercial success with the former's street corner to boardroom mantras and the latter's "bling bling" aspirations.

As hip-hop's influence was growing exponentially, Wu-Tang Clan was increasingly looking from the outside in. As *Time Magazine* reported in 1999, before *Iron Flag*'s release hip-hop had surpassed country as the biggest selling music genre: "In 1998, for the first time ever, rap outsold what previously had been America's top-selling format, country music. . . . Rap sold more than 81 million CDs, tapes and albums last year, compared with 72 million for country. Rap sales increased a stunning 31% from 1997 to 1998, in contrast to 2% gains for country, 6% for rock and 9% for the music industry overall."[8]

While Wu-Tang Clan had a hand in hip-hop's meteoric rise in popularity, thus revenue generation for labels, the Staten Island rappers did not fully reap its benefits. Wu-Tang Clan's bestselling album, *Wu-Tang Forever*, was released in 1997. Yes, Wu-Tang Clan had grown rich off of solid sales and enterprising business ventures, but compared to their peers they had been eclipsed. A clear example of this is Will Smith's *Big Willie Style*, also released in 1997, that would end up being certified nine times platinum. RZA was obviously disdainfully aware of this when he told *Time Magazine* in 1999, "I don't think the creativity has been big. I think the sales have been big, and the exposure has been big. Will Smith is *rap*. That's not hip-hop. It's been a big year for rap. It's been a poor year for Hip-Hop."[9]

Wu-Tang Clan found success making decidedly underground hip-hop music, which has its own rewards. "The Wu-Tang Clan has accrued cultural capital rare in Hip-Hop. The Wu-Tang style is sui generis," wrote pop culture critic Sasha Frere-Jones in the *New Yorker* in 2006.[10] But underground music could never compete for long with commercial rap sales-wise, which continued its rise with acts such as OutKast, Jay-Z, and even DMX whose gritty, urban-infused music owed some credit to the inroads Wu-Tang Clan began making in 1993. But despite all the respect and acknowledgment given, the reality was that Wu-Tang had to contend with fans looking for a new favorite artist to idolize. As *Rolling Stone* noted in its positive review of the *Iron Flag*, "Fashionable thugs have switched from Wu Wear to Jay-Z's Rocawear."[11]

Interestingly, Jay-Z's *The Blueprint* album, which was released a couple of months prior to *Iron Flag*, on September 11, 2001, features production manned dominantly by Kanye West and Just Blaze. Hailed as a classic album even before its release, *The Blueprint*'s production relies heavily on soul samples. In recent years hip-hop production had generally strayed away from sampling with rising cost of clearances being the reason. Thus producers such as Swizz Beatz, the Neptunes, and Timbaland thrived with production dominantly based on live keyboard playing. But *The Blueprint*'s success—it would go on to be certified triple platinum—swung the needle back to sampling. The production style, particularly the use of soul vocal samples sped up to the point where they sounded like Alvin & the Chipmunks records, was obviously influenced by RZA. Passing hip-hop listeners might not have made this connection, but Kanye West, who came to prominence using the technique, was quick to admit his influence. "West admits he took the idea from the Wu-Tang Clan's The RZA; he insists on giving credit where it's due," said a glowing profile of West in a 2005 issue of *Time Magazine*.[12]

For the time being RZA, despite no longer ruling by dictatorship, had managed to sew together another distinguished album from the Wu-Tang Clan. No easy feat considering that with three previous group albums and 15 solo albums between its individual members to date, the "Wu-Tang Clan sound" could no longer be easily pegged. This was made more difficult when considering *Iron Flag* was only a dozen tracks and clocked in at a shade under an hour in length. Yet all the members of Wu-Tang Clan were well represented on *Iron Flag*, which was received with open arms by critics. "Known for its various personalities, the Clan offers a little something for everyone on this concentrated list," wrote *Billboard Magazine* of the album.[13]

On its release, consumers were not as enthused with *Iron Flag*. Wu-Tang Clan's fourth album only managed to debut at #6 on the *Billboard* R&B/Hip-Hop Albums chart where their previous two albums had debuted at #1. Worse yet, the album only entered the *Billboard* Hot 200 chart at #32. It would be six long years before Wu-Tang Clan would return and release another album, *8 Diagrams* (2007). Until then, there still plenty of Wu-Tang Clan projects from individual members to be released, with wildly varying levels of success.

NOTES

1. "Wu-Tang Clan Album This Year?; New Wu?," *New Musical Express*, June 29, 2001.

2. "Upfront: In the News," *Billboard Magazine*, March 19, 2002, 8.

3. Wilson, Elliott, "RZA's Iron Flag Guide," *XXL Magazine*, March 2002, 94.

4. Ibid.

5. Ibid.

6. Ibid.

7. Wilson, Elliott, "Wrath of the Math," *XXL Magazine*, March 2002, 91.

8. Farley, Christopher John, "Hip-Hop Nation," *Time*, February 8, 1999, 56 (54–64).

9. Ibid.

10. Frere-Jones, Sasha, "Ghost's World," *The New Yorker*, March 20, 2006, 154.

11. Pareles, John, "Wu-Tang Clan: Iron Flag," *Rolling Stone Magazine*, January 31, 2002, 51.

12. Tyrangiel, Josh, and Mendez Berry, Elizabeth, "Why You Can't Ignore Kanye," Time Magazine, August 29, 2005, 54.

13. Hall, Rashaun, "Reviews & Previews: Wu-Tang Clan," *Billboard Magazine*, January 12, 2002, 21.

CHAPTER 11
Group Hiatus, Solos Still Flow

GZA/GENIUS, *LEGEND OF THE LIQUID SWORD*

Although the Wu-Tang Clan as a collective did not reconvene for several years after 2001's *Iron Flag* album, there was still music to be made. During this period more individual Wu-Tang acts tried to assert themselves as soloists, which positively or negatively affected the overall Wu-Tang brand, depending on their success. It would be a year's time almost to the day, December 10, 2002, before the next release from an official Wu-Tang Clan member—GZA/Genius's *Legend of the Liquid Sword*. The album is full of GZA's cerebral wordplay with some rapping guests that include Ghostface Killah on "Silence," RZA and Masta Killa on "Fam (Members Only)," and Inspeactah Deck on "Sparring Minds." Production on the album is handled by a number of producers including Allah Mathematics, GZA, and Arabian Knight.

RZA only contributed one track to *Legend of the Liquid Sword*: the abrasive, horn littered "Rough Cut," which incredulously only featured GZA on its chorus with the rhymes handled by rappers Armel (signed to GZA's Liquid Swords Entertainment at the time) along with 12 O'Clock and Prodigal Sunn. RZA's minimal contribution was attributed to "busy schedules."[1] *Legend of the Liquid Sword*'s standout cuts include "Animal Planet" where GZA incorporates the animal kingdom into his rhymes ("Porcupines have a rep for sticking everything in sight") and "Fame," where he name checks celebrities throughout his rhymes similarly to *Liquid Sword*'s "Labels" and *Beneath the Surface*'s "Publicity." "Larry's Bird flew out of Nicholas' cage," he raps on "Animal Planet."

Though the lead single, "Knock Knock," didn't even chart, the album was still received with a good deal of enthusiasm by critics.

The general consensus was that GZA's rhymes are still on point, but his accompaniment on the beats is occasionally lacking. *The Source Magazine* rated the album an above average four out of five mics and *XXL Magazine* rated it an L (large) out of XXL (extra extra large).[2] Other outlets including *Billboard* and *Rolling Stone* gave positive reviews of the album, the latter pointing to GZA's use of metaphors and soul music samples as redeeming factors.[3] The praise didn't carry over to retail sales, though. On its release, *Legend of the Liquid Sword*, GZA's fourth album, only reached #75 on the *Billboard* 200 chart and #21 on the *Billboard* R&B/Hip-Hop Albums chart.

For tried-and-true fans of Wu-Tang Clan and GZA, *Legend of the Liquid Sword* is one of those albums they point to as being criminally underrated. In its 2003 year-end issue *Source Magazine* listed it as one of the year's most slept-on albums, saying, "Even without a radio banger, the Wu's premier lyricist's third [*sic*] opus offered an intoxicating mix of wordplay and top-notch beats—check 'Animal Planet' and 'Fame.' "[4] While most of the public snoozed on GZA, Inspectah Deck readied his follow-up to 1999's much delayed *Uncontrolled Substance*.

INSPECTAH DECK, *THE MOVEMENT*

Inspectah Deck released his sophomore album, *The Movement*, on May 20, 2003, almost six months after GZA released *Legend of the Liquid Sword*. Independently released via Koch Records, *The Movement*'s lead single was "City High," a nimble offering that contained Deck's precise flow over a hypnotizing vocal sample. The track is produced by Hassan aka Phantom of the Beats, a member of 1990s rap group UMC's and the same team behind the production of Ghostface's "Apollo Kids." Hassan would split most of *The Movement*'s production duties with Ayatollah, a then up and coming producer who gained acclaim after helming rapper/actor Mos Def's 1999 hit "Ms. Fat Booty." After a short intro where Deck boldly declares, "This is for hood!," "City High" kicks off as the album's lead track, but unfortunately it is also the album's musical peak. The album's beats just aren't nearly dynamic enough, on the average, to help sustain Deck's relentless flow.

The Movement is by no means totally lacking in redeeming moments. "Framed" features original crime rapper Kool G. Rap and

Killa Sin relaying misdemeanor tales over swift drum kicks and ringing bells from producer Phantom of the Beat. Another pair of songs worth seeking out are the title track and "Who Got It," which features Ayatollah's keen use of swelling chords and atmospheric vocal samples. Quizzically, besides Streetlife appearing on "Shorty Right There," there are no other appearances from Inspectah Deck's Wu-Tang Clan band mates on *The Movement*.

The album was met with general indifference from critics and the public alike. *The Source Magazine* gave the album a rather generous three and a half out of five mics review but made sure to note that "Deck needs a compass," while describing the album as scattershot and full of weak beats.[5] *XXL Magazine* gave the album an M (medium) out of XXL (extra extra large) rating, citing Deck's lack of personality, experiments with his delivery, and the songs' hooks as flaws.[6] The charts were not any kinder to Deck with *The Movement* landing way down at #132 on the *Billboard* 200 chart and #7 on the *Billboard* Top Independent Albums chart when it was released.

A summer would pass before RZA released his third solo album, *Birth of a Prince*, on October 7, 2003. While his previous album was released via Koch Records, RZA now slid over to a new label home in Sanctuary Records (with distribution by BMG Records) for his latest album. *Birth of a Prince* also has the distinction of being the Wu-Tang Clan head honcho's first album billed as RZA, not Bobby Digital. But since the album at least partially relays the concept of RZA shedding his libidinous alter ego, Bobby Digital still rears his head on the project. The album features the usual RZA mélange with copious amounts of guest verses and avant-garde beats. While he does produce the majority of the album, additional producers include Megahertz, Bronze Nazareth, and True Master.

RZA, *BIRTH OF A PRINCE*

Bob 'n I/The Grunge/We Pop/Grits/Fast Cars/Chi Kung/You'll Never Know/Drink, Smoke + Fuck/The Whistle/The Drop Off/ Wherever I Go/Koto Chotan/A Day to God Is 1,000 Years/ Cherry Range/The Birth/See the Joy

Before *Birth of a Prince* came to fruition, RZA was busy making strides in Hollywood by scoring movies. In April 1999 he released the *Ghostdog: Way of the Samurai Soundtrack*, a compilation album with songs appearing in the film as well as a score, *Music from the Motion Picture Ghost Dog: The Way of the Samurai*. The latter was only released in Japan and includes a number of Wu-Tang Clan songs that were not in the film.[7] The movie *Ghostdog: Way of the Samurai*, released in May 1999, is about a modern-day samurai retained by the mafia in an unnamed city and was written and directed by Jim Jarmusch. Jarmusch began writing the script in 1998 and was listening to Wu-Tang Clan and RZA (along with Dub music—Lee Scratch Perry, King Tubby—and 1980s era Miles Davis) during the process.[8] Naturally Jarmusch, who has called RZA the Thelonious Monk of hip-hop, approached the rapper/producer with the idea and RZA, who was already getting deep into the study of Eastern philosophy, felt like it would be a natural fit.[9] RZA even made a small cameo in the film.

After RZA's success on *Ghostdog*, renowned film director Quentin Tarantino sought him out to score his two-part *Kill Bill* series of films, released in 2003 and 2004. By taking an eclectic mix of musical genres for the scores—the *Kill Bill Vol. 1 Original Soundtrack* was released September 23, 2003, and *Vol. 2* on April 13, 2004—RZA gained even more accolades for his work. The attention RZA was getting for his score and soundtrack projects was beneficial to the promotion of *Birth of a Prince*, which was released three days before *Kill Bill Vol. 1* premiered in the United States.

While for years he had been extolling the differences between RZA and Bobby Digital, by the time *Birth of a Prince* was released that line of distinction was increasingly blurred. *Birth of a Prince* opens with "Bob N' I" and begins with a sample of soul and jazz songstress Freda Payne's "Feeling Good" (1966) before abruptly cutting short to let Bobby Digital channel his inner B-Boy. He immediately starts rhyming over a breakbeat style instrumental rhythm full of bongos produced by longtime Wu-Tang Clan engineer Jose "Choco" Reynoso. The song then segues into "The Grunge," another breakbeat style track thanks to its use of Tom Jones's funky "Looking Out My Window" (1968). The Bobby Digital braggadocio continues on with the Megahertz produced "We Pop," which was the album's lead single. The song features a stuttering mix of synth and percussion and after RZA delivers an animated first verse, he gives up the mic to a pair of MCs from CCF Division, yet another Wu-Tang Clan affiliate group. Before going on to the next track, a hidden song titled "Hood Rats" is heard where RZA once again castigates a promiscuous and shiftless woman.

With "Grits" we finally seem to get RZA rhyming as RZA. However, there has never been much distinction in the cadence and vocal delivery of Bobby Digital and RZA. Equally mournful and soulful singing from Allah Real pounds home the song's lyrics of persevering despite limited means; in this case, food. "One pound box of sugar, and a stick of margarine/A hot pot of Grits kept my family from starvin,' " biographically raps RZA. The lilting baseline and piano riff also bolster the monotone Masta Killa's second verse that deals more with childhood reminiscing than grits. Nevertheless, the song is one of *Birth of a Prince*'s strongest. The rest of the album is hit or miss, mostly due to inconsistencies in the guest artists or rote topics. "Drink, Smoke + Fuck" is an ode to baser behavior that has been previously done by The Beatnuts ("Psycho Dwarf") in 1993, and others. "Wherever I Go" is marred by amateurish rhymes from CCF Division. "You'll Never Know" with its spaghetti Western guitar lick and "The Whistle," which uses a flute sample from Bernard Wystraete's "Daydream" (1969), are excellent songs stuck in the middle of the album's logjam.

Birth of a Prince doesn't regain the consistency displayed in its beginning until "A Day to God Is 1000 Years," which finds RZA incorporating the teachings of the Nation of Gods and Earths, as well as Eastern philosophy and various religions he has been studying, into his rhymes. "Whether, black or white, more shapes than snowflakes/ Existing, everywhere but you still can't locate," is how RZA rhymes about the ubiquity of God in the first verse. By the third verse he's ruminating on mortal matters when he utters, "Yo, the pen is mightier than the sword, as I face my worldly challenge/In the scale of justice and my heart remains balanced and neutral, my respect for all men is mutual." RZA's reflections are made further palatable by the track's serene horn sample taken from "Memories of Scirocco" (1982) by Chuck Mangione. On the remainder of the album RZA performs with a decidedly more methodical tone, whether it be promoting more Five Percent Nation rhetoric on the Bronze Nazareth–produced "The Birth" or rhyming from the perspective of a sperm cell, seriously, on the album's closer "See the Joy."

Thanks to RZA maintaining a higher public profile than those of GZA and Inspectah Deck, *Birth of a Prince* fared slightly better at retail than his Wu-Tang Clan brethren's respective albums. The album landed at #49 on the *Billboard* 200 chart and #20 on the *Billboard* R&B/Hip-Hop Albums chart. The critical reception to *Birth of a Prince* was mixed. Traditional press heaped on the praise. The *Boston Globe* called it a "powerful collection from one of hip-hop's most unique voices," and the *Village Voice* said, "Birth of a Prince grows on you as the sequencing reveals itself, each song a building block of an allegory about his spiritual nativity."[10] Hip-hop press was already keen on RZA; *The Source Magazine* rated the album four out of five mics.[11]

Birth of a Prince assured fans that RZA and Wu-Tang Clan were still capable of releasing appealing music. It also was yet another album that was not *The Cure*, the proposed title RZA intended his original solo album to be before choosing to get Bobby Digital out of his system. As usual, RZA was unsure of the public's readiness for the release of *The Cure*, telling *The Source Magazine*, "I just don't know if Hip-Hop is ever ready [for it]. The first time I thought about putting *The Cure* out was after 9/11, but it was Wu-Tang time, so I just chilled."[12] Surely RZA had not intended for the public to cool on Wu-Tang Clan, which was seemingly the case.

RAEKWON, *THE LEX DIAMOND STORY*

Raekwon's third album, *The Lex Diamond Story*, hoped to close out a relatively lackluster year in the Wu-Tang Clan music history book on a brighter note. Like the Wu-Tang Clan group, Raekwon was signed to Loud Records and in turn ended up out of a record deal when the label closed for business as a standalone entity in March 2002. By early 2003, Raekwon secured a new recording home for himself and his Ice Water Inc. imprint with Universal Records.[13] *The Lex Diamond Story* was released on December 13, 2003, to mixed but mostly optimistic reviews.

Raekwon is one of Wu-Tang Clan's most talented lyricists, so *The Lex Diamond Story* still managed to achieve a decent amount of sonically enjoyable moments. Ghostface makes the most of his two appearances on the album, particularly on "The Missing Watch," a quasi-sequel to his own "The Watch," which was removed from *Bulletproof Wallets* due to sample clearance issues. Produced by Mizza, on "The Missing Watch" Raekwon and Ghostface describe the hunt for a misplaced time-piece that cost close to six figures with the usual studied and savvy detail. After rushing back to the club where he suspects the watch was lost, Raekwon raps that he's "Eyeballing every fake Frankie Lymon in the joint/Break out, find my shit!," over cavernous drums from producer Mizza.

"All Over Again" is an autobiographical number where Raekwon lyrically recounts the creation of Wu-Tang Clan and his development into a successful rapper. Raekwon gives RZA credit for the vision to convince him to leave the drug-dealing game for the rap game. But the nod in rhyme would be RZA's only appearance on the album because for his second solo project in a row, Raekwon chose not have any of his production. Raekwon was steadfast in his determination to succeed without RZA's help; the producer received just as many kudos for the opus that is *Only Built for Cuban Linx . . .* as the rapper.

At the start of the skit that precludes "Smith Brothers," Raekwon is heard getting aggravated enough to call an interviewer an "asshole" for harping on the past, clearly a representation of the rapper's occasional resentment at fans and critics for constantly referring back to *Cuban Linx* while disregarding the music he was presenting now. "Smith Brothers" further drives Raekwon's point home as he delivers asphalt-colored tales over a steady barrage of piano chords and drum kicks from producers the Smith Brothers (rapper/producer, and brothers, Smooth the Hustler and Trigger the Gambler). "Musketeers of Pigs Alley" is another notable track featuring aggressive raps from Masta Killa and Inspectah over industrial tinged, minimalist production that could have made the song fit comfortably in the early Wu-Tang Clan discography.

Also in line with the usual Wu-Tang Clan maneuvers, Raekwon uses *The Lex Diamond Story* to showcase the a crew of artists he was grooming called Ice Water Inc. that consisted of rappers Polite (a long-time friend of Raekwon's), Cigar, P. C. (Paulie Caskets), and Stumik who hailed from Staten Island's Park Hill Projects. "I just wanna give them the opportunity to be successful as well," Raekwon told *The Source Magazine* in 2004.[14] Unfortunately also true to Wu-Tang Clan form, despite the best intentions, Ice Water Inc.'s debut (as Ice Water), *Polluted Water*, would be released in 2007 not through Universal Records but via the independent label Babygrande Records.

Polite is the best of the Ice Water bunch and excels when playing a complimentary role as in the aforementioned "Missing Watch" as well as "Clientele Kidd," which also features Ghostface's only other verse on the album. However, songs with prominent Ice Water Inc. contributions—"Robbery" and "Wyld in da Club"—are some of the album's weakest. Ice Water shouldn't shoulder all the blame, though. "Pa-blow Escablow" has a beat of little more than ascending guitar chords that make it sound amateurish and causes what is another great narrative rap from Raekwon to be a difficult listen. But "Ice Cream Pt. 2" produced by DJ Khalil, who would go on to produce much better fare as part of Dr. Dre's production camp, delivers a limp beat that, despite Method Man and Cappadonna contributing verses, is still a poor sequel to the original.

The Lex Diamond Story is a more palatable listen than *Immobilarity*, but when compared to Raekwon's overall body of work, it is not the resounding return to form that fans and critics hoped for. There were glimpses of past greatness but a total package was not properly pieced together. *Rolling Stone* pointed out that Raekwon's "middling verse drowns in a sea of underwhelming guest appearances and beats even a corner boy wouldn't rap over."[15] Interestingly, some outlets such as the *Boston Globe* and *Entertainment Weekly* gave the album positive reviews, mostly due to the enthusiasm at getting new Wu-Tang Clan–related material.[16] Hip-hop press was warier; *The Source Magazine* rated the album a respectable three and half out of five mics but in its L out of XXL review of the album, *XXL Magazine* made sure to mention that Raekwon stumbled when going for mass appeal with radio-friendly records.

The Lex Diamond Story would be Raekwon's worst performing album on the charts to date, peaking at only #102 on the *Billboard* 200 chart and #18 on the *Billboard* R&B/Hip-Hop Albums chart. The album was purportedly the close of a trilogy, setting the stage for a proper *Only Built 4 Cuban Linx . . .* sequel.[17] Fans would have to remain patient; thanks to numerous delays, *Only Built 4 Cuban Linx . . . Pt. II* would not be released for another six years.[18]

Besides RZA, none of 2003's records from the Wu-Tang Clan family of artists offered much difference from other hip-hop releases. Wu-Tang Clan were no longer underground heroes or underdogs to rally behind, and coupled with little radio support, the albums stalled out at shelves with none of the 2003 releases cracking the Top 10. The year 2004 would be slightly better for Wu-Tang Clan, mostly thanks to the talents of Ghostface. But it would take more than one member of this league of extraordinary rappers to defend their honor in the court of new-age MCs and fans less interested in past exploits.

NOTES

1. Johnson, Gregory, "Urban Legend," *The Source Magazine*, January 2003, 76 (74–76).

2. Samuel, Anslem, "Record Report: GZA/Genius," *The Source Magazine*, January 2003, 143–44. Osborne, Ben, "GZA/Genius: Legend of a Liquid Sword," *XXL Magazine*, December 2002, 173–74.

3. Blashill, Pat, "GZA," *Rolling Stone*, January 23, 2003, 66. Paoletta, Michael, "Legend of the Liquid Sword (Music release)." *Billboard* 115, no. 2 (January 11, 2003): 29. *Academic Search Premier*, EBSCO*host* (accessed July 22, 2010).

4. "Slept on Albums of 2003," *The Source Magazine, February 2004*, 51.

5. Barrow, Jerry L., "Record Report: Inspectah Deck," *The Source Magazine*, July 2003.

6. Aku, Timmhotep, "Inspectah Deck: The Movement," *XXL Magazine*, 2003. 157, 178.

7. http://www.soundtrackcollector.com/catalog/soundtrackdetail.php?movie id=45896.

8. Rubin, Mike, "Ways of the Samurai," *Spin Magazine*, March 2000, 123 (122–24).

9. Ibid.

10. Capobianco, Ken, "RZA: Birth of a Prince," *Boston Globe*, November 2, 2003. http://www.proquest.com.dmvgateway.nysed.gov/ (accessed July 23, 2010). Kim, Serena, "RZA: Birth of a Prince," *The Village Voice*, November 5, 2003 http://www.proquest.com.dmvgateway.nysed.gov/ (accessed July 23, 2010).

11. Perry, Daryl, "Record Report: RZA: Birth of a Prince," *The Source Magazine*, December 2003, 168.

12. Golianopoulos, Thomas, "Name Dropping," *The Source Magazine*, December 2003, 127 (126–27).

13. Ice Water Inc. was the name of Raekwon's new venture and one of his partners was Randy Spelling, son of storied TV producer Aaron Spelling.

14. Wilkes, Joseph, "Off the Radar: Ice Water," *The Source Magazine*, March 2004, 81.

15. Caramanica, Jon, "Raekwon: The Lex Diamond Story," *Rolling Stone Magazine*, February 5, 2004, 60.

16. Capobianco, Ken, "Raekwon: The Lex Diamond Story," *Boston Globe*, January 2, 2004, C13. Endelman, Michael, "Raekwon: The Lex Diamond Story," *Entertainment Weekly*, January 9, 2004, 80.

17. Golianopoulos, Thomas, "Chain Reaction," *Scratch Magazine*, March/April 2006, 80 (76–82).

18. Golianopoulos, Thomas, "Record Report: Raekwon," *The Source Magazine*, March 2004, 160–161. Aku, Timmhotep, "Raekwon: The Lex Diamond Story," *XXL Magazine*, November 2003, 173.

CHAPTER 12
Goodbye Ol' Dirty Bastard, Wu-Tang Marches On

The year 2004 and the next couple of years would be bittersweet for the Wu-Tang Clan. There would still be a relatively steady trickle of individual albums. After spending two years at Clinton Correctional Facility in upstate New York, in April 2003 Ol' Dirty Bastard was transferred to a mental facility in New York City to finish his sentence.[1] On May 1 of the same year Ol' Dirty Bastard was released from Manhattan's Psychiatric Center and was driven directly to a press conference at the Rhiga Royal Hotel to announce that he had signed with Roc-a-Fella Records.[2] Despite Ol' Dirty Bastard's extended and involuntary hiatus from the music industry, there was still anticipation for new material from the rapper. There was an album called *The Trials and Tribulations of Russell Jones*, mostly previously recorded material, that was remixed and released in 2002 without Ol' Dirty Bastard's knowledge. On his return to free society a proper *Dirt McGirt* album was slated to have five to seven RZA tracks.[3]

While Ol' Dirty Bastard, now going officially by Dirt McGirt, was recording his Roc-a-Fella Records debut, the Wu-Tang Clan reunited for a tour in November 2004. But in that same month, after missing a reunion show in New Jersey the night before, Ol' Dirty Bastard would pass away, leaving an indelible legacy with the Wu-Tang Clan and hip-hop, but also leaving a void within the group. Fortunately, succeeding amid adversity is as Wu-Tang Clan as a kung-fu sample, and the group and its members would eventually reach the light after these dark times. Also in 2004, RZA released all of Wu-Tang Clan's members from the individual recording contracts he signed them to in 1993. As usual, how various members fared without RZA's musical input varied. But one member who seems to thrive even without the Abbot's guiding hand is Ghostface Killah.

GHOSTFACE KILLAH, *THE PRETTY TONEY ALBUM*

Just as RZA and Raekwon before him, Ghostface moved to a new recording home for his next album. The rapper's first three albums were released on RZA's Razor Sharp Records via Epic/Sony Records. But with each album selling progressively less than the previous, Ghostface deemed it time for a change. Ghostface always possessed an uncanny amount of star power, even among his uber-talented and gregarious Wu-Tang Clan brothers, that eclipsed the moderate commercial success he had received (*Ironman* sold platinum, *Supreme Clientele* sold gold). In November 2003 Ghostface performed a remix of Beyonce's "Summertime Remix" with the R&B/pop singer in New York's Madison Square Garden during Jay-Z's "farewell" performance to a rousing ovation. Shortly thereafter Ghostface put in a call to long-time record business executive Lyor Cohen, then the head of Universal Music Group Island Def Jam label, about coming over to Def Jam from Epic. The deal was made, though Cohen would leave Def Jam to become North American Chairman and CEO of the Warner Music Group before Ghostface released his Def Jam debut, *The Pretty Toney Album.*

Ghostface Killah was in a new recording home for a fresh start. To make his name more palatable for stodgy retailers, he started formally going by just "Ghostface" as seen on the album's cover art.[4] The move to Def Jam worked out in Ghostface's favor with regard to sample clearances. A litany of highly esteemed hip-hop producers on the album, including No I.D and K-Def, use elaborate and majestic samples on nearly every track while Ghostface rhymes on every song as if his life depended on it. Also, for the first time Ghostface's album track listing coincides with the songs on the actual album.

With all the pieces in place, the question was, Could Ghostface deliver a fourth, highly acclaimed album in a row? The album's unofficial "street" single, the RZA-produced "Run," tilted the odds in the rapper's favor. Featuring a grating, sped-up, and distorted harmonica sample snatched from Les Baxter's "Hogin' Machine" (1969) laid over galloping drums that won't quit, Ghostface sprints over the track with a frenzied verse detailing when running from the police is the best play. In the song, Ghostface name-checks his friend Un, who he has mentioned in previous songs, who is serving a 25 years to life sentence because the rapper believes Staten Island police lost the evidence that would prove he didn't commit the crime (murder).[5] Rapper Jadakiss guests on the song, tacking on a second verse that matches wits with Ghostface's first. "Run" didn't chart but was a mix tape hit and built anticipation for the release of *The Pretty Toney Album* on April 20, 2004.

From the start of *The Pretty Toney Album* listeners can feel his swagger and confidence. Listeners hear Ghostface answering questions over a loop of the chords of Tommy Youngblood's 1969 version of "Tobacco Road" and he says, "I'ma do it how I been doing it. Ain't nothing but a different label." The first proper song "Biscuits," produced by Wu-Elements member True Master, only confirms that Ghostface's fiery flow is still ample as he shares the mic with guest Trife Diesel. Ghostface and his Theodore Unit protégé take turns rocking over the rugged beat that utilizes a filtered horn sample from R&B duo Sam & Dave's version of "I Can't Stand Up for Falling Down" (1984).

It is appropriate that the first song utilizes a sample from an artist/group that worked for the storied Stax label that specialized in R&B/soul music as Ghostface has constantly stated his love for 1960s and 1970s soul music to the press. His previous three albums featured songs with plenty of soul samples and *The Pretty Toney* album is no different.

K-Def samples another Stax Record alumni—David Porter's "I'm Afraid the Masquerade Is Over"—for the spine-tingling "Over" and Ghostface himself is credited for producing "Save Me Dear," which uses a fresh portion of the same Freddie Scott "(You) Got What I Need" (1968) record, famously sampled by rapper Biz Markie.

The album's crescendo, which also illuminates Ghostface's status as an "Old Soul," is "Holla." Not settling for rapping over a two-bar loop or breakbeat, on "Holla" Ghostface decided to simply rhyme over the Delfonics' "La La Means I Love You" (1968), vocals and all. Rapping about his quandaries in the rap music industry, it is another stirring performance from Ghostface, who at times seems to be on the verge of bursting into tears. In a 2004 interview, the rapper explained to *The Source Magazine*, "In Hip-Hop, in order to be a real MC you gotta really know how to maneuver. You gotta know how to make a nigga cry some-time. You gotta make a nigga really feel the pain. You [also] gotta make a nigga laugh."[6]

Ghostface certainly seems to have had fun while making this album, constantly hitting his tried-and-true formulas, besides the soul samples. A classic hip-hop breakbeat, in this case Esther Williams's "Last Night Changed It All" (1976), gets blessed with Ghostface's rap bars on the K-Def produced "Keisha's House," which, due to its brevity, is labeled a skit. Ghostface teams with the decidedly blue-collar, but hungry, rappers such as Sheek Louch and Styles P on the brassy "Metal Lungies." The collaboration with Missy Elliott, "Tush" on the other hand is an obvious play for radio. Produced by D. Trotman & Dub Dot Z, it uses the harmony, melody, and just about everything else from the disco friendly "Naked Truth" (1975) by Best of Both Worlds. The reception to "Tush," sanitized as "Push" when presented as a single, was divisive. *Billboard Magazine* called the song a "club anthem" but the *Boston Globe* wrote it "may sound great in theory but it falters in execution."[7]

The rhymes on "Tush"/"Push" are slickly delivered, but lines such as, "Come with me and just leave your friends/Cause we don't need no cock blocking," meant the usually lyrically dexterous rapper was dumbing it down. Ghostface explained to *Vibe Magazine* in 2004, "Ain't no disrespect, but the average person don't wanna hear lyrics no more. They just wanna shake their ass. So if you wanna play dumb, I can play dumb too. I'm not gonna bust my brain, actin' like I gotta write a Malcolm X dart, because right now, the people are simple-minded."[8] "Tush"/"Push" was Ghostface's volley at radio, which was critical to sales. The single would reach #1 on the *Billboard* Dance Music/Club Play Singles chart and #12 on the *Billboard* Hot Dance Singles chart, but only hit #53 on the *Billboard* R&B/Hip-Hop Singles chart. Also, in spite of Ghostface's comments that listeners weren't into lyrics, *The Source Magazine* still deemed his verse on "Be This Way" deserving of a "Hip-Hop Quotable" in its April 2004 issue.[9]

Lesser talented acts had surpassed Ghostface in sales (not exactly anything new when considering the history of American music). He is keenly aware of this when he raps, "It's like they love garbage, for God's sake, I'm the real artist," on the bubbly "Ghostface," an ode to "AJ Scratch" from Kurtis Blow's *Ego Trip* (1984) album. On its release, *The Pretty Toney Album* did slightly better on the charts than its predecessor, landing at #6 on the *Billboard* 200 chart and #4 on the *Billboard* R&B/Hip-Hop Albums chart. But despite seemingly better promotion from Def Jam, *The Pretty Toney Album* only sold about 69,000 units its first week compared to *Bulletproof Wallets*' 76,000.

Critics, and fans who purchased the album, were enthused with the project in spite of its lackluster sales. Urban press including *Vibe Magazine*, *The Source Magazine*, and *XXL Magazine* all gave *The Pretty Toney Album* enthusiastic reviews.[10] While *Pretty Toney* is a solid, even elite, Ghostface album, the proverbial elephant in the CD packaging cannot be ignored; there are no Wu-Tang Clan appearances on the album. RZA only contributes a pair of beats—"Run" and the minute-long though profound "Kunta Fly Shit"—and would no longer retain the executive producer handle he kept on all previous Ghostface albums. Wu-Tang Clan members did appear on a few records that were leaked but didn't make the final cut on the album such as "The Drummer," which features Method Man as well as Streetlife and Trife. Even without assistance from his Wu-Tang Clan brothers, Ghostface still manages to deliver another quality piece of work, further cementing his status as Wu-Tang Clan's premier artist.

METHOD MAN, *TICAL 0: THE PREQUEL*

Ghostface's first foray under the Def Jam flag didn't transform him from underground herald to mainstream rap champion. His new labelmate and Def Jam veteran Method Man had enjoyed a higher profile thanks to his appeal to women, Grammy-winning hits ("You're All I Need"), as well as his burgeoning acting career. But music was still the charismatic rapper's first love and on May 18, 2004, just one short month after Ghostface *The Pretty Toney Album* Method Man released his third solo album, *Tical 0: The Prequel*, five years after his last album.

Method Man had not been completely gone from the music scene since his last album. Besides the two Wu-Tang albums since he released his sophomore album, 1998's *Tical 2000: Judgement Day*, he collaborated with Redman to release the critically acclaimed *Blackout!* album in 1999. All of these titles were at least platinum sellers. Method Man was always prolific when it came to cameo appearances on albums from artists outside of the Wu-Tang Clan family whether they be hip-hop (LL Cool J, Cypress Hill, and Run-DMC) or R&B (Mary J. Blige, Ginuwine, and Missy Elliott) acts.

While previously Raekwon was focused on moving forward with his latest release, Method Man was looking at the past as inspiration for his most recent work. By adding *The Prequel* to his third album's title it signified an attempt at recapturing some of the sonic resonance of his debut—1994's *Tical*—10 years later. "This shit is the prequel, the shit that should've been on the first: beats, thoughts and all that," explained Method Man to *The Source Magazine* in 2003 while he was in the midst of recording the album.[11] Method Man also felt that *Tical* was too unscripted. In the same interview he told *The Source*, "None of that running into the studio to drop a verse. Cause when it came to my albums, my shits sounded like freestyle tapes. I had to get right with myself and become more focused—because this shit is a business."[12]

Despite Method Man's intentions, *Tical 0: The Prequel* possesses a number of key differences from *Tical* that are evident before the album is even played. Most obvious, its predecessor in namesake was completely produced by RZA. *Tical 0* features production from an assortment of some of the hottest hip-hop producers of its day, including Rockwilder, Denuan "Mr. Porter" Porter of Eminem-endorsed rap group D-12, and Sean "Diddy" Combs, but only one RZA-produced track. There is also an extensive list of guest artists on *Tical 0*, including Ludacris, Missy Elliott, Busta Rhymes, and Snoop Dogg.

For such a star-studded album, getting *Tical 0* into stores wasn't a smooth task. Method Man has always had a love/hate relationship with his Def Jam label, and in 2004 it was no different. According to the rapper, *Tical 0* was done as early as February 2004, but the album was held up because the label didn't have faith in him (and lacked any singles).[13] *Tical 0*'s lead single ended up being "What's Happenin,' " which is produced by Busta Rhymes's tour DJ, Scratchator, and also features the animated rapper. Method Man and Busta Rhymes take turns dropping party instigating rhymes over a sample of a fuzzy, muddled bass line stripped from "Dum Maro Dum," a Hindi Indian song by Bollywood singer Ashla Bhosle. Despite the attempt at a rousing, club-friendly song, "What's Happenin' " only managed to enter the *Billboard* R&B/Hip-Hop Songs chart at #64.

It is no wonder no other song from *Tical 0* made it to the charts; there are few songs that inspire repeated plays in this set. *Tical 0*'s problem is that it is too ambitious. Too many guest producers and too many guest artists leave the listener no entry point to figure out where Method Man is exactly coming from or where he exactly wants to go musically. The song "Rodeo," produced by Boogz, features Ludacris, a Def Jam labelmate of Method Man's and a celebrated lyricist from Atlanta. But the chemistry he and Method Man share on this electric guitar–driven track is minimal and further sabotaged by a lame hook that hears the rappers chanting, "Come up out of them dirty clothes, bend on over and touch them toes/Uh-oh, wee-oh, wee-oh!/Come on and ride this rodeo," square dance announcer style.

Songs with Snoop Dogg ("We Some Dogs," which also features Redman) and Kardinal Offishall ("Baby Come On") also fail to resonate, due mostly to generic sounding beats. The result is Method Man, whose gravelly baritone has long been one of his assets, lets his voice get lost in his overcrowded guest list. At different points in the album's first two songs ("The Prequel" and "Say What"), Method Man raps "he gets it crunk." The reference is noteworthy because producer Lil Jon had found great success the previous couple of years with his "Crunk" hip-hop, and in turn many purveyors of the hip-hop subgenre of music were coming to prominence. While Method Man certainly had created songs that did get the party crunk or hyped up, in these songs' context it denotes that the rapper was hopping on trends rather than creating them.

Pandering to mainstream expectations is the reason Method Man recruited Sean Combs and longtime Bad Boy Executive Harve Pierre (who is credited for "A&R Direction" on the album) to help with *Tical 0: The Prequel*. However, after the album received backlash on its release, Method Man publicly second-guessed that decision.[14] "I didn't know that when people look at me, they didn't just look at me as a performer who goes around and has fun all day. . . . They want me to say something. I got [so] caught up in the other hoopla that I stopped saying anything. I just got wrapped up in trying to make hit records and SoundScan," Method Man admitted to MTV.com's Shaheem Reid in 2006.[15]

In its review of *Tical 0*, *Entertainment Weekly* pointed out that "Meth's rugged rhymes still flow with effortless finesse, but for the first time, he loses his identity," while also noting that maybe Method Man was too busy with his upcoming role in the feature film *Soul Plane* and his short-lived sitcom on the FOX Network.[16] Method Man disagreed with this possible reasoning, insisting that his music never suffered because of his other commitments; it's just that the listening public was no longer as interested in the Wu-Tang Clan.[17]

While demand for all things Wu-Tang Clan certainly cooled since their late 1990s height, adding to the malaise Method Man's album elicited from the listening public was its mediocrity in comparison to his Wu-Tang Clan buddy Ghostface's *The Pretty Toney Album* released just a month before. Whereas Ghostface delivered an album attuned to his personal tastes (emotive rhymes over soul sample heavy production), Method Man delivered an album that had as many different hip-hop styles as its guests. Ironically, some of *Tical 0*'s best musical moments occur with Wu-Tang Clan assistance.

RZA's production on *Tical* had a raw, almost lo-fi quality to it, but on *Tical 0* the beats are clean and polished. This isn't a bad thing but the beats are broad and cliché to the point of boredom. RZA's lone contribution, besides introducing Method Man and his many aliases, on the album's intro is the brooding "The Turn." RZA outfits splices of piano chords and vocals from 1975's "Where Are You Going to Love" by Smokey Robinson and the Miracles with lithe drums for Method Man and Raekwon to attack with focused rhyme energy. Another standout track is "The Afterparty," a duet with Ghostface where the old friends rhyme about the remains of a wild party the previous night and the ungrateful, freeloading partygoers left in its wake. Produced by Qu'Ran "Q" Goodman, the instrumental flips strings from the beginning of 1978's "I Just Don't Know about This Girl" by the Detroit Emeralds and is one of the rare moments on *Tical 0* where Method Man fluidly matches his underrated rap talents with an alluring track.

"The Motto," produced by Lee Stone and Nyshiem Myrick, features a static-y base line and spare key notes—making it a track that could have fit seamlessly into *Tical*—and is another stand-out track, but ultimately it is not enough to save the album's multiple shortcomings. Most media outlets couldn't say enough about how much of a disappointment *Tical 0: The Prequel* turned out to be. *Spin Magazine* (which also pointed out the album's too many guests) went as far to say that Method Man had "jumped the shark."[18] Even the traditional hip-hop press, always careful to not critique Wu-Tang Clan members too harshly, was unimpressed.[19] *The Source Magazine* gave *Tical 0* a generous three and half out of five mics review but made sure to point out that the album's production was not up to par.[20] In giving the album a two and half out of five mics record review, *Vibe Magazine* wrote that "Method Man does not bring the pain on his latest album," a tongue in cheek nod to *Tical*'s lead single "Bring the Pain."

Despite the bruises critics were administering, *Tical 0* managed a respectable entry into the charts; the album debuted at #2 on the *Billboard* 200 chart, #1 on the *Billboard* R&B/Hip-Hop Albums chart, and #3 on the *Billboard* Rap Albums chart. *Tical 0* was the third Method Man album (fourth if we count *Blackout!* with Redman) to debut at #1 on the *Billboard* R&B/Hip-Hop Albums chart. However, while his previous two albums were certified platinum, to date *Tical 0: The Prequel* has only been certified gold. Going back in time had not been kind to Method Man.

MASTA KILLA, *NO SAID DATE*

While everyone was taking Method Man to task for his third solo album, one of his Wu-Tang Clan partners quietly released his solo debut a couple of weeks later. Masta Killa was the last official Wu-Tang Clan member to join the Shaolin fold and would also have the distinction of being the last member to release an official solo album when he released *No Said Date* on June 1, 2004.[21] Since first appearing on "Da Mystery of Chessboxin'" on *Enter the Wu-Tang (36 Chambers)*, the Brooklyn native built an impressive resume of verses on subsequent Wu-Tang Clan group albums and on albums from individual members as well. Songs such as Ghostface's "Winter Warz," Raekwon's "Glaciers of Ice," and Wu-Tang Clan's "One Blood Under W" contained performances from Masta Killa that proved he was not an "also ran" in the collective. While many of his Wu-Tang Clan cohorts sought to assert themselves as soloist as a means to prove to the public or themselves that they could succeed without using their group affiliation as a crutch, Masta Killa cherished and thrived on being part of a team.[22]

Masta Killa was the last Wu-Tang Clan member to release a solo album but he didn't seem to hold any bitterness over that fact. Instead, in various interviews surrounding the release of the recording he stated that he used the time to learn all he could from his eight big brothers.

Masta Killa wasn't merely sounding cliché. His lone contribution to *Enter the Wu-Tang Clan*, the last verse on "Da Mystery of Chessboxin,' " was the first rhyme he had ever seriously written.[23] Masta Killa's role as a team player came in handy because though there is only one extended posse cut on *No Said Date*, he manages to get every Wu-Tang Clan member to make an appearance on the album. As the culmination of years of experience as one of Wu-Tang Clan's chess pieces, some of the material on *No Said Date* was already up to five years old.[24] The album's title is a furtive reference to its delayed release, having been in the works and nearly completed for a number of years. The lead single was the RZA-produced title track, which features a haunting brass sample of composer Henry Mancini's "Police Woman Theme" (1976), which is familiar to fans of OutKast as it is similarly used on their song "Skew It on the Bar-B" (1998), featuring Raekwon.

Masta Killa possesses a monotone flow that makes his words and lyrics easy to hear and understand. While his lyrics are highly stylized, his deadpan delivery sometimes prevents them from having lasting impact on listeners when the beat is not engaging. Thankfully, Masta Killa displays a sharp ear for beats throughout *No Said Date*. RZA contributes, and also rhymes on, two more tracks; a concept song called "School" where Masta Killa details his upbringing over stark drums that switched at the beginning the producer's verse to a galloping groove, and "Old Man," which samples Quincy Jones's "The Streetbeater" (1973) (also known as the theme from 1970s sitcom *Sanford & Son*) and features an animated Ol' Dirty Bastard on the chorus and ad libs. Most of the remainder of the album's production is handled by Wu-Elements producers True Master and Mathematics.

Mostly thanks to Masta Killa's strict adherence to the Wu-Tang Clan musical aesthetic, there was praise for *No Said Date* with critics and devoted fans still interested in the Staten Island rap outfit. The biggest hang-up with *No Said Date* was that it was a throwback record. *The Source Magazine* lamented that the album hadn't been released 10 years earlier in its three and a half out of five mics review of the album.[25] *XXL Magazine* was less enthused, writing that Masta Killa's "ability to bring the ruckus is waning."[26] But the notoriously picky Pitchfork.com gave the album an 8.3 out of 10 rating while noting, "But Masta Killa has delivered one the most urgent, straightforward Wu releases since the group's debut over a decade ago."[27]

Focused first and foremost on dynamic beats and lyrical wordplay, it didn't mess with the predominant hip-hop music of the day's penchant for tales of big money spending, fancy cars, and expensive tastes. This type of popular hip-hop music was not the rule, but it nevertheless tended to be the best selling and most recognizable by mainstream listeners.

Masta Killa's *No Said Date* was released via an independent label (Nature Sounds Records). Besides being one of the quietest and low-key Wu-Tang members, this can help partially explain the album's weak showing on the charts. The album entered at #136 on the *Billboard 200* chart and #31 on the *Billboard* R&B/Hip-Hop Albums chart while none of its singles charted. Nevertheless, with all the Wu-Tang Clan methods in place, Masta Killa executed an album full of quality hip-hop music. *No Said Date* is loaded with Wu-Tang Clan appearances in the same manner as the first wave of solo releases from the group, in effect making it a "Wu-Tang Clan album" as well.

REQUIEM FOR OL' DIRTY

Ol' Dirty Bastard appears on Masta Killa's "Old Man"—as well as its video—but sadly it would be his last on a Wu-Tang Clan record, besides posthumous releases. On his release from a mental facility the previous year, he peculiarly signed with Dame Dash's Roc-a-Fella Records, about as far removed from a Wu-Tang Clan entity as one could get. Ol' Dirty saw Roc-a-Fella as the best situation to get back into the music industry while Dame Dash saw the rapper as an opportunity to further expand his label's global brand.[28] Ol' Dirty immediately got to recording, with his usually ambitious predilections. In 2003, Ol' Dirty told *XXL Magazine*, "I wrote a lot of lyrics when I was in jail, but I'm not using any of them. I'm starting fresh. I want to record hardcore material, commercial material and crossover material. Whatever suits the needs of the public, that's what I'll put out."[29]

With the rapper hoping to put all his legal troubles behind him, besides new music Ol' Dirty Bastard also started taping a reality show for VH1. Within a couple of weeks Ol' Dirty managed to record a new song with Pharrell of the Neptunes ("Pop Shit" from *The Neptunes Present . . . Clones* [2003]) and a song with Roc-a-Fella singer Nicole Wray called

"Welcome Home" was sent to radio. But despite initial interest, mostly because of the novelty of his recent release from a mental facility, the music did not leave a lasting impression on fans and critics alike.

By the summer of 2003, the title of Ol' Dirty Bastard's third official album was revealed to be *Dirt McGirt*, named after his new official moniker, with an intended release date of October 2004 that came and went.[30] Production on the album was to be handled by RZA, Swizz Beatz, and the Neptunes. RZA was still involved in his cousin's project because Ol' Dirty remained signed to his production company.[31] While RZA cosigned Ol' Dirty Bastard's move to Roc-a-Fella, other Wu-Tang Clan members including Inspectah Deck and Raekwon were wary of the maneuver. On the flipside, Ol' Dirty Bastard felt that Wu-Tang Clan abandoned him during the height of his legal troubles. By February 2004 Ol' Dirty Bastard was performing shows to promote *Dirt McGirt*, which was now slated for a March release date that also came and went. A duet with Macy Gray called "Don't Go Breaking My Heart," a cover of the Elton John song, was released in July 2004. By this time there was no release date for the *Dirt McGirt* album at all.

In the summer of 2004 the Wu-Tang Clan reunited for a show in California. A DVD of the show, titled *Disciples of the 36 Chambers: Chapter 1*, was released for sale in September 2004. The Wu-Tang Clan performed a show in New Jersey on Friday, November 12, 2004. Ol' Dirty Bastard was the only Clan member who did not make the show. The next day, EMS workers were unable to revive the rapper after he passed out in the lounge of 36 Records LLC, Wu-Tang Clan's studio, located on 34th Street in New York City. It would be discovered that Ol' Dirty had a combination of cocaine and the prescription pain-killer Tramadol in his system. The untimely death hit the hip-hop and music community at large profoundly. "The great [artists] tread that fine line between genius and pain. Dirty has experienced a fair share of both," said Sylvia Rhone, the head of Elektra Records while Ol' Dirty was on the label, to *The Source Magazine* in 1999, years before his death.[32]

Despite Ol' Dirty Bastard's weary soul finally being at peace, there was still plenty of unreleased music to be heard. An official mix tape called *Osirus*, yet another of Ol' Dirty Bastard's monikers, was released in January 2005 and was officially sanctioned by the late rapper's manager, Jared Weisfeld, and mother, Cherry Jones. *Osirus* featured the DJ Premier–produced "Pop Shots," which features a focused ODB ably rapping to the track's chopped piano chords and stuttered production. The *Osirus* mix tape was not part of the material Ol' Dirty Bastard was recording for his Roc-a-Fella debut. Interestingly, "Pop Shots" was also to serve as the lead single to the official *A Son Unique* album that was scheduled to be released on June 21, 2005, by Roc-a-Fella/Def Jam Records. However, the album inexplicably never made it to store shelves. *XXL Magazine* ran an L out of XXL review of the album, noting that ODB's chemistry with his Wu-Tang Clan mates was fine but lacking when matched with his Roc-a-Fella/Def Jam cohorts.[33] *Vibe Magazine* and *Rolling Stone Magazine* also gave the album mostly positive reviews, yet to this day it remains unreleased.[34]

Ol' Dirty Bastard may have had trouble getting his final album released in death, but a living and breathing U-God alleged to have issues getting his music out for public consumption, too. On September 13, 2005, U-God released his second solo album, *Mr. Xcitement*, to little if any fanfare. U-God had taken to the press the previous year, while promoting a compilation album he released called *U-Godzilla Presents the Hillside Scramblers*, with disparaging remarks aimed mostly at RZA about feeling like a slave within the Wu-Tang Clan.[35] RZA retaliated in earnest, noting that despite U-God being the least acclaimed of Wu-Tang Clan's rappers he still insisted on keeping him in the group.[36]

Needless to say, despite executive producing U-God's previous album, the producer was totally absent from *Mr. Xcitement*. There also were no appearances from any Wu-Tang Clan members, with Wu-Elements producer 4th Disciple's "A Long Time Ago" being the only song with any Wu-Tang DNA besides U-God himself. The rapper told New York City's *Amsterdam News*, "Basically my objective is to prove to people that me, myself, U-God, can stand on his own and sell records."[37] Noble intentions, but *Mr. Xcitement* was panned by critics and largely by everyone except the most diehard of Wu-Tang Clan fans. The album failed to even chart.

A month after U-God's *Mr. Xcitement* came and went, GZA released a collaborative album with DJ Muggs of Cypress Hill that many consider to be the rapper's fifth album. Billed as DJ Muggs vs. GZA, and the first of an ongoing series between the producer and different MCs, the title of the project was *Grandmasters*. The title is a reference to the game of chess, GZA being an avid fan of the ancient game. The majority of the album's song titles refer to chess terms including "Exploitation of Mistakes," "Queen's Gambit," and "Unprotected Pieces." RZA continues his playful use of associated words on "Queen's Gambit (N.F.L.)," managing to mentions every NFL football team's mascot in the rhyme, except for the Atlanta Falcons. Apparently GZA did want to throw in "Falcon Crest" somewhere in the rhymes but thought about it after the song was completed.[38]

GZA and Muggs became acquainted after the rapper appeared on the renowned producer's *Soul Assassins* (1997) compilation album. Like RZA, Muggs is known for production driven by grim, dusky samples and stark moods, making his beats a natural complement to GZA's elaborate rhymes. After agreeing to the project, GZA received a dozen or so beats from Muggs to get acquainted with and rhyme to. GZA then flew out to LA a month or so later to record the album. A notable song on the *Grandmaster* project, with a familiar title, is "All In Together," a dedication to Ol' Dirty Bastard. The rhymes were originally written for ODB and with RZA on the song's intro their All In Together group is once again together in spirit.

Grandmasters was released on October 25, 2005, on the independent Up Above Records label. The album quietly entered at #189 on the *Billboard* 200 chart and #69 on the *Billboard* R&B/Hip-Hop Albums chart. Critics were endeared with *Grandmasters*; *XXL Magazine*, in giving the album an XL rating in its review, went as far to as to say GZA has been as consistent as Ghostface, just without all the fanfare.[39]

GHOSTFACE KILLAH, *FISHSCALE*

Coincidentally, the next album in the Wu-Tang Clan discography would be Ghostface Killah's *Fishscale*. But before its release, in February 2006 Wu-Tang Clan reunited for a month-long East Coast tour, their first since 1997, partly in dedication to the late Ol' Dirty Bastard. At the time Ghostface wasn't too sure if the Wu-Tang Clan's tour would lead to another group album, though other members such as GZA hoped it would increase its possibility.[40] Thanks to his uncanny consistency at releasing quality music that satiated his core fan base, Ghostface maintained his rank as Wu-Tang Clan's most dependable artist. 2004's *The Pretty Toney Album* was not the commercial success he hoped his then new Def Jam label would grant him, but it was no fault of the music he presented. So without skipping a beat, but after the successful reunion tour with Wu-Tang Clan, Ghostface readied the release of his fifth solo album, *Fishscale.*

Fishscale is a colloquial term for uncut cocaine, and its use as an album title was intentional. On *The Pretty Toney Album* Ghostface was in more of a celebratory, boasting, and bragging mode of rhyme. But on *Fishscale*, the album's content is more in line with the grand tales of criminal enterprise and gangster life reflections that harken back to the themes on *Only Built 4 Cuban Linx . . .* Ghostface's rationale for this shift backward was because it was what the public wanted to hear since nefarious drug dealing stories seem to be better received than righteous preaching.[41] For example, at the time Virginia hip-hop duo the Clipse were getting critical acclaim for their music soaked in cocaine tales and references. Also, then upcoming Atlanta rapper Young Jeezy who called himself "The Snowman" was liberal with the drug references in his music. As one of the architects, with Raekwon, of the style of hip-hop—after Kool G. Rap—who better to thrive off its popularity than Ghostface?

Even if it quenched the public's thirst for sex, drugs, and hip-hop, no matter the album's theme, the project needed a radio hit to drive sales. Each subsequent solo release from Ghostface had sold fewer records than its predecessor, with the most recent of the bunch, *The Pretty Toney Album*, only selling 69,000 records its first week in stores. Ghostface was frustrated with this trend, to the point where he even started thinking, though not for long, that maybe he was losing his touch.[42] For *Fishscale*'s lead single, Ghostface released the Pete Rock–produced "Be Easy." The beat was able enough, featuring a flamboyant horn sample and vocal snippet from "Stay Away from Me" (1973) by The Sylvers. However, it didn't perform well enough—it peaked at only #91 on the *Billboard* R&B/Hip-Hop Songs chart—to push sales of *Fishscale.*

For *Fishscale*'s second single Ghostface resorted to one of his old formulas. He released "Back Like That," a syrupy R&B styled rap song that features the crooning of singer/songwriter Ne-Yo, an eventually Grammy-winning artist just coming into his own. The song is eerily similar to *Bulletproof Wallets*' "Never Be the Same Again," except this time Ghostface's rhymes reveal him to be less forgiving of an adulterous lover whose misgivings were in retaliation to his own infidelity. The beat of "Back Like That" is constructed of a sample of the opening piano notes of "Baby Come Home" by Willie Hutch and produced by Xtreme. In its chorus "Back Like That" Ne-Yo interpolates a portion of Jay-Z's "Song Cry" from *The Blueprint* album, singing, "Yeah, what I did was wack/But you don't get a nigga back like that."

"Back Like That" performed better than "Never Be the Same Again," peaking at #61 on the *Billboard* Hot 100 Singles chart, #14 on the *Billboard* R&B/Hip-Hop Songs chart, and #11 on the *Billboard* Rap Songs chart. Fans who preferred that Ghostface not delve into too many R&B friendly rap songs didn't have to worry for too long. On listening to *Fishscale* it is readily evident that Ghostface again adhered to his method of creating an album he would want to listen to. The album is loaded with soul samples that Ghostface has a field day rhyming over with unfettered passion. Ghostface owes a debt to Def Jam—figuratively, but probably literally, too—for the label's willingness to clear so many samples. Not every sample could be cleared, though. "The Champ," produced by Just Blaze, went through several permutations before the final version that is heard on the album. The original version contained dialogue from the film *Rocky III* (1992) and sampled a version of Peggy Lee's "Fever" (1958). A version of "The Champ" with a new melody appeared on mix tapes, while the final version has studio musicians replaying the Lee sample.[43]

The rest of the album's vocal guests are minimal but potent. While Raekwon was absent on *The Pretty Toney Album*, the Chef appears on the *Fishscale* disc four times, every contribution reinforcing the chemistry the duo shares when performing together. This is particularly evident on "R.A.G.U.," where producer Pete Rock uses the drums and sharps piano stabs of one of Ghostface's favorite groups and collaborators—1968's "The Look of Love" by The Delfonics—to create a sinister sounding instrumental. The duo run through an urban gangster tale about a kid that Raekwon decides not to shoot because he is friends with Ghostface. However, during Ghostface's verse he reveals that he no longer associated with the once loyal friend because he stole clothes from him.

Raekwon isn't the only specially invited guest. Ghostface's Theodore Unit, particularly Trife, appear throughout the album. The entire

Wu-Tang Clan, including a posthumous performance from Ol' Dirty Bastard as well as Cappadonna, all appear on the pulsating "9 Milli Bros." Produced by MF DOOM, the beat is all throbbing organs and major chords. RZA is heard at the beginning of the song, naming almost everyone on the track save for Cappadonna. But RZA's vocals are actually a sample taken from shout-outs at the end of "Fast Cars" from his *Birth of a Prince* album. RZA neither rhymes nor contributes any production to *Fishscale*. Nevertheless, RZA's beats aren't missed much thanks to multiple producers that include MF DOOM, Pete Rock, Just Blaze, and the late Jay Dee/J Dilla, a multidimensional sampling of some of the day's most esteemed hip-hop producers. This team of beat-smiths softens the blow of RZA's glaring absence with their tracks all complementing Ghostface's brand of music.

MF DOOM, formerly known as Zev Love X of early 1990s rap group KMD, besides his production is also known for off-kilter rhyme gymnastics, making him and Ghostface kindred hip-hop spirits. Many of their mutual fans anticipated and celebrated their musical union and none of their collaborations on *Fishscale* disappoint. Besides the afore-mentioned "9 Milli Bros.," DOOM also produces the synth soaked "Clips of Doom," the trippy "Jellyfish," and the psychedelic "Under-water." Interestingly all of DOOM's beat contributions were previously available as instrumentals on his *Special Herbs* series of instrumental albums.[44]

The late Jay Dee/J Dilla's contributions are especially notable since the heralded underground producer passed away from complications from the disease lupus in February 2005, only a month and a half before *Fishscale*'s release. Ghostface grimly recounts getting a duly deserved beating from his mother as a child on the Dilla produced "Whip You with a Strap"; its instrumental version, known as "One for Ghost," was available on Dilla's *Donuts* released in February 2005. On "Whip You with a Strap" and "Beauty Jackson," Dilla utilizes soul vocal samples—singer Luther Ingram's "To the Other Man" (1972) and female Philadelphia group The Three Degrees' "Maybe" (1970), respectively—in such a manner that they elicited emotions from Ghostface he is all too happy to express with his rhymes.

According to Ghostface there was a lot of turmoil at Def Jam during the album's release, which made him understand the issues his label-mates such as LL Cool J and Method Man had with the label.[45] It didn't seem to effect Ghostface's project since *Fishscale* sold 110,000 units its first week in stores, debuting at #4 on the *Billboard* 200 chart, #2 on the *Billboard* R&B/Hip-Hop Albums chart, and at #2 on the *Billboard* Rap Albums chart. Also, showing Ghostface was capable of thriving in the digital age, the album entered at #4 on the *Billboard* Digital Albums Chart. Praise for *Fishscale* was ubiquitous in the hip-hop press, with *XXL Magazine*, *The Source Magazine*, and *Vibe Magazine* all giving the album fervently positive reviews.[46] The mainstream press was just as enthused, with *Time Magazine*, *Entertainment Weekly*, and *People Magazine* singing *Fishscale*'s praises.[47] In 2006, *Time Magazine* called Ghostface "Wu-Tang Clan's last reliably great member," while also mentioning, "The production puts equal value on melody and tension and even has room for nostalgia . . . the truth is Ghostface is better on his own."[48]

Despite *Time*'s willingness to forsake the rest of Wu-Tang Clan, Ghostface's success, along with the short tour the group embarked on earlier in 2006, meant the inevitable calls for another Wu-Tang Clan group album from the media and fans. But before a reunion could take place there were still a several individual albums from Wu-Tang members, including two more from Ghostface alone, to be released. None of these forthcoming releases achieved anywhere near the success of *Fishscale*. In some cases it was due to inferior material while in others it was proficient music that was unfortunately and unworthily overlooked.

INSPECTAH DECK, *THE RESIDENT PATIENT*

Inspectah Deck independently released his third album, *The Resident Patient*, on June 25, 2006, via his own Urban Icon Records, distributed by Traffic Entertainment. At the time of its release it was considered a mix tape and supposedly a teaser for his third album—a proper sequel to *The Movement* called *The Rebellion*.[49] However, Deck still has yet to release an album by that title. *The Resident Patient*, named after one of author Arthur Conan Doyle's Sherlock Holmes stories, has some decent moments despite minimal Wu-Tang Clan participation. Only Masta Killa and U-God make appearances on the album while RZA is nowhere to be found. Songs worth noting include the swinging

"Get Ya Weight Up" produced by Inspectah Deck himself, and the string-infused "A Lil Story" produced by Cilvaringz. As usual, Inspectah Deck's rhymes are still capable, but the overwhelming majority of his musical accompaniment is lackluster and sabotages the gifted rapper's efforts.

MASTA KILLA, *MADE IN BROOKLYN*

In August 2006 the Wu-Tang Clan again struck out on tour, this time headlining the fourth annual Rock the Bells Festival along with other spot dates. Masta Killa managed to release his second album, *Made in Brooklyn*, on August 8, 2006. Released independently again via Nature Sounds Records, on *Made in Brooklyn* the Brooklyn-born rapper decided to include more elements from his native borough via producers and guest artists. As on his previous album, Masta Killa squeezed in a number of Wu-Tang Clan guest including Raekwon and Ghostface on the album's second single "It's What It Is."

Produced by P. F. Cuttin', a Brooklyn producer who was a member of short-lived rap group Blahzay Blahzay, the three MCs attack a wave of horns and punishing drums. RZA, U-God, and Method Man drop guest verses on "Iron God Chamber," and GZA and Inspectah Deck lend verses to "Street Corner" to round out the rest of the Wu-Tang Clan cameos. RZA, who was an executive producer on *No Said Date*, doesn't produce any tracks for *Made in Brooklyn*. However, Masta Killa does an admirable job of selecting beats from producers including Bronze Nazareth and Pete Rock—to rhyme over beats that are firmly rooted in the Wu-Tang Clan design of intense sound collages and soulful loops. In 2006, Masta Killa explained in an interview with MVRemix.com, "My style comes from all of the eight. All of that is what makes me. That's why I'm the ninth. It takes nine to be complete. . . . I took all of my brothers as a lesson. It was fortunate that I was able to sit in the cut and study, both talent and business wise."[50]

Thanks to the lessons Masta Killa picked up as a member of Wu-Tang Clan, *Made in Brooklyn* earned its fair share of praise. *The Source Magazine* in its three and half mic review of the album called it a throwback to the Wu-Tang era.[51] The *Village Voice* also playfully called the album "immensely appealing in that classic martial arts vs.

cracked soul vs. random threats of violence vs. earnest spiritual advice Wu-Tang way."[52] The album is not without missteps. "Let's Get Into Something" is a milquetoast attempt at a R&B flavored rap record and the guest rappers on "East MCs," save for Killa Sin, are not quite ready for prime time. Nevertheless, *Made in Brooklyn* is one of the better post–*Iron Flag* efforts from the Wu-Tang Clan that is too often overlooked by fans.

METHOD MAN, *4:21 . . . THE DAY AFTER*

With Ol' Dirty Bastard gone physically the Wu-Tang Clan lost one of its most recognizable mainstream figures. Besides RZA and increasingly Ghostface, Method Man was the third most prominent artist in the group, though lately it was likely to be more because of his acting credits than for his music. With the specter of not living up to his musical expectations on his mind Method Man hoped to win back the rap public's affection with *4:21 . . . The Day After*, his fourth solo album.

The overwhelming consensus was that on Method Man's previous album, *Tical 0: The Prequel*, the rapper tried to fit too many superfluous sounds, styles, and hip-hop trends on the album, which inevitably made it sound scattershot and unfocused. *4:21 . . . The Day After* remedies that early in the album's coalescence by Method Man in 2005 connecting with RZA, whose role on *Tical 0* was negligible, to assist with the new album. RZA, as confident as ever, told MTV.com in 2005, "When the RZA and Meth get together, it's like peanut butter and jelly. They taste good by themselves, but they're great together. That's what we're doing with this album: [matching] his great lyrical talent, personality and style with my hard beat-making and song-making."[53]

Fans wouldn't get to sample Method Man's latest meal until over a year later when *4:21 . . . The Day After* was released on August 29, 2006. RZA ended up producing only four of the album's 17 tracks, though he is credited as an executive producer on the album along with Method Man and Erick Sermon. Already having worked with Method Man on his *Blackout!* album with Redman, Sermon was also brought in to help correct the musical transgressions of *Tical 0*, contributing four tracks to *4:21*. It is Sermon that produced the album's lead single, the Lauryn Hill sampling "Say."

Utilizing acoustic guitars and a vocal sample of Lauryn Hill's voice from "So Many Things to Say" from her *MTV Unplugged No. 2.0* (2002) album, on "Say" Method Man rhymes with his heart on his sleeve. Over three verses he squarely aims his ire at the media and fans that turned on him by saying he went Hollywood or lost a lyrical step. On the last verse Method Man raps, "The last album wasn't feeling my style/This time my foot up in they ass bet they feeling me now/Cause Tical, he put his heart in every track he do/But somehow y'all find some way to give a wack review."

"Say" was received well by fans because of Method Man's sincerity but it would be *4:21 ... The Day After*'s only single. There was controversy surrounding Method Man saying he felt "Say" should not have been the lead single for the album, which may have contributed to Def Jam dialing back on the promotion of the project. "Say" didn't make much of a dent at radio, only making it to #66 on the *Billboard* Hot R&B/Hip-Hop Singles chart.

4:21 ... The Day After gets it title from April 20 being considered "Weed Day" among marijuana aficionados, with Method Man taking the day after to recover and see things clearer. On the first few songs of the album Method Man is clearly on a mission to prove he is still a high-caliber MC as he raps with a chip on his shoulder. "Y'all was dumb enough to think that Method numbers up," he sneers on the album's RZA-produced opener, "Intro," over claustrophobic keys and spooky chords and flutes.

The album contains fine work including "Dirty Mef," which features a posthumous appearance from Ol' Dirty Bastard over sharp drums and banging piano keys produced by Erick Sermon and Allah Mathematics. The street records, created without regard for radio accessibility, are some of the album's best moments. "The Glide" includes verses from Raekwon, U-God, and Wu-affiliate La the Darkman over a deliberate, four-note synth riff, and on "Konichiwa Bitches," Method Man handles the song by himself, rapping over thick drums kicks and sweeping string sounds. Both of these aforementioned songs are produced by RZA. The rest of the producer's contributions to the album are the marijuana ode "4:20" featuring Streetlife and Carlton Fisk and the grim "Presidential MC" with Raekwon, which also features a verse from RZA for good measure.

More help from Wu-Tang Clan mates—producer Allah Mathematic also contributed a couple of tracks—further facilitates *4:21*'s sonic consistency. But things go wayward with songs that are marked for female listeners or radio playlists, such as the saccharine "Let's Ride" featuring R&B singer Ginuwine's singing or the slickly produced "4 Ever" with singer Megan Rochell, which fail to gel as repeated listening material. This is especially apparent when compared to past successful collaborations between Method Man and singers such as "You're All I Need" with Mary J. Blige or "Break Ups 2 Make Ups" with D'Angelo.

According to Method Man, he's never had a problem with constructive criticism about his music. It is just when he felt writers were assassinating his character that he considered the media to have gone too far.[54] Ironically, a perturbed Method Man led to the creation of an album that is definitely better in terms of quality listening material than his previous effort. But whether the expectations are fair or unfair, *4:21 . . . The Day After* is not as entertaining a listen as *Tical* or *Blackout!* On its initial release the album performed decently, entering at #8 on the *Billboard* 200 chart, #4 on the *Billboard* R&B/Hip-Hop Albums chart, #8 on the *Billboard* Digital Albums chart, and #3 on the *Billboard* Rap Albums chart. But with little additional promotion after its release, and short attention spans from fans, the album was soon forgotten.

GHOSTFACE KILLAH, *MORE FISH*

There would be one more project from Wu-Tang Clan in 2006, from Method Man's labelmate. Ghostface released his second album of the year, aptly titled *More Fish*, on December 12, 2006. Def Jam needed another fourth quarter release and the prolific Ghostface had plenty of songs to patch together an album's worth of material. The lead single was the celebratory themed "Good," produced by P-Nut & Kool Ade, who sampled and turbo boosted, regal horns from 1978's "Love Music" by R&B icons Earth, Wind & Fire. "Good" would be the closest recording to a commercial song on *More Fish* since the rest of the album is loaded with street friendly songs and the usual soul samples but with a rawer edge.

More Fish plays more like a commercial mix tape, especially with the opening song, "Ghost Is Back," on which Ghostface lyrically lets loose over the instrumental to rapper Rakim's "Know the Ledge" (1991). Ghostface only appears on three songs by himself since the album is stocked with guests including Redman and Sheek Louch as well as his Theodore Unit team that includes Trife, Cappadonna, Shawn Wigs, Solomon Childs, and his literal son, Sun God. A pair of songs are sans Ghostface entirely including "Miguel Sanchez," which features only Trife and Sun God blistering the instrumental's brazen horns, filched from Earth, Wind & Fire's "Love Is Life" (1971) by producer Fantom of the Beat, the standout. Other notable producers lending production to *More Fish* include MF DOOM, Mark Ronson, and Hi-Tek.

Some of the songs on *More Fish* were previously released. The bluesy "Josephine" appeared on Hi-Tek's *Hi-Teknology*^{2}: *The Chip* released in October 2006. Also, a remix of Ghostface's hit single, "Back Like That," is included that adds a verse from rapper/producer Kanye West. One song that was actually a preview, to most U.S. listeners, was the Mark Ronson–produced "You Know I'm No Good" featuring Amy Winehouse. The song originally appeared on Winehouse's second album, *Back to Black*, which though released in October 2006 in the United Kingdom, would not be released stateside until March 2007.

More Fish barely registered at retail on its release, selling only about 36,000 units its first week and peaking at #71 on the *Billboard* 200 chart, #13 on the *Billboard* R&B/Hip-Hop Albums chart, and #6 on the *Billboard* Rap Albums chart. But as usual, critics and fans felt that Ghostface had once again delivered another terrific album. Hip-hop attuned outlets including *The Source Magazine*, *XXL Magazine*, and *Vibe Magazine* gave the album kudos.[55] Mainstream media titles such as *Rolling Stone* and *Entertainment Weekly*, and also Pitchfork.com heaped praise on Ghostface's work as well. While most artists, particularly Wu-Tang Clan members as of late, had trouble generating enthusiasm for albums they took considerable time to assemble, Ghostface reaped more applause with an album that seemed to be rushed out at the end of the year.

What's even more remarkable, and a testament to Ghostface's work ethic, is that there is an entire set of songs from the *Fishscale/More Fish* time period that didn't appear on either album. Prior to *Fishscale*'s release, a song called "Charlie Brown" was leaked; it appeared as a snippet on a promotional album sampler supplied by Def Jam, which was produced by MF DOOM. "Charlie Brown" featured a prominent sample of 1969's "Alfomega" by Brazilian composer/singer guitarist Caetano Veloso and his Tropicalias, but the label was unable to clear its use. After ineffectively attempting to replay the loop with studio musicians, the song was scrapped.[56] Another song called "Can Can," which samples The Pointer Sisters' "Yes We Can" (1973), was supposedly for a future project but was leaked as well.[57]

The year 2006 was a nice up-tick for the Wu-Tang Clan. Ghostface remained the most reliable member in terms of quality musical output, Method Man managed to partially bounce back with a coolly received fourth album, while Masta Killa's sophomore album enjoyed a generally warm critical reception. The brief tour dates Wu-Tang Clan embarked on throughout the year also received positive feedback. The momentum may not have been steamrolling, but it was there. After seeing their collective influence essentially fade with each passing release, the question everyone was asking was, Can the Wu-Tang Clan again reign over the hip-hop world? While the Clan seemed as fractured as ever, RZA was still confident that they could and was willing to try.

NOTES

1. .Oh, Minya, "ODB Rejoins Society (Kind Of); Set To Drop New LPs, 'Ol' Dirty Drawers,' " MTV.com, April 7, 2003, http://www.mtv.com/news/articles/1471091/20030407/ol_dirty_bastard.jhtml.

2. Ganz, Caryn, "Dirty Comes Clean," *Spin Magazine*, August 2003, 36.

3. Golianopoulos, Thomas, "Name Dropping," *The Source Magazine*, December 2003, 127 (126–27).

4. He would return to "Ghostface Killah" by his next album, 2006's *Fishscale*.

5. Aku, Timmhotep, "Train of Thought: Ghostface Killah," *XXL Magazine*, Jan./Feb. 2004, 164.

6. Gotti, "Jesus Walks," *The Source Magazine*, June 2004, 125.

7. Hall, Rashaun, "Ghostface Killah: The Pretty Toney Album," *Billboard Magazine*, May 1, 2004, L.501.Capobianco, Ken, "Ghostface Killah: The Pretty Toney Album," *Boston Globe*, May 14, 2004, C13.

8. Kwak, Donnie, "Holy Ghost," *Vibe Magazine*, May 2004, 142 (140–144).

9. "Hip-Hop Quotable: Ghostface Killah 'Be This Way,' " *The Source Magazine*, April 2004, 126.

10. Barrow, Jerry L., "Record Report: Ghostface Killah," *The Source Magazine*, April 2004, 123–24. [four out of five mic review] Markman, Robert, "Ghostface Killah: The Pretty Toney Album," *Vibe Magazine*, April 2004, 156. [four out of five record review]Samuel, Anslem, "Ghostface Killah: The Pretty Toney Album," *XXL Magazine*, April 2004, 204. [XL out of XXL rating]

11. Ratcliffe, Fahiym, "Back to the Lab: Method Man," *The Source Magazine*, February 2003, 54.

12. Ibid.

13. Linden, Amy, "Tough Luv," *XXL Magazine*, May 2004, 106 (100–106).

14. Reid, Shaheem, "Method Man Drops Diddy, Seeks Clarity On New LP, 4:21 . . . The Day After," MTV.com; http://www.mtv.com/news/articles/1533408/20060601/puff_daddy.jhtml.

15. Ibid.

16. Fiore, Raymond, "Tical 0: The Prequel," *Entertainment Weekly*, May 14, 2004, 68.

17. Linden, "Tough Luv."

18. Ryan, Chris, "Across the Wuniverse," *Spin Magazine*, December 2007, 94.

19. Samuel, Anslem, "Method Man: Tical 0: The Prequel," *XXL Magazine*, June 2004, 152. [L out of XXL rating]

20. Golianopoulos, Thomas, "Record Report: Method Man," *The Source Magazine*, June 2004, 149–150.

21. Valdes, Mimi, "Right and Exact," *Vibe Magazine*, September 1997, 116.

22. Paine, Jake, "Masta Killa Interview," originally in AllHipHop.com; http://www.wutang-corp.com/news/article.php?id=526.

23. Bernard, Adam, "Masta Killa Interview," October 3, 2006. http://www.rapreviews.com/interview/mkilla06.html.

24. Paine, "Masta Killa Interview."

25. Burgess, Kimberly, "Record Report: Masta Killa," *The Source Magazine*, June 2004, 156.

26. Kondo, Toshitaka, "Record Report: Masta Ace," *XXL Magazine*, May 2004, 172.

27. Ubl, Sam, "Album Review: Masta Killa: No Said Date," August 18, 2004, http://pitchfork.com/reviews/albums/5605-no-said-date/.

28. Reid, Shaheem, "Ol' Dirty Bastard Now Dirt McGirt, Signs To Roc-A-Fella," MTV.com, May 1, 2003, http://www.mtv.com/news/articles/1471665/20030501/ol_dirty_bastard.jhtml.

29. Gonzales, Michael A., "Fighting Temptations," *XXL Magazine*, January/February 2004, 129 (126–130).

30. Reid, Shaheem, "ODB's Roc-A-Fella Deal Rocks The Boat For Some Wu Members," MTV.com, August 7, 2003, http://www.mtv.com/news/articles/1475978/20030806/ol_dirty_bastard.jhtml.

31. Ibid.

32. Byers, R. K., "Get Dirty," *The Source Magazine*, December 1999, 224 (176–182, 224).

33. Crosley, Hillary, "Ol' Dirty Bastard: A Son Unique," *XXL Magazine*, July 2005, 147. [L out of XXL rating]

34. Rodriguez, Jayson, "ODB: A Son Unique," *Vibe Magazine*, June 2005, 157. [4 out of 5 record review]Sheffield, Rob, "Ol' Dirty Bastard: A Son Unique," *Rolling Stone Magazine*, November 30, 2006, 114. [3 out of 5 star review]

35. Reid, Shaheem, "Wu-Tang Clan's U-God Blames RZA for No New Wu Output, MTV.com, March 1, 2004, http://www.mtv.com/news/articles/1485454/20040301/u_god.jhtml.

36. "RZA responds to U-God and clears Aftermath rumor," WuTang Corp.com, March 2, 2004, http://www.wutang-corp.com/news/article.php?id=428.Reid, Shaheem, "RZA Responds To U-God's Wu-Tang Allegation," MTV.com, March 8, 2004, http://www.mtv.com/news/articles/1485608/20040 308/wu_tang_clan.jhtml.

37. Strickland, L. Nzinga, "And on the 7th Day," *New York Amsterdam News*, September 1, 2005, 19, 40.

38. Golianopoulos, Thomas, "Train of Thought: GZA," *XXL Magazine*, December 2005, 166.

39. Barone, Matt, "Muggs vs. GZA: Grandmasters," *XXL Magazine*, December 2005, 169. [XL out of XXL rating.]

40. Breihan, Tom, "Return of the Ruckus," *The Village Voice*, February 14, 2006, 34.

41. Callahan-Bever, Noah, "Sincerely Yours," *XXL Magazine*, May 2006, 74.

42. Callahan-Bever, "Sincerely Yours," 72.

43. Wang, Oliver, "Phantom Tracks," *Scratch Magazine*, July/August 2006, 32.

44. All available on *Metal Fingerz presents Special Herbs: The Box Set Vol. 0–9*; Ghostface's "Jellyfish" is the same instrumental as Metal Fingerz (MF) DOOM's "Sumac Berries"; Ghostface's "9 Milli Bros." instrumental is the same as MF DOOM's "Fenugreek"; Ghostface's "Clips of Doom" instrumental is the same as MF DOOM's "Four Thieves Vinegar"; Ghostface's "Underwater" instrumental is the same as MF DOOM's "Orange Blossoms."

45. Heinzelman, Bill, "Walking through the Darkness," *The Source Magazine*, December 2006, 52–55.

46. Barone, Matt, "Ghostface Killah: Fishscale," *XXL Magazine*, April 2006, 171–172. [XL out of XXL rating] Heinzelman, Bill, "Record Report: Ghostface Killah," *The Source Magazine*, May 2006, 97. [4 out of 5 mic rating] Detrick, Ben, "Ghostface Killah: Fishscale," *Vibe Magazine*, April 2006, 151. [4 out of 5 record review]

47. "5 of Our Favorite Picks," *Time Magazine*, April 24, 2006, 72. [positive album review] Arnold, Chuck, "Ghostface Killah," *People Magazine*, May 1, 2006, 45. [4 star album review]Fiore, Raymond, "Ghostface Killah; Fishscale," *Entertainment Weekly*, March 31, 2006, 64. [A- rated album review]

48. "5 of Our Favorite Picks," *Time Magazine*, April 24, 2006, 72. [positive album review]

49. Variano, Michael, "Inspectah Deck ... Icon," HipHopDX.com, February 1, 2005, http://www.hiphopdx.com/index/interviews/id.370/title./p.all.

50. Fowle, Noah, "Masta Killa," MVRemix.com, August 2006, http://www.mvremix.com/urban/interviews/masta_killa_06.shtml.

51. Dre, A. L., "Record Report: Masta Killa," *The Source Magazine*, June 2006, 101.

52. Harvilla, Rob, "SXSW Preview Hoedown," *The Village Voice*, March 7, 2007–March 13, 2007, 127.

53. Reid, Shaheem. "RZA Happy to Once Again Be the Peanut Butter to Method Man's Jelly," MTV.com, May 12, 2005, http://www.billboard.com/news/masta-killa-keeps-wu-tang-close-for-new-1002912699.story#/news/masta-killa-keeps-wu-tang-close-for-new-1002912699.story.

54. Jay, Lil, "Interviews: Method Man," DubCNN.com, October 2006, http://www.dubcnn.com/interviews/methodman/.

55. Diva, Amanda, "Critical Beatdown: Ghostface Killah," *XXL Magazine*, March 2007, 136. [XL rating album review] Heinzelman, Bill, "Record Report: Ghostface Killah," *The Source Magazine*, December 2006, 113–114. [3 ½ out of 5 mic rating album review] L.Oficial, Peter, "Ghostface Killah: More Fish," *Vibe Magazine*, January 2007, 110. [positive album review]

56. Wang, Oliver, "Phantom Tracks," *Scratch Magazine*, July/August 2006, 32.

57. Ibid.

CHAPTER 13
Wu-Tang Redux

Ever since Loud Records folded in March 2002, Wu-Tang Clan, one of hip-hop music's most profoundly influential collectives of the 1990s, were free agents without a recording home. In 2004, there were rumors that the Staten Island rappers were in talks with Dr. Dre's Aftermath Records about aligning with the West Coast titan who helped Eminem become an international star. RZA confirmed the gossip, saying the idea was the late Ol' Dirty Bastard's and further revealed that negotiations were being made.[1] However, a move to Dr. Dre's label never came to fruition. Chatter about a reunion also began getting louder in 2005, shortly after Ol' Dirty Bastard's untimely passing.

In February 2005, the group recorded a song called "I Go Through Life" that was purportedly to be included on ODB's *A Son Unique* album, which at the time was due in stores March 2005.[2] Technology eased the song's creation with Method Man recording his verse in California, Masta Killa, GZA, and Raekwon recording their parts in New York City, while Cappadonna and other members in different cities emailed their verses in to RZA, who then completed the song. However, the song wasn't completed in time to make the *A Son Unique* album. Also in 2005, RZA stated that Raekwon's album, at this juncture being executive produced by Busta Rhymes, and Method Man's album (the eventual *4:21 ... The Day After*, which didn't arrive until 2006) were going to come before a Wu-Tang Clan album.

In December 2006, the Wu-Tang Clan signed a one-album deal with SRC Records. SRC is distributed by Universal Motown Records and is owned by Steve Rifkind, who signed the Wu-Tang Clan to their original recording deal. The wheels were now set in motion for Wu-Tang Clan to release their fifth album, titled *8 Diagrams*. The title was an ode to *8 Diagram Pole Fighter*, one of the key kung-fu movies influential to

RZA when he was formulating the idea of the Wu-Tang Clan. As early as 1998, shortly before the second wave of Wu-Tang Clan individual albums, RZA toyed with the idea of calling Wu-Tang Clan's third album *The Eighth Diagram.*[3]

The group didn't start recording the album until April 2007 but there were still some individual projects to attend to before *8 Diagrams'* release. *RZA presents Afro-Samurai: The Album* was released on January 30, 2007. *Afro Samurai* was a five-episode anime TV series adopted from the Japanese *Afro Samurai* manga comic by artist Takashi Okazaki. The Afro Samurai character searches for the killer of his father, whose murder he witnessed as a young child. Okazaki created the character, an African American samurai, partly as an ode to his love of hip-hop music and culture. RZA was the ideal choice to create a soundtrack and score for the film after his success at handling the same duties for Jim Jarmusch's *Ghostdog: The Way of the Samurai* and Quentin Tarantino's *Kill Bill Vol. 1 & 2.* GDH, the parent company of the *Afro Samurai*'s anime studio Gonzo, contacted RZA about creating the *Afro Samurai* soundtrack. The producer jumped at the opportunity once told that one of the project's directors had worked on *Ninja Scroll* (1993), a cult favorite anime film of which RZA was already a fan.

Afro Samurai: The Album is a commendable effort even if one were oblivious to the film, though it surely helps to have seen it. The album's performers include artists recognizable to anyone familiar with RZA's Bobby Digital albums, including Beretta 9 and Suga Bang as well as pleasant surprises such as rappers Q-Tip and Talib Kweli. The album's lead single was "Cameo Afro," which features GZA and Big Daddy Kane—interestingly, the two rappers were labelmates over 15 years earlier on Cold Chillin' Records. The mix of instrumentals from the cartoon with songs that remain on topic with its plot are all highlights of the album. It also made for the perfect outlet for RZA to use all the quirky sounds he could get out of his keyboards without the distraction of having to worry about a rapper's lyrics as much.

After the success of the *Afro Samurai* project, attention was turned to the possibility of Raekwon finally releasing the proper sequel to *Only Built 4 Cuban Linx . . .* Raekwon at this time was signed to Dr. Dre's Aftermath Entertainment, and in late 2006 Wu-Tang Clan's official Web site announced that Raekwon had revealed at a Rock The Bells show that *Only Built 4 Cuban Linx . . . Pt. II* would be released in the summer of 2007. However, by the fall of 2007 it was obvious the album would not be arriving anytime soon. The Wu-Tang Clan went out on tour again over the summer, increasing the prospects of their album coming to a realization and being released that year.

In October 2007, Wu-Tang Clan's legacy was paid tribute by the third annual VH1 Hip-Hop Honors award show. While the accolades were surely appreciated, the Wu-Tang Clan didn't want it to be considered a swan song or a pat on the back for a job well done; they still had plenty of music to create and share with the world. There were two albums released by the Wu-Tang camp before the year was up: *8 Diagrams*, their first in a long six years, and Ghostface Killah's *The Big Doe Rehab*.

GHOSTFACE KILLAH *THE BIG DOE REHAB*

"In the six years the Clan were on hiatus, Ghostface Killah was busy becoming one of the greatest MCs ever," said *Rolling Stone* in 2007.[4] Indeed Ghostface was in peak form and after releasing two albums the previous year, he began working on his seventh album, *The Big Doe Rehab*, in the spring of 2007. But Ghostface put the recording process on hold to go out on tour with the Wu-Tang Clan that summer.

By October 2007, the Wu-Tang Clan announced that *8 Diagrams* would be released on December 4, 2007. Unfortunately this was also the same date Ghostface was scheduled to release *The Big Doe Rehab*. Ghostface was not happy with this turn of events, telling MTV.com that he had December 4 locked in as his release date for months. However, delays with Wu-Tang Clan's album pushed its release date back, which now conflicted with Ghostface's album release. Further adding to Ghostface's ire was the fact that he previously delayed the recording of *The Big Doe Rehab* to go on tour with Wu-Tang Clan as well to record *8 Diagrams*, only to not be compensated for his work in a timely fashion.[5]

Ghostface was adamant that he was not changing his release date. RZA blinked first, moving *8 Diagrams*' release date back a week to December 11, 2007. Fans shouldn't have been complaining too much; they were getting a back-to-back dose of Wu-Tang music to digest before the year was up. Ghostface's *The Big Doe Rehab* was the first album up and was fitted with more of the usual mélange of male libido, big money ambitions, and urban crime noir, with a guest list of like-minded artists along to help. *More Fish* featured predominantly Theodore Unit artists. On *Big Doe Rehab* Theodore Unit rappers including Trife Da God and Cappadonna are well represented as are Wu-Tang Clan members Raekwon, Method Man, Masta Killa, and U-God. Rappers Beanie Sigel and Styles P appear on "Barrel Brothers," which rounds out the rest of the album's rapping guests.

Just as important as the lyrical content, Ghostface again recruits a cadre of producers that give him beats mined from mostly soul and R&B sample sources that cater to his tastes for melodic and epic-sounding grooves. Bad Boy Records producers Sean C & LV—who had recently earned a boost in acclaim for producing a chunk of music on Jay-Z's latest "comeback" album *American Gangster* (2007)—produce a handful of tracks on *Big Doe Rehab*. Other contributors on the production side include Baby Grand, Scram Jones, and Anthony Acid. By now, listeners should have grown accustomed to their being no contributions from RZA on a Ghostface album, which is again the case on *Big Doe Rehab*. Fortunately for Ghostface, he is the only Clan member able to create albums with no input from RZA that are as appealing as the projects on which the two shared executive producer duties.

Big Doe Rehab's lead single was the Sean C & LV produced "We Celebrate." The song considerably samples the melody and drums of 1972's "I Just Want to Celebrate" by rock band Rare Earth, which is itself a popular hip-hop break. Kid Capri is heard on the song's chorus, along with the refrain of "I just want to celebrate" sampled from the original record, hyping up the song between Ghostface's amped up verses. Most of Sean C & LV's beats use familiar samples; "Killa Lipstick," which uses Faze-O's "Riding High" (1978), is another example. Allmusic.com saw this as a detriment in its review of the album, noting that the production duo "make passable but not extraordinary beats, with short, overly simple samples that do nothing to bring attention to Ghost's rhymes."[6]

AllMusic.com's assertion is debatable. Tracks such as the sultry "Paisley Darts," which feature precise rhymes from Cappadonna, Trife, Raekwon, Sun God, and Method Man, and the threateningly tranquil "Shakey Dog starring Lolita," a crime tale with Raekwon that acts as a loose sequel to "Shakey Dog" from *Fishscale*, are standout tracks that use relatively obscure samples. Meanwhile, "Supa GFK" is another top-notch song where Ghostface is again basically rhyming over an entire song—in this case the familiar "Superman Lover" (1976) by Johnny Guitar Watson. The Watson sample has been used numerous times by hip-hop acts—and in Ghostface's "Supa GFK" similarly to Redman's "A Day of Sooperman Lover"—but this is not enough to adversely affect the current song's appeal. While critical response to *The Big Doe Rehab* was not as overwhelmingly favorable as prior releases, especially the highly applauded *Fishscale*, the album was seen as another winner from Ghostface. But when the first-week numbers of albums sold came back at only about 35,500 units, Ghostface became distressed. *The Big Doe Rehab* was a full-fledged album and didn't fare any better than December 2006's *More Fish* (it sold approximately 36,000 its first week in stores), which many considered to be an album of glorified bonus tracks.

Ghostface even took to the Internet, releasing a video on his MySpace page a week after *Big Doe Rehab*'s release; thanking his supporters but expressing bewilderment—he says early in the clip, "I thought y'all loved me"—at having 115,000 "friends" on the social networking site but only 30,000 or so people actually went and purchased the album. He places the blame on illegal downloading while also urging viewers to not only support his album but to go out and buy Wu-Tang Clan's *8 Diagrams* as well. Ironically, commentary that Ghostface and other Wu-Tang Clan members, including Raekwon and Inspectah Deck, gave the press about the music on Wu-Tang Clan's *8 Diagrams* could not be considered beneficial to its prospects at record stores.

WU-TANG CLAN, *8 DIAGRAMS*

Campfire/Take It Back/Get Them Out Ya Way Pa/Rushing Elephants/Unpredictable/The Heart Gently Weeps/Wolves/Gun Will Go/Sunlight/Stick Me for My Riches/Starter/Windmill/Weak Spot/Life Changes

---

Wu-Tang Clan built anticipation for *8 Diagrams* when it was announced in October 2007 that "The Heart Gently Weeps" would be the album's first single. A new Wu-Tang Clan album was big news but just as intriguing was the song's use of 1968's "My Guitar Gently Weeps" by the Beatles as its sonic foundation. The Wu-Tang Clan had announced this via their MySpace page, while also mentioning that *8 Diagrams'* release date had been moved from November 13 (which itself was a shift from an intended September release) to December 4. The group also claimed they formally cleared the use of the Beatles sample, a first in history. However, a day later the Wu-Tang Clan quickly clarified, again via their MySpace page, that they actually interpolated "While My Guitar Gently Weeps."

Ghostface recorded a song called "My Guitar" that was intended to be on *The Pretty Toney Album*, in which he raps over the original song, but it was unable to be cleared for inclusion on the project. However, what added to the buzz of Wu-Tang Clan's "The Heart Gently Weeps" was that it features RZA's friend Dhani Harrison, son of the late Beatle George Harrison, playing rhythm guitar on the song while former Red Hot Chili Peppers member John Frusciante plays lead guitar. With Neo-soul singer Erykah Badu in the mix on the song's chorus, along with the familiarity of the Beatles tune that serves as its template, on paper "The Heart Gently Weeps" appeared to be a can't-miss hit. But while the song is well constructed, it didn't possess the indelible quality of tracks such as *Enter the Wu-Tang*'s "Can It Be All So Simple" or *The W*'s "I Can't Sleep." The verses from each rapper also didn't mesh topically with Raekwon relaying a cryptic street corner tale, Ghostface depicting a trip to the supermarket that ended up with him punching out a would-be assailant, and Method Man quickly recounting his days as a low-level drug dealer. Nevertheless, despite never charting, "Heart Gently Weeps" was still voted #50 on *Rolling Stone Magazine*'s "100 Best Songs of 2007" list.

As previously noted, at Ghostface's behest, RZA convinced SRC Records to push back the release of Wu-Tang Clan's first album in six years by a week to December 11, 2007. Around the time Ghostface first expressed concern about conflicting release dates, Raekwon made public his dissatisfaction with the beats on *8 Diagrams*. Over the years Wu-Tang Clan had gone from being tight-lipped about any turmoil within the group to making disparaging comments about RZA and other Wu-Tang Clan executives in the public sphere. U-God infamously said he felt like a slave because RZA had not green-lit the release of solo projects while on-again, off-again member Cappadonna felt he was not getting his proper due within the group. At different points, Method Man had also mentioned to the press that a Wu-Tang Clan album wasn't likely until inner group issues were reconciled.

Raekwon told journalist and radio personality Minya Oh (Miss Info) in early November 2007 that there was severe discontent within Wu-Tang because the creative direction RZA wanted to take *8 Diagrams* was not in line with the type of music members wanted to record after a six-year hiatus.[7] Raekwon went on to say that RZA was using too many pianos and guitars, which didn't match the rappers' desire to make "punch you in the face music." Ghostface and Inspectah Deck would chime in to different media outlets as well, generally saying they were not 100 percent behind the music on *8 Diagrams*. Needless to say, the participants' lack of full support for their own project was not a good sign for consumers who were deciding whether or not to throw their support behind the album by purchasing it. Despite the situation looking like it was RZA versus the rest of the Wu-Tang Clan, *8 Diagrams* would still be released on December 11, 2007, and it was then that the public and critics would be able to hear for themselves the musical product of this dysfunction.

Despite the Wu-Tang Clan's inner turmoil that became public, RZA never lost confidence in his abilities as a producer. A glance at his track record showed that he knew how to make multiple classic albums. This surely was on the minds of people who purchased the album despite a lack of endorsement from some of its main players. *8 Diagrams* begins with "Campfire" where a weary but wise voice—sampled from kung-fu film *Shaolin and Wu-Tang*—is heard recounting that kindness, faith, and justice are the traits needed to be a good person and lead a good life. After about a minute the low, sorrowful singing that began at the track's start is more clearly heard; it is a sample of 1978's "Gypsy Woman" sung by a cappella group the Persuasions. Powerful drums kick in with an intermittent horn that along with the beat's rhythm makes it sound like a call to arms. Method Man is the first Wu-Tang voice heard and he sounds all business, closing his rhyme by sneering, "I'm like Barry Bonds on anything that RZA throw." Ghostface picks up where Method Man left off with his own tense verse followed by a return to just the Persuasions' vocals that serves as an interlude before Cappadonna closes with the third and last verse. Considering the Wu-Tang Clan's own story was filled with more drama than most

Greek tragedies, the intro track sets an appropriate tone for the rest of the album.

On "Take It Back," Raekwon, Inspectah Deck, Ghostface, and U-God handle microphone duties. Their rhymes are straight ahead battle rhymes with no clear direction beyond witty one-liners and threats to would-be foes. The song's title alludes to the Wu-Tang Clan returning to a rap game that may have forsaken their talents. "Before you even had a name you was screaming Wu-Tang," says Method Man on the latter part of the chorus. The song's beat incorporates the familiar bass line of Bob James's "Nautilus." Though the same sample was used for Ghostface's "Daytona 500," on "Take It Back" producer Easy Mo Bee (RZA is credited as a co-producer) uses a shorter, clipped portion of sample that gives the song a darker character.

After "Take It Back" ends, the flippant drums and cascading keys of "Get Them Out Ya Way Pa" are heard. The track has a spare feel to it since it is made up of little more than drum fills, a distorted base line, and hi-hats. The rhymes from Raekwon, U-God, and Masta Killa are fine enough but the rather drab beats makes for a forgettable song. Before listeners lose any more interest, rousing horns are answered by shiny strings and mark the arrival of "Rushing Elephants." The song possesses the marching rhythm of early Wu-Tang Clan posse cuts and has the necessary personnel with Raekwon, GZA, RZA, and Masta Killa contributing verses.

A couple of songs prior, "Get Them Out Your Way Pa" was reminiscent of early RZA beats since it was made of minimal sound elements. "Rushing Elephants" too harkens back to early beats from RZA discography since it relies on a loop of a horn blast and nimble strings, sampled from 1982's "Marcia in LA (Alzati spia)" by Italian composer Ennio Morricone. Both songs also demonstrate RZA's development as a producer since they are so cleanly produced with little distortion. "Unpredictable" exhibits more of RZA's refinement and is also further akin to his soundtrack work because of its use of so many sonic elements. On "Unpredictable" guitar riffs, dissonant piano chords, and harsh synth notes all get laid over a mechanized drum track. The bass on the song is played by Shavo Odadjian of rock band System of a Down with whom RZA has formed a group called Achozen.

More live playing is incorporated on "The Heart Gently Weeps." The song's mellow vibe serves as a rest stop in the album's progression.

"Wolves" shifts the momentum to a faster pace since it sounds more like an event than a song. After film dialogue from *8 Diagram Polefighter* that describes the best way to fight wolves, the voice of Parliament/ Funkadelic's maestro George Clinton comes on before the beat launches. Clinton is heard throughout the track, serving as a hypeman between verses. In a feature story on the Wu-Tang Clan in *Spin Magazine* that ran in 1997, Clinton commented on Wu-Tang Clan, telling the magazine, "If you try and control somebody, they're going to rebel like a mother-fucker," when discussing how he reigned in the natural chaos of the many talented musicians he was surrounded by and orchestrated in Parliament/ Funkadelic.[8] RZA could have used that advice 10 years later.

Raekwon leads off "Gun Will Go" with a smooth but sinister verse over haunting piano chords, followed in turn by Method Man and Masta Killa. The chorus is sung by male vocalist Sunny Valentine. The song is a rock-solid album cut, though Valentine's crooning isn't going to win any awards. The next song, "Sunlight," is *8 Diagrams'* only solo song, performed by RZA. Over somber female vocals and lush chords, RZA waxes poetic on spirituality, be it God or Allah. "Who gives you all and never ask more of you/The faithful companion that fights every war with you," raps RZA.

Singing from Gerald Alston, former lead singer of R&B group The Manhattans, is how "Stick Me for My Riches" begins. The song is produced by Mathematics and has a bouncy groove to it, which Raekwon surely wasn't too appreciative of. Nevertheless, Method Man, Inspectah Deck, RZA, and GZA ably handle the rhythmic track, despite the copious amount of singing. Sunny Valentine, along with a female vocalist, come back for more chorus singing duties on "Starter." Streetlife, who along with Cappadonna are the only rappers who aren't core members of the Wu-Tang Clan to appear on *8 Diagrams*, provides the lead-off verse. Over a bubbly track that features a three-note horn loop, all of the song's rappers—GZA, Inspectah Deck, and U-God—kick cunning lyrics focused on courting women. GZA maintains his deadpan flow on his technically proficient verse, rapping, "Whatever situation or the circumstances/Outdoor, indoor, she's taking the chances/Hotel, motel or Holiday Inn/Overlooking that bible, she continued to sin." Even GZA's highbrow wordplay can't make a listener overlook the reality that "Starter" is a deliberate attempt at a peppy club/party track from the gritty rappers from the slums of Shaolin.

While "Starter" is an upbeat number, the next track, "Windmill," is emphatically somber because of its use of a sample of Nancy Sinatra's "Bang Bang (My Baby Shot Me Down)" (1966)—the same song also happened to be included on the RZA-produced *Kill Bill Vol. 1 Soundtrack*. RZA lifts the haunting guitar with a tremolo effect from Sinatra's song for "Windmill," which starts with a vocal sample of Johnny Mathis's "Warm & Tender" (1957). The song's beat feels repetitive and though it includes spirited verses from its participants—Raekwon, GZA, Masta Killa, Inspectah Deck, Method Man, and Cappadonna—it would not rank high on a list of the best Wu-Tang Clan posse cuts. The orchestral horns of the next song, "Weak Spot," also do little to complement the above average verses from RZA, Raekwon, and GZA.

8 Diagrams comes to a close, not including a pair of bonus tracks, with "Life Changes," a song dedicated to the late Ol' Dirty Bastard first recorded in 2005 (then titled "I Go Through Life"). The song takes its chorus directly from the opening lines sung by Freda Payne on "The Road We Didn't Take" (elements of its bass line and chords are used for the beat as well) from her album *Contact* (1971). The sung lament—"I've gone through life pretending/That time will change the ending"—is especially poignant since Ol' Dirty Bastard's untimely death had friends and family asking what they could have done to save him from his fate. All surviving members, except for Ghostface, perform verses that express the pain they felt after learning of their friends passing while also celebrating his life. After RZA's verse, the song comes to a close with Sifu Shi Yan-Ming, a Shaolin monk RZA befriended in 1995, reciting the Heart Sutra, a Buddhist scripture, in his native tongue.

Some versions of *8 Diagrams* contain two bonus tracks. "Tar Pit" features U-God, Cappadonna, and Streetlife rapping over drums and spectral guitars as well as extensive blustering from George Clinton as background vocals. "16th Chamber (ODB Special)," which appears on international versions of the album, features Method Man and Ol' Dirty Bastard rhyming over filtered drums and its raw feel is a give-away that it is a song that was recorded during the Wu-Tang Clan's nascent period. Method Man's verse can be previously heard as the second verse on "Release Yo' Delf" (from his *Tical* debut) and Ol' Dirty Bastard used his verse, save for the first few lines, on the previously released "Protect Ya Neck II The Zoo" (from his *Return to the 36 Chambers* debut).

The music on *8 Diagrams* thoroughly showcases RZA's masterful production sensibilities. Unfortunately at this point, his Wu-Tang bandmates no longer trusted his vision. RZA's production skills are refined, his ear for melody is acute, and the album is seamlessly sequenced. It does have a lot of guitar, strings, and orchestration—which Raekwon and Ghostface were against—but it is almost always used appropriately with thoughtful nuance. RZA's production aesthetic had evolved, and there lies the rub. The desolate and stark sounds RZA reintroduced to hip-hop in 1993 began being augmented with each subsequent, and successful, album release that had his guiding production hand. His sonic aesthetic was further tempered when he began incorporating music theory into his production. All this meant that RZA's sound was perpetually changing, and in the late 1990s and early 2000s most welcomed his development. But in 2007 others—fans and Wu-Tang Clan members themselves—were not as willing to accept his progression.

Despite anti-promotion, at least to start, from Ghostface and Raekwon, *8 Diagrams* managed to sell 68,478 copies its first week in stores.[9] The number was good enough for the album to land at #25 the *Billboard* 200 chart and #9 on the *Billboard* R&B/Hip-Hop Albums chart. The critical reception was divided between those who thought RZA had strayed too far from the established Wu-Tang template and those who thought his expansion was nothing short of production wizardry. *Billboard Magazine* and *Rolling Stone Magazine* expressed surprise at how good the album was in their reviews.[10] The *New York Times* called the album "quirky and uneventful," and *Spin Magazine*, placing the blame on RZA's production, said, "It's a relatively solid record, but without any of the spectacularly gritty flashes the Wu are known for."[11]

Raekwon was right. RZA's production flourishes didn't jibe with the aggressive music the rapper felt Wu-Tang Clan fans wanted to hear. Raekwon would get his turn when he finally released *Only Built 4 Cuban Linx . . . Pt. II* in 2009. But the public feud between RZA's avant-garde approach to rhythms and Raekwon's and Ghostface's desires for a back-to-basics approach left *8 Diagrams* dead in the water. In addition to Ghostface and Raekwon, fans wanted vintage Wu, while RZA was steadfast in progressing with the Wu-Tang Clan's sound. With the inroads he'd made in scoring films—and acting, as he appeared in Ridley Scott–directed *American Gangster* (2007)—RZA had no intentions to look to the past. The backlash *8 Diagrams* received even before its release is regretful because in retrospect it is one of RZA's and Wu-Tang Clan's better works.

NOTES

1. Reid, Shaheem, "RZA Responds To U-God's Wu-Tang Allegations," MTV.com, March 8, 2004, http://www.mtv.com/news/articles/1485608/2004 0308/wu_tang_clan.jhtml.

2. Vineyard, Jennifer, "Wu-Tang Regroup for ODB Tribute Track, RZA Brings Pink the Grunge," MTV.com, February 10, 2005, http://www.mtv.com/news/articles/1496808/20050210/rza.jhtml.

3. Diehl, Matt, "Wu World Order," *Rolling Stone Magazine*, October 15, 1998, 23.

4. Hoard, Christian, "Wu's Next," *Rolling Stone Magazine*, December 13, 2007, 132.

5. Reid, Shaheem, and Rodriguez, Jayson, "Mixtape Monday: Ghostface Mad Over Owed Money, Drop-Date Duel with Wu-Tang; Jay-Z Talks 'Dead Presidents 3' Leak," MTV.com, http://www.mtv.com/bands/m/mixtape_monday/101507/.

6. Brown, Marisa, "The Big Doe Rehab," AllMusic.com, http://allmusic .com/cg/amg.dll?p=amg&sql=10:dvftxzehldke.

7. "Miss Info Exclusive: Raekwon reveals the turmoil within the Wu-Tang Clan," November 8, 2007, http://www.missinfo.tv/index.php/miss-info-exclusive -raekwon-reveals-the-turmoil-within-the-wu-tang-clan/.

8. Smith, RJ, "Phantoms of the Hip-Hopera," *Spin Magazine*, July 1997, 74.

9. Ewing, Aliya, "Hip Hop Album Sales: Week Ending 12/16/07," HipHopDX.com, December 19, 2007, http://www.hiphopdx.com/index/news/ id.6123/title.hip-hop-album-sales-week-ending-12-16-07.

10. Hoard, Christian, "Wu's Next," *Rolling Stone Magazine*, December 13, 2007, 132. Vrabel, Jeff, "8 Diagrams," *Billboard Magazine*, December 15, 2007, 36.

11. Sanneh, Kelefa, "Critic's Choice: Wu-Tang Clan," December 10, 2007, E7. Golianopoulos, Thomas, "Et Tu, Wu?," *Spin Magazine*, January 2008, 96.

CHAPTER 14
Shaolin Still Runs It

In 1997 RZA told *Rolling Stone Magazine*, "We're one in the heart and one in the mind. That's the power of Wu-Tang."[1] If that concept still held true, then the Wu-Tang Clan's powers were considerably weaker in 2008. The fascination fans showed while witnessing the Wu-Tang Clan's public feuding in late 2007 during the run-up to the release of *8 Diagrams* proved that the group was still a viable and influential entity in the hip-hop world and music world as a whole. But the tepid reception to the album's release was also clear evidence that the group's popularity had atrophied considerably since its peak in the late 1990s. Nevertheless, RZA, GZA, Method Man, Ghostface Killah, and Raekwon were still highly regarded artists who would continue to release new material all the way into the new millennium. Masta Killa, U-God, and Inspectah Deck, though not as revered by the general public, would deliver new material as well.

RZA, *DIGI SNACKS*

Digi Snacks Intro/Long Time Coming/You Can't Stop Me Now/ Straight Up the Block/Booby Trap/Try Ya Ya Ya/Good Night/No Regrets/Money Don't Own Me/Creep/Drama/Up Again/Put Your Guns Down/Love Is Digi/Part II/O Day

---

After the release of *8 Diagrams*, the Wu-Tang Clan went on tour without RZA, while making sure not to perform any songs from the album. With the promotion of *8 Diagrams* a lost cause—Raekwon and Ghostface did not appear in the video for its lead single "The Heart Gently Weeps"—RZA stepped into an opportunity to release new music when Koch Records offered him a deal for another solo album. In 2008, there would be only two releases from the Wu-Tang Camp. RZA would return as Bobby Digital to release his fourth album, *Digi Snacks*, on June 24, 2008, and GZA would release his sixth album, *Pro-Tools*, on August 19, 2008. The former would receive middling reviews with pointed jabs while the latter would receive generally positive reviews from critics. Both would receive only nominal attention from the public.

Digi Snacks only managed to enter at #111 on the *Billboard* 200 chart and peaked at #29 on the *Billboard* R&B/Hip-Hop Albums chart on its release. While RZA was lambasted for refusing to stop tinkering with his production on *8 Diagrams*, his continuous use of orchestral production, found sounds, and minor chords are what critics were fond of on *Digi Snacks*. On *Digi Snacks*, Bobby Digital is up to his usual hypersexualized antics, but likely thanks to RZA's own headaches with Wu-Tang Clan, his alter ego is more contemplative. "Drama" is an example of this restrained Bobby Digital who raps a conversation with the Rugged Monk that revolves around the latter venting about the vulnerability a young ghetto dweller feels when he thinks there are minimal options for upward mobility. The song is beautifully produced with lush, plodding chords and female vocalist Thea van Seijen's singing. "I'd like to live my life in peace/And have, not to worry about all the dramas of the day," she coos on the song's chorus with a voice whose timbre sounds like a poor woman's Billie Holiday.

The album's lead single was the bluesy "You Can't Stop Me Now" whose beat was constructed of a replayed version of 1970's "Message from a Black Man" by the Whatnaughts. Nas featured the same sample on a song called "You Can't Stop Us Now" from his *Untitled* album, released about a month after *Digi Snacks*. "You Can't Stop Me Now" features Inspectah Deck, the only Wu-Tang Clan member to make an appearance on the album. The two rappers spend their time recalling Wu-Tang's climb from the streets to the studio. Raps RZA, "Making beats for the streets, so the family could eat/In '93, Wu-Tang Clan dropped their first LP." The song was previously mentioned in the press as being part of *8 Diagrams* and probably was considering its content.

Now 16 years since Wu-Tang Clan debuted and 11 years since his *Bobby Digital in Stereo* solo debut, RZA again chooses to use his platform to spotlight artists he is grooming. The rapper Crisis, of Wu-Tang affiliate group The Black Knights (along with the Rugged Monk), who hail from California, and female vocalist Thea van Seijen, who is from the Netherlands, both appear prominently throughout *Digi Snacks*. A track that sticks out, sorely, is the David Banner–produced "Straight Up the Block" that sounds forced because of RZA's dumbed-down lyrics ("Who got the biggest dick, who got the phattest whip") that make it sound more like a parody of Southern rap music than an attempt at club play. The track uses a repeated vocal sample of Jay-Z for its chorus, a technique popularized by producer Swizz Beatz a few years prior, that also makes it sound humdrum.

RZA has always been a capable rapper but he is a producer first and foremost. The atmospheric harmonies of "Good Night" might lead some to miss that it is an attempt at sexual seduction in song if they don't pay close attention. But too many guest verses and production that is either loved or hated, with little gray area in between, is the reigning idiosyncrasy that marks *Digi Snacks*. *Time Out New York Magazine* succinctly summed up the critical dichotomy of *Digi Snacks* in its review of the album: "Through a fan's eye it's sometimes heavy-going, with occasionally brilliant production flourishes and inspired verses. And from a mainstream, chart-oriented point of view, it's ultimately inessential."[2] But when RZA raps, "But if you decipher my lyrics, truthfully and not critically/You'll see I influence the world mentally as well as physically" on "O Day" it is clear that what may be RZA's greatest trait—confidence that can border on arrogance—is still intact.

GZA, *PRO-TOOLS*

RZA went out on his own tour to support *Digi Snacks*, with most stops touting special Wu-Tang Clan guests. While inner Wu-Tang relations weren't at their best, GZA could still count on RZA and Masta Killa. The two rappers were the only members who came through when he announced he was in the studio working on *Pro-Tools*, and both appear on the searing "Pencil." Produced by Mathematics, the song samples a sped-up portion of 1970's "I'll Always Love You" by Velma Perkins to create a sprinting rhythm for the MCs to blister with their "darts." "Pencil" is the first song heard on *Pro-Tools* and is representative of the album's throwback Wu-Tang Clan vibe.

Though RZA produces only one song—the mechanized "Life Is a Movie," which samples singer/composer and electro pioneer Gary Numan's "Films" (1979)—Wu-Elements producers Mathematics, True Master, and Bronze Nazareth make contributions that naturally contain the Wu-Tang musical DNA of fuzzy, filtered samples and steady drums to keep the rappers on beat. As for the rhymes, the guests are minimal and GZA is up to his usual rhyme tricks that seem to be done more to keep himself entertained than impress fans. On "Alphabets," over a glum guitar loop with an occasional soul vocal flourish, a couple of smooth verses get stylistically trumped by a chorus where he effortlessly manages to include every letter in the alphabet. On "0% Finance" he mentions a myriad of automobile makers as metaphors for a story about a model and her suitor with multiple twists and turns. "A temp at the Ford modeling agency/Suburban area where the Caucasians be/Her great-grandfather was a Cherokee Indian/Explorer and navigator traveling then begin," raps GZA, cleverly mentioning Ford Motor Company's Suburban and Explorer model of SUVs, Jeep's Cherokee model, and Lincoln's Navigator model in a few lines.

Despite adhering closely to the traditional Wu-Tang Clan template, *Pro-Tools* got most of its attention for its lead single, "Paper Plate," a dis track aimed at rapper 50 Cent. There had been a long simmering feud between 50 Cent and the Wu-Tang Clan since the rapper's 1999 single "How to Rob" where he playfully described robbing some of the day's more prominent rappers, Wu-Tang Clan members included. A volley of vitriol was fired at 50 Cent on Ghostface's *Supreme Clientele* and "Paper Plate"—a paper plate is flimsy and a throwaway; get it?—was GZA's swipe at the commercially successful rapper. In 2007 GZA began calling 50 Cent's music "disposable" during his performances. 50 Cent eventually responded to GZA in an interview on the Shade 45 Internet radio station by saying he was "irrelevant" and mocking his age. "Paper Plates" is a decent song by itself with plenty of slick jabs at 50 Cent and G-Unit—at one point GZA says he'll "spray the flea unit with pesticides"—but the album had better songs that deserved attention for their quality rather than controversy.

GZA's *Pro-Tools* actually did better on the charts than RZA's album. *Pro-Tools* entered the *Billboard* 200 chart at #52, the *Billboard* R&B/Hip-Hop Albums chart at #13, and the *Billboard* Independent Albums chart at #2. Critics warmly received the album. In its review, the

Associated Press gushed, "Slinging 'glorious slang' over stark beats that spotlight the Wu-Tang vet's frigid flows, his fifth full-length continues to sharpen the shatterproof wordplay first introduced on 'Words From The Genius.' "[3] Though GZA didn't possess the commercial visibility of Ghostface—*Pro-Tools* also had the additional hurdle of being released through independent label Babygrande Records—the elder statesmen of Wu-Tang proved that he could be as consistent when it came to delivering technically proficient albums.

Pro-Tools would be the last album from a Wu-Tang Clan member in 2008. Fans would have to wait until January 2009 was almost over for RZA to release the *Afro Samurai Resurrection: Original Soundtrack* on January 27. Arriving nearly two years to the day after its predecessor, *The RZA Presents Afro Samurai: The Original Soundtrack*, the new album features some of the previous album's same players including Q-Tip, Suga Bang Bang, and The Black Knights. Newer artists to RZA's fold including Thea van Seijen, Stone Mecca (a band RZA has toured with), and System of the Down bassist Shavo Odadjian appear as well. Even Ghostface manages to participate on "Whar," along with Kool G. Rap, which uses the same bass line last heard at the beginning of "Clan in da Front" from Wu-Tang Clan's *Enter the Wu-Tang* debut. Female rapper Rah Digga makes a distinguished contribution to the album, appearing on two songs ("Bitch Gonna Get Ya" and "Girl Samurai Lullaby"). But the same qualms with RZA's recent releases—disparate themes, lack of cohesion between songs—plague the album.

Another Wu-Tang Clan–affiliated project would not be released for another four months when Method and Redman released *Blackout! 2*, the sequel to their platinum-selling *Blackout!* album, on May 19, 2009. But a decade later, unlike on *Blackout!* where he served as an executive producer and produced a pair of tracks, RZA had no involvement in *Blackout! 2*. Ghostface and Raekwon do manage to appear on the Bink! produced "4 Minutes to Lockdown," one of the album's better cuts and the only proper Wu-Tang Clan guests, unless we include Streetlife's appearance on a song called "How Bout Dat." On "4 Minutes to Lockdown," Method Man curiously raps, "Same way I live it how I spit in the booth, next to RZA, ain't no nigga bigger than the group." The line can be taken many ways but it seems that Method Man still has respect for RZA's role as leader of Wu-Tang Clan, no matter the circumstances.

U-GOD, *DOPIUM*

U-God would release his third album, *Dopium*, on June 23, 2009. Ironically, because little regarded past work created low expectations for this album, *Dopium* was the most Wu-Tang Clan–loaded album of the year to date. The album starts strong, with RZA'esque production from Teddy Ted & J. Serbe and help from his Clanmates on the first few songs; Ghostface ("Train Trussle"), Cappadonna and Killah Priest ("God Is Love"), and GZA ("Stomp da Roach"). Raekwon also checks in for precocious drug raps, a precursor to his upcoming *Only Built 4 Cuban Linx . . . Pt. II*, on the Da Beathoven produced "Coke," which also features Irish American rapper Slaine. However, a few questionable "house mixes" of three songs that are tacked onto *Dopium* as bonus tracks as well as the chopped and screw styled "Wu-Tang," featuring Method Man, mar the album. As critics love to point out, U-God could have used RZA's production assistance because besides the Large Professor–produced "New Classic," the production is generally listless. But considering their past financial squabbles, it is no surprise RZA has no involvement in the *Dopium* album. The Wu-Tang presence only helps U-God's case, and his rhymes are still potent in doses, but *Dopium* does not make the cut on any lists of essential Wu-Tang Clan albums.

WU-TANG CLAN, *WU-TANG CHAMBER MUSIC*

An unofficial Wu-Tang Clan album called *Wu-Tang Chamber Music* was released on June 30, 2009, only a week after U-God's *Dopium*. The album was released by E1 Records (formerly Koch Records) and the Wu-Tang Music Group, and RZA served as the project's executive producer. RZA was adamant that this was not an official Wu-Tang Clan album, particularly since all of its members do not appear on the album. A band of musicians called The Revelations were charged with creating a vibe similar to the sounds of *Enter the Wu-Tang (36 Chambers)* but by utilizing live instrumentation. Fans and critics were receptive to *Chamber Music* with the Wu-Tang and guest MCs delivering heady performances.

Not including intros, outros, and RZA's philosophical sermonizing between tracks, *Chamber Music* has only eight songs. Lushly produced and despite its unofficial tag, the album was a welcome reprieve from recent suspect releases from Wu-Tang Clan members. The label pushed "Harbor Masters" featuring RZA, Ghostface, AZ, and Inspectah Deck and "Ill Figures" featuring RZA, Raekwon, and Kool G Rap, both credible songs. The latter is especially interesting since we hear two "coke rap" masters, Raekwon and Kool G. Rap, collaborating on the same song. Throughout the album Wu-Tang Clan members Ghostface, Raekwon, Inspectah Deck, U-God, as well as RZA appear on songs with rappers who share New York City roots including Cormega, Sean Price, and Sadat X. According to RZA, producer Bob Perry brought him the idea of creating an album of Wu-Tang–inspired music that lacked any sampling.[4]

RAEKWON, *ONLY BUILT 4 CUBAN LINX ... PT. II*

In hindsight, *Wu-Tang Chamber Music* only whetted the appetites of Wu-Tang Clan fans not for another group album, but for Raekwon's long-delayed *Only Built 4 Cuban Linx ... Pt. II*.

One of the jabs 50 Cent aimed at GZA during their verbal scuffle was that at a then 41 years of age, GZA was too old to still be rapping. Even if 50 Cent's taunts are disregarded, hip-hop fans are notorious for losing faith in their heroes as they age. Rappers don't help their case by constantly mentioning how they plan on moving to other careers since they "can't rap forever." Or, like Jay-Z and Too Short, older rappers announce their retirement, which usually means an eventual return from retirement. So instead of being accommodating to new material, these fickle fans increasingly cherish the vintage material while treating newer material with aloofness. The new material has the added misfortune of being held to a higher, often unrealistic, and almost unattainable standard.

Raekwon was able to sidestep this scenario in 2009. Now pushing 40 years old himself (he was born January 12, 1970), Raekwon "The Chef" could not have picked a more perfect time to finally release *Only Built 4 Cuban Linx ... Pt. II*. The last Wu-Tang Clan album, *8 Diagrams*, was met with indifference by the public. *Only Built 4 Cuban Linx ... Pt. II* had been supposedly on the cusp of release for years. In a 2004 interview with *Source Magazine*, RZA told the publication, "I've been talking to [Ghost and Raekwon] about doing another *Cuban Link*. I think the fans deserve another *Cuban Link*. I think the fans deserve another Wu-Tang Clan album, too. After that I think we did our job."[5] Hints like these of *Cuban Linx ... Pt. II* being perpetually in the works had given the album a mythic aura, similar to Dr. Dre's still unreleased *Detox*. Raekwon was even signed to Dr. Dre's Aftermath Records for a short stint in 2007, with Busta Rhymes on board to executive produce the album. By 2009, Busta Rhymes was no longer a part of the project, but the album was finally coming to fruition.

In 2007 RZA famously butted heads with Raekwon about the type of sound the latter wanted to use. By 2009, the two old friends were on better terms. RZA only contributes two tracks to *Only Built 4 Cuban Linx ... Pt. II*, but they are both exceptional songs on one of 2009's best albums. Earlier in the year (February 2009), Raekwon leaked "Wu Ooh," which would eventually become *Cuban Linx ... Pt. II*'s lead single. The song, whose title was changed to "New Wu," features Raekwon, Method Man, and Ghostface flowing over a mesmerizing, hastened sample of vocal harmonizing lifted from 1971's "I've Changed" by Detroit R&B group The Magictones. RZA outfits the song with pounding drums and the three rappers joyously perform on the song with Method Man handling the hook. The song is a perfect mesh of Wu-Tang street appeal with a groove docile enough for radio. But inexplicably, the song received minimal radio support.

RZA's other contribution to the album is "Black Mozart," which also features rhymes from Inspectah Deck. The song samples the spine-chilling "Theme from *The Godfather*" (1974), which is a cover of Nino Rota's "Speak Softly Love (Love Theme from *The Godfather*)," by Belizean group The Professionals. Both of RZA's songs feature distinct samples that haven't been overly tweaked with the pianos and guitars Raekwon previously abhorred. The beats are counter to RZA's music of late, but credit Raekwon's assertiveness in insisting that vintage beats from the Wu-Tang Clan's leader is what he needed on *his* album.

Putting *Only Built 4 Cuban Linx ... Pt. II* together was a four-year plus effort for Raekwon and fortunately every delayed step along the way managed to benefit its eventual release. For example, he had been able to secure production from J. Dilla before he died in February 2006 and his short stay on Aftermath Records left him with a pair of Dr. Dre–produced tracks. The album also contains all the crucial elements of Wu-Tang's glory days: deft lyricism, outstanding production, kung-fu samples, and a sense of urgency that Raekwon's last couple of albums did not possess. As the album's release date loomed, "House of Flying Daggers" was released as a single. It is a true Wu-Tang Clan posse cut that features a commanding lead-off verse by Inspectah Deck, who is swiftly followed by Raekwon, Ghostface, and Method Man. The song's hook interpolates Wu-Tang Clan's own "Clan in da Front" from *Enter the Wu-Tang*. The song, produced by the late J. Dilla, uses a marching synth pattern and vocal clip from a cover of the Beatles' "Eleanor Rigby" by R&B greats the Four Tops, and it is a clear homage to RZA's production. J. Dilla would also produce "Ason Jones" on *Cuban Linx ... Pt. II*, a touching song dedicated to the late Ol' Dirty Bastard.

Media that were privy to an early listen to *Only Built 4 Cuban Linx ... Pt. II* excitedly reported that the album was one of Raekwon's best, coming close to matching the verve of the original. On its release the album sold a hefty, for the times, 68,000 units, enough for it to enter at #4 on the *Billboard* Top R&B/Hip-Hop albums chart and #2 on the *Billboard* 200 chart. This was a triumphant return for Raekwon, especially considering the album was independently released on his own Ice H20 Records label, with distribution by EMI. The album that claimed the #1 spot on the *Billboard 200* was Jay-Z's *Blueprint 3*, which had a considerably larger promotional budget.

Raekwon went on a grassroots campaign, beginning well before its release, to promote the album, particularly making sure his name stayed in rotation on popular blog sites. After the album's release, he would release singles and videos for the Scram Jones–produced "Walk Wit Me" (an iTunes bonus track), the Alchemist-produced "Surgical Gloves," the Ice Water Productions–helmed "Canal Street," the Dr. Dre and Mark Batson–produced "Catalina," and the Marley Marl–produced "Pyrex Vision."

Critics and fans loved *Only Built 4 Cuban Linx ... Pt II*. Fourteen years after the release of the original, Raekwon delivered a worthy sequel. Among its many accolades the album was ranked the fifth best album of 2009 by Pitchfork Media and the seventh best album of the year by *Time Magazine*. *Source Magazine* named it the Album of the Year. Raekwon told UK newspaper *The Guardian*, "The whole main purpose of the album is to make you reminisce. ... But at the same token, you still gotta show some kind of growth, and we did that, too.

My mind is thinkin' in both directions at the same time—on makin' a classic album and still managin' to make it sound like how we was feelin' when we made music way back when."[6] Rappers always talk a good game about their album harkening back to their glory days. But Raekwon's rhetoric differs in that he actually delivers.

As with any successful Wu-Tang Clan release, there was soon talk of the album being a springboard to a Wu-Tang Clan reunion. Hopes were only raised with Ghostface releasing his eight album, *Ghostdini: Wizard of Poetry in Emerald City*, a few weeks later on September 29, 2009. Ghostface originally drew skepticism because when *Ghostdini: Wizard of Poetry in Emerald City* was announced he told the press that it was an R&B album. He went on to clarify that the album would feature a hefty amount of R&B hooks, similar to a number of such collaborations on all his previous albums, going all the way back to "All That I Got Is You" with Mary J. Blige on his 1996 debut *Ironman*. Once again RZA was completely absent from the project. The album is a solid work from Ghostface but failed to make much of a mark commercially, landing at #6 on the *Billboard* Top R&B/Hip-Hop albums chart and #28 on the *Billboard* 200 chart.

2010 AND BEYOND

Despite the lukewarm reception at retail to Ghostface's *Ghostdini: Wizard of Poetry in Emerald City*, his label Def Jam Records still saw the recent success of Raekwon (who was still actively promoting *Only Built 4 Cuban Linx . . . Pt. II* as well as releasing singles that didn't make the album and mix tapes) as an opportunity. All of the Wu-Tang Clan members on Def Jam—Ghostface and Method Man—would release a collaborative album with Raekwon titled *Wu-Massacre*. The album's lead single was the RZA-produced "Our Dreams," which features a sample of Michael Jackson's 1975 ballad "We're Almost There."

Released March 30, 2010, *Wu-Massacre* was rushed into stores to take advantage of the attention Raekwon was getting for *Only Built 4 Cuban Linx . . . Pt. II*. But before it was released, Method Man expressed dismay that the project was hastily created and therefore not as good as it could have been. The three rappers, who are also credited as executive producers, only appear together on three of the album's 10 songs (the album is only a half hour long). The album's opening track, "Criminology 2.5," inadvertently alludes to its ad hoc construction because it is an amended version of the song, which had previously leaked, and was thought to be part of *Cuban Linx . . . Pt. II* but was not included on it final track list. Allmusic.com noted in its review of the album that its producers (Scram Jones, Emile) "take their cues from RZA's playbook." This is to be expected of producer Mathematics, who handles some of the album's best tracks including "Meth vs. Chef 2," a sequel to the original from Method Man's *Tical* debut, and "Miranda," which features all three of the album's costars lyrically serenading a woman over a sublime piano and vocal loop taken from 1972's "Let It Be Me" by Soul singer Linda Jones.

Wu-Massacre turned out not to be the major release Def Jam was banking on. Inspectah Deck was probably hoping it would have made more ripples, too, since he released his third album, *The Manifesto*, the week before on March 23, 2010. Besides the lead single "The Champion," produced by Alchemist, the independently released album (on Inspectah Deck's own Urban Icon Records) made little noise beyond hip-hop Web sites and the hip-hop blogosphere. Inspectah Deck's album only managed to peak at #69 on the *Billboard* Hip-Hop/R&B albums chart while *Wu-Massacre* opened at #6 on the *Billboard* Hip-Hop/R&B albums chart and #12 on the *Billboard* 200 chart. *Wu-Massacre* also entered the *Billboard* Top Rap albums chart at #2. Before 2010 came to an end, Ghostface Killah released his ninth album, *Apollo Kids*, to the usual critical kudos but with minimal commercial recognition. *Apollo Kids* only entered the *Billboard* Hip-Hop/R&B albums chart at #28 and the *Billboard* 200 chart at #120.

Raekwon has already recorded his next album, titled *Shaolin vs. Wu-Tang*, to be released March 2011, and also has plans to release another album the same year. *Shaolin vs. Wu-Tang* is the same title of the album he proposed members of Wu-Tang Clan record sans RZA during the run up to the release of *8 Diagrams*. Raekwon has also gone on the record to say that it will not feature RZA. However, RZA was probably busy anyway since besides contributing production to Kanye West's *My Beautiful Dark Twisted Fantasy* (2010) album, he is on board to participate in the sequel to GZA's *Liquid Swords*. Ghostface revealed his plans to release a proper sequel to his *Supreme Clientele* album, too.

The success of *Only Built 4 Cuban Linx . . . Pt. II* naturally extended as a victory for Wu-Tang Clan. What Raekwon was able to accomplish wasn't a new phenomena. Old school sensibilities—the original *Only Built 4 Cuban Linx . . .* was released over 14 years before its successor—with a new age twist was long a Wu-Tang staple. In 1994, RZA told *Urb Magazine* of the group's initial albums, "Wu-Tang Clan is bringin' niggas back to 1987. We was there in the Old School, we're the product of the Old School. . . . So now we're showin' them what they showed us, but in a new form."[7]

One particular song on *Only Built 4 Cuban Linx . . . Pt. II*, "Black Mozart," illustrates RZA's motivation. The song samples "The Godfather Theme" by the Professionals. RZA revealed that he studied *The Godfather* while he was creating the Wu-Tang Clan, modeling himself after Vito Corleone, head of the fictional Corleone crime family.[8] Knowing when and when not to administer his power and influence over the rest of the Clan was something RZA did with aplomb, at least early in the group's history. Then there was the title "Black Mozart" itself. In a 1998 story in *USA Today*, RZA told the newspaper, "I want to leave something here. I want to create a sound. Mozart is still living through his music. I want to bring something new to the planet where people will say that the only reason it's here is because we brought it here."[9]

There is no question that RZA has already accomplished his mission. The Wu-Tang Clan, and by default RZA because we truly can't have one without the other, has left an ineffaceable imprint on hip-hop music and culture. Hip-hop crews made up of individual artists such as Cam'ron's Dipset, 50 Cent's G-Unit, and Lil' Wayne's Young Money owe their success to the Wu-Tang Clan blueprint. While the Golden Age of Wu-Tang Clan (1993–1998) is long gone, Wu-Tang Clan has been able to remain relevant for 17 years. Their new releases may no longer shake the foundation of the music world but they still manage to generate interest in their music from a legion of fans. While Wu-Wear has long lost its luster among the fashionable set, Wu-Tang Clan teamed with A-Life for a line called "A Wu-Tang Life" in 2006 that was well received.

The Wu-Tang Clan brand, no matter how diluted it may have become through the years, is still Gibraltar like. The Clan's lofty ambitions for world domination were tempered with a grassroots sensibility in their music that endeared them to listeners of all creeds and colors. "White kids are getting their beat on what hipness is from black kids again," reported record executive John McClane to the *New York Times* in 1998 while Wu-Tang Clan mania was still fresh.[10] Whether an inner-city Black kid, or a college student that lives in the suburbs, Wu-Tang Clan's music always managed to be relatable to broad swath of society. "A good lyric is like a parable, where you can hear one line and take it in five different ways," RZA told *Rolling Stone Magazine* in 2001.[11]

But RZA also told *XXL Magazine*, "I always tell people our lyrics aren't really for this generation, it's for the next generation to come across and study."[12] Fortunately Wu-Tang Clan and RZA have managed to create music that has a shelf life of indeterminable expiration date. To be a true hip-hop fan means being at least fleetingly aware of Wu-Tang Clan's accomplishments. There is always the incessant talk of hip-hop culture being a youth culture. This is only partly true. The youth are the driving force whether it is determining the latest trends or deciding the rapper du jour. But ironically, more often than not, those select rappers haven't been teenagers in years. Jay-Z, Puff Daddy, and Dr. Dre are all over 40 years old. Eminem and 50 Cent are both way past 30 years old. Wu-Tang Clan were not exactly spring chickens when they first entered the record business. At the time of *8 Diagrams*' release, GZA was Wu-Tang Clan's oldest member at 41 years old while Method Man, at 36 years old, was its youngest. But on a daily basis, younger fans are getting acquainted with the Clan's older material, often after listening to their more recent work.

Journalist Elliott Wilson described RZA as Willie Mitchell meets Albert Einstein.[13] The match of soul music and science makes it a fitting comparison. RZA found a way to take his limited resources and craft a masterpiece in *Enter the Wu-Tang (36 Chambers)*. In *The Wu-Tang Manual* RZA says, "The limitations of technology can become artistic tools themselves."[14] As RZA added more tools to his arsenal, whether via acquiring more advanced production equipment, studying music theory, and soaking up everything around him, his production gifts grew exponentially. At first the fans cheered him on and he could do no wrong. Being responsible for seven Top 10 albums as well as scores of imitators were evidence of that. "In between Wu-Tang albums, I took the time to become a trained musician. I always felt that my music was cinematic anyway," says RZA in his *Wu-Tang Manual*.[15] But in a real-life plot twist, as he kept going, kept experimenting with orchestral arrangements, found sounds and new techniques, fans and his own Wu-Tang Clan wanted him to dial the progression back. The same fixation on creating sound collages that shattered the norm is the same trait that drove many, but not all, fans away.

However, RZA was steadfast, some would say hardheaded, in his belief that his way was the best way. For RZA, reinvention and expansion is survival. Under his guidance the Wu-Tang Clan was making Fortune 500–worthy business moves while keeping a fresh-off-the-project block mentality. This is a far cry from the tailored, boardroom posturing of present-day Jay-Z, for example. "What these guys have done—without taking a single business school course—is to go right to the head of the class in terms of strategy development," said James I. Cash, then a professor of business administration at Harvard Business School, to the *New York Times* in a 1996 story on Wu-Tang Clan's entrepreneurial ventures.[16]

The only means by which Wu-Tang Clan could once again shock the world was to advance, not retreat back into the ground they had long since tread. But with his dictatorship long gone and other Clan member asserting themselves enough to scale a full-out mutiny, the once steely Wu-Tang Clan armor was visibly cracked. Infighting continues with the Wu-Tang Clan to this day. Despite their recent successes, or maybe because of them, Ghostface sued RZA over unpaid royalties. In late August 2009, Ghostface reached a settlement with Wu-Tang Clan Production for over $158,000 in unpaid royalties, stemming from a 2005 lawsuit. RZA is currently appealing the case, citing that the contract he and all the other Wu-Tang Clan member signed with Wu-Tang Productions stipulated the producer receive a 50 percent share of royalties with the other 50 percent split between the songwriters. Considering most times there was one producer, RZA, and eight or more lyricists in Wu-Tang Clan, this is where things get dicey.

Such bickering only puts the prospect of another Wu-Tang Clan album further out of reach, though it is not totally impossible. Business relationships can be dissolved and friends can grow apart, but family bonds are infinite. Familial disagreements are a way of life and the Wu-Tang Clan has a history that goes back years before the 1993 debut album. So when they call each other "brothers" it isn't lip service. If the Clan truly hated RZA's guts, there is no way he would have produced "Our Dreams," the lead single to *Wu-Massacre*, released after Ghostface's lawsuit. In early August 2010, the entire Wu-Tang Clan reunited for a few tour stops in the United Kingdom. Though RZA did not participate, in late 2010 and early 2010 the Wu-Tang Clan embarked on the Rebirth Tour throughout the United States.

Seems like Method Man was being prophetic when in a 1995 *Source Magazine* cover story he said, "The only way out of the Wu is death. Word up. You can quote me on that shit."[17] It's the continuation of the cycle of life. Fans, young and old—and even some dead and gone—have grown up on Wu-Tang Clan. RZA once told *Vibe Magazine*, "Even with all that knowledge right there and reading all these books, I never gave my childhood up." With a legacy that only continues to grow and ripen with time, Wu-Tang Clan and RZA are big kids that will perpetually stay in the hip-hop picture.

NOTES

1. DeCurtis, Anthony, "Wu Tang Family Values," *Rolling Stone Magazine*, July 10, 1997–July 24, 1997, 86.

2. Lawrence, Eddy, "Music—Album Reviews—RZA," *Time Out New York*, June 24, 2008, 16.

3. O'Connell, Jake, "Music Review: Wu-Tang's GZA Shows Lyrical Genius," *The Associated Press*, August 19, 2008.

4. Graff, Gary, "RZA Returns to the 'Chamber,'" Billboard.com, June 25, 2009, http://www.billboard.com/news/rza-returns-to-the-chamber-1003987701 .story#/news/rza-returns-to-the-chamber-1003987701.story.

5. Gotti, "Jesus Walks" *The Source Magazine*, June 2004, 125.

6. Batey, Angus, "The Return of Raekwon," *The Guardian*, September 11, 2009, 13.

7. Dookey, Spence, "5 Cycles and 20 Seasons of Wu-Tang," *URB Magazine*, Vol. 7, No. 53 (52–55).

8. RZA and Chris Norris, *The Wu-Tang Manual* (New York: Riverhead Books, 2005), 102.

9. Jones, Steve, "Wu-Tang Clan's RZA Fits Pieces Into 'Digital' World," *USA Today*, December 8, 1998, 4D.

10. Strauss, Neil, "Crossing Racial Boundaries, Rap Gains Ground," *The New York Times*, October 15, 1998, E1.

11. Diehl, Matt, "Microphone Fiend," *XXL Magazine*, August 2001, 114.

12. Wilson, Elliott, "Victory," *XXL Magazine*, October 2000, 106.

13. Wilson, "Victory," 103.

14. RZA and Chris Norris, *The Wu-Tang Manual*, 191.

15. Ibid., 113

16. Diehl, Matt, "Brash Hip-Hop Entrepreneurs," *The New York Times*, December 8, 1996, 34.

17. Hinds, Selwyn Seyfu, "The Wu-Gambinos," *The Source Magazine*, October 1995, 85 (84–88).

Index

"0% Finance" (GZA/Genius), 216

"4:20" (Streetlife, Carlton Fisk), 193

4:21. The Day After (Method Man), 192–94

4 Ever (Megan Rochell), 194

"4 Minutes to Lockdown" (Ghostface, Raekwon) Bink! producer for, 217

"4 Minutes to Lockdown" (Ghostface, Raekwon, Method Man), 217

"4th Chamber" (Ghostface, RZA, Killa Priest), 54

4th Disciple, 32, 55, 126; producer, "A Better Tomorrow," 76; production, "Impossible," 77; sound production, *Tical 2000: Judgment Day*, 89; sound production, *Wu-Tang Clan Forever*, 74

6 Feet Deep (RZA, Gravediggaz), 28, 85

8 Diagram Polefighter (film dialogue), 209

8 Diagrams (Wu-Tang Clan), xiv, 202, 205–7; production sensibilities on, 211; productions in, RZA, 208; reception for, 211

"9 Milli Bros" Wu-Tang clan, 188–89

9th Prince of Killarmy, 97

12 O'Clock, 38, 163

"16th Chamber (ODB Special)" (Method Man, Ol' Dirty Bastard), 210

The 36th Chamber of Shaolin (film), 35

36th Chamber of Shaolin (Shaw Borthers Films), 1–2

50 Cent's G Unit, 224

50 Cent vs. GZA/Genius, 216, 220

60 Second Assassin, 38

"100 Rounds" (Raekwon), 109

"111" (GZA, Masta Killa, Killa priest, Njeri Earth), 99

"260" (Ghostface and Raekwon), 59

Achozen, 208

Afro Samurai (Anime TV series), 202

Afro Samurai: The Album (RZA), xiv, 202, 217

"After the Laughter" (Wu-Tang Clan), 10–11, 22–23

"The Afterparty" (RZA and Ghostface), 181

"After the Smoke is Clear" (Delfonics, Ghostface, Raekwon, RZA), 58, 62

"Ain't No sunshine" (Michael Jackson), 44

"Airwaves" (RZA), 94

album track lists: *Birth of a Prince* (RZA), 165; *Bobby Digital in Stereo* (RZA), 92; *Bulletproof Wallets* (Ghostface with Raekwon), 144; *Digi Snacks* (RZA/Bobby Digital), 212; *Digital Bullet* (RZA as Bobby Digital), 142; *Iron Flag* (Wu-Tang Clan), 153; *Ironman*(Ghostface Killah), 57; *Nigga Please*, 102; *Only Built 4 Cuban Linx (Raekwon and Ghostface Killah)*, 40; *Return to 36 Chambers (The Dirty Version)*, 34; *Return to the 36 Chambers (The Dirty Version)* (Ol' Dirty Basterd), 34; *RZA as Bobby Digital in Stereo*, 92; *Supreme Clientele* (Ghostface Killah), 111; *The W* (Wu-Tang Clan), 133; *Wu-Tang Forever*, 72

Allah Mathematics, 140, 193. *See also* Mathematics

Allah Mathematics production, *Beneath the Surface*, 100

"All I Got Is You Pt. 2" (Raekwon), 109

"All I Need" (Method Man), 30

All in Together: crew as Wu-Tang Clan forerunner, 7; GZA/Genius, RZA and Ol' Dirty Bastard, 3–4

"All In Together" (GZA/Genius and Mugs), 186

"All In Together Now" (Ol' Dirty Bastard), 106

"All Over Again" (Raekwon), 169

"All That I Got Is You" (Ghostface, Mary J. Blige, Popa Wu), 62–63

"Alphabets" (GZA/Genius), 216

Ameraycan Studios, 73

American Cream Team (Raekwon Rappers), 110

"American Gangster" (film) (RZA), 211

"Andalu" (Spheeris), 109

"Animal Planet" (GZA/Genius), 163

anti-white themes, 105

AOL Online, 82

Apollo Kids (Ghostface Killah), 223

"Aries" (Cannonball Adderly), 53

Armel, 163

ASR-10 beat machine, 35

"Assassination Day" (Inspectah Deck, RZA, Raekwon, Masta Killa), 59

"Assassin with Son" (from *Shogun Assassin* soundtrack), 54

ATC, 54

Ayatollah, 164

"Babies" (Ghostface, Raekwon, GZA, RZA), 157

"Baby Come On" (Ol' Dirty Bastard), 35

"Back in the Game" (Wu-Tang Clan), 157–58

"Back Like That" (Ghostface), 187–88

"Back Like That" (Remix)
(Ghostface), 195

Bad Boy Records, 77, 82

Bad Boys, x

Badu, Erykah, 206

"Ba-Lue Bolivar Ba-Lues-Are"
(Thelonius Monk), 39

"Bang Bang (My Baby Shot Me
Down)" (Nancy Sinatra), 210

Banner, David, 215

"Barrel Brothers" (Beanie Sigel,
Styles P), 204

"Be Easy" (Ghostface), 187

"Bells of War" (Ghostface, U-God,
Method Man, RZA, Masta Killa,
Ghost Man and Raekwon), 78–79

Beneath the Surface (GZA/Genius),
xiii, 88, 98; Allah Mathematics,
production, 99; Arabian Knight,
production, 99; RZA
contribution, 99

Beretta 9, 202

"A Better Tomorrow" (Inspectah
Deck, Masta Killa, U-God, RZA,
Method Man), 76

"B.I.B.L.E." (Killa priest), 55

The Big Doe Rehab (Ghostface
Killah), 203–4

Biggie Smalls, 73

Big Willie Style (Will Smith), 82

Bink! 217

Bink! production, "Bizarre," 107

"The Birth" (RZA), 167

Birth of a Prince (film) (RZA), 165

Birth of a Prince (film) (RZA),
reception for, 168

Birth of a Prince (RZA), 166

"Biscuits" (Ghostface), 174–75

"Biscuits" (Method Man), 29

"Bitch Gonna Get Ya" (Rash
Digga), 217

"Bizarre" (U-God), 107

"Black Bach" (Lamont Dozier), 114

"Black Jesus" (Papa Wu), 62

The Black Knights, 215, 217

Black Knights of the North Star, 128

"Black Mozart" (RZA, Inspectah
Deck), 220, 224

Blackout! (Method Man,
Redman), 141

Black out! (Redman, Method
Man), 177

Blackout! (Wu-Tang Clan and
Redman), xiii, 99, 137

Blackout! 2 (Wu-Tang Clan and
Redman), 217

"Black Shampoo" (U-God), 80

"Black Widow Pt. 2" (Ol' Dirty
Bastard), 143

Blige, Mary J., 30–31; on "All I
Need," 30; "All That I Got Is You"
(Ghostface), 62–63

The Blueprint Album (Jay-Z), 160

Blue Rasberry, 30, 32, 33, 44,
49, 128

BMG, 82

"B.O.B.B.Y." (RZA), 93–94

"Bobby Did It" (RZA, Ghostface,
Timbo King, Islord, Jamie
Sommers), 96

Bobby Digital. *See also* RZA

Bobby Digital (RZA), 92–93.
See also RZA

Bobby Digital in Stereo (film), 94

As Bobby Digital in Stereo (RZA), xii

Bobby Digital in Stereo (RZA/
Bobby Digital), 87, 142;
production, 97; reception for, 97–98

Bobby Digital Presents Northstar
(Northstar), 128

Bobby Steele (RZA), 55.
See also RZA

"Bob N' I" (Bobby Digital), 166

Bone Thugs-N-Harmony, 65

Booster, 30

"Box in Hand" as "Deadly Darts," 60–61

"Box in Hand" on *Ironman* (Raekwon, Ghostface, Method Man), 60–61

"Breakdown (Part 2)" (Rufus Thomas), 114

"Breaker, Breaker" (Gza/Genius), 100

"Break Ups 2 Make Up" (Method Man), 90

"Bring the Pain" (Method Man), 29–30

"Bring the Ruckus" (Wu-Tang Clan), 18

Bronze Nazareth producer on *Pro-Tools*, 216

"Brooklyn Babies" (RZA as Bobby Digital), 143

"Brooklyn Zoo" (Ol' Dirty Bastard), 35–36

"Brooklyn Zoo II (Tiger Crane)" (Ghostface and Ol' Dirty Bastard), 38

"Buck 50" (Ghostface Killah), 115

Buddha Monk, 38

Bulletproof Wallets (Ghostface with Raekwon), 142, 144–45, 145–46, 148, 149

Busta Rhymes, 201

Call Me (Al Green), 59

"Camay,"61

"Cameo Afro" (GZA, Big Daddy Kane), 202

"Campfire" (Method Man, Ghostface, Cappadonna), 207–8

Cam'ron Dipseet, 224

"Can It Be All So Simple" (Remix) (Ghostface and Raekwon), 45

"Can It Be All So Simple" (Wu-Tang Clan), 20, 206

"Can't Wait" (Ol' Dirty Bastard), 103, 104

"can't We Try?" (Teddy Pendergrass), 61

Cappadonna, 61, 195; absence from *Iron Flag*, 154; *The Big Doe Rehab*, 204; "Fish," 61; "Ice Cream," 48; "Ice Water," 46; incarceration, 127; "Little Ghetto Boys" (Raekwon), 77; misogyny, 76; and perception of Wu-Tang Clan, 154; *The Pillage*, 101; prison, 101; on Razor Sharp Records, 127; as true Wu-Tang Clan member, 127; "Winter Warz" (posse cut), 60; with Wu-Tang Clan, 48

"Careful (Click, Click)" (Wu-Tang Clan), 136

Carey, Mariah, 39

Carlito's Way (film), 64

Caruso, Mike, 154

"Cash Still Rules/Scary Hours (Still Don't Nothing Move But the Money)" (Wu-Tang Clan), 74

"Cash Still Rules/Scary Hours (Still Don't Nothing Move But the Money)" (Wu-Tang Clan), 74

CCF Division, 167

"Cereal Killer," 141

"Chamber Music" (Wu-Tang Clan), 136

"A Change is Gonna Come" (Otis Redding), 61

"A Change is Gonna Come" (Sam Cook), 64

the Chef, xi

"Cherchez La Femme"
(Dr. Buzzard's Original Savannah
Band), 118
"Cherchez LaGhost" (Ghostface),
117–18
Chess, in "Da Mysterry of
Chessboxin," 21
Childs, Solomon, 195
"Child's Play" (Ghostface), 117
"Chrome Wheels" (RZA, Madam
D, Raekwon, 12 O'Clock,
Prodigal Sunn), 155–56
The Chronic (Dr. Dre),
17–18, 64
Cigar, 169
Cilvaringz, 190
"The City" (Inspectah Deck), 78
"City High" (Inspectah Deck), 164
"Clan in da Front" (Wu-Tang Clan), 19
Clarence 13X (Smith, Clarence), 2, 3
Clarks Wallabee Shoes, 46, 123
"Clientele Kidd" (Raekwon and
Ghostface), 170
Clinton, George, 209
Clipse, 187
"The Closing" (Raekwon), 81
"Clyde Smith" (Skit) (Raekwonn),
118
"Cobra Clutch" (Ghostface Killah),
114
"Coke" (Raekwon, Slaine), 218
"Cold Blooded" (Ol' Dirty Bastard),
104
Cold Chillin' Records, 4, 56
Cold Crush Brothers, 52
"Cold World" (Inspectah Deck),
53, 56
"Come Do Me" (GZA/Genius), 4
"Conditioner" (Ol' Dirty Bastard),
137, 141
Cormega, 219

"Could I Be Falling in Love?"
(Syl Johnson), 49
Cowan, Denys, 51
"Cracker Jack" (Ol' Dirty Bastard),
106
"C.R.E.A.M." (Wu-Tang-Tang
Clan), 21, 35
crime themes: "Criminology"
(Ghostface Killah, Raekwon),
204; *Fishscale*, 187; "Shakey Dog
starring Lolita" (Raekwon), 204
"Criminology" (Ghostface Killah
and *Raekwon*), 43
The Cure, 142
Cuttin', P. F., 192
"Cuttin' Headz" (Ol' Dirty Bastard
and RZA), 38
"Cuttin' Headz" on *Wu-Tang Clan
Demo Tape*, 39

Da Beathoven, 218
"Daily Routine" (RZA and Kinetic
9), 97
"Damage" (Ol' Dirty Bastard and
RZA), 36
"Da Mystery of Chessboxin' "
(Wu-Tang Clan), 21
D'Angelo, 90
"Dat Gangsta" (U-God), 107
"A Day to God is 1000 Years"
(RZA), 167
"Daytona 500" (The Force MDs), 61
"Deadly Darts" as original "Box in
Hand," 60–61
"Deadly Melody" (Wu-Tang clan),
76–78
"Deadly Venoms" (RZA as Prince
Rakeem), 5
Death Row Records, 53–54
"Deck's Beat" (Inspectah Deck,
producer), 116

Def Jam Records, xi, 27, 30, 174, 189, 194, 222

Delfonics, 62

Dennis Cole (Ghostface), 57. *See also* Ghostface Killah

Detox (Dr. Dre), 220

Diggs, Mitchell, 124

Diggs, Robert Fitzgerald, x, 1. *See also* RZA

Digi Snacks (RZA/Bobby Digital), 214–15

Digital Bullet (RZA/Bobby Digital), 142, 144

"Dirt Dog" (Ol' Dirty Bastard), 105

Dirt McGirt (Ol' Dirty Bastard), 184

"Dirty Dancin' " (Ol' Dirty Bastard and Method Man), 39

"Dirty Mef" (Method Man and Ol' Dirty Bastard), 193

Disciples of the 36 Chambers: Chapter 1 (Wu-Tang Clan), 184

"The Documentary," 42

Dogg Pound, 65

Doggystile (Snoop Dogg), 17–18, 64

"Domestic Violence" (RZA and Jamie Sommers), 96–97

"Don't Go Breaking My Heart" (Ol' Dirty Bastard, Macy Gray), 184

"Don't U Know" (Ol' Dirty Bastard), 36–37

dope themes: "Criminology," 43; "Faster Blade" (Raekwon and Ghostface), 59; *Fishscale*, 187; "Gold" (GZA/Genius), 52–53; "Hells Wind Staff/Killa Hills 10304" (GZA/Genius), 55; "Ice Water," 46; "Knowledge God," 42; "Maxine," 146; "Spot Rusherz" (Ghostface, Raekwon), 47

Dopium (U-God), 218

"Do You Really (Thang, Thang)" (DJ Kay Slay and posse), 139

"Drama" (Bobby Digital, Rugged Monk, Thea vana Seijen), 214

Dr. Doom, 96

Dr. Dre, x, 17–18, 64

"Drink, Smoke + Fuck" (RZA), 167

"Drunk Game (Sweet Sugar Pie)" (Ol' Dirty Bastard), 37, 39

"Duck Seazon" (Wu-Tang Clan), 80

"Duel of the Iron Mic" (Wu-Tang Clan), 52

East Coast hip-hop and *Only Built 4 Cuban Linx*, 50

East/West Records, 54

Easy Mo Bee, 208

Eddie Murphy Delirious (film) (Eddie Murphy), 47

Education of Sonny Carson, 59

The Education of Sonny Carson (blaxploitation era film), 58

Eight-Diagram Pole Fighter (Shaw Brothers film), 2

Elektra Records, xi, 27

"Elevation" (Inspectah Deck), 101

El Records, 218

EMU SP 1200, 14

"The End" (The Doors), 80

Ensoniq EPS 16 Plus Sampler: for "Brooklyn Zoo," 35; for "C.R.E.A.M" (Wu-Tang Clan), 35; and keyboard based samplers, 93; for "Method Man" (Method Man), 35; for "Protect Ya Neck" (Wu-Tang Clan), 35

Ensoniq EPS sampling workstation, 15, 20

Enter the Wu-Tang (36 Chambers) (Wu-Tang Clan), 11, 15–16, 17; first group album, xi

Enter the Wu-Tang (36 Chambers) (Wu-Tang Clan), and the game of chess, 21

Enter the Wu-Tang (36 Chambers) (Wu-Tang Clan): rhyming dexterity, 19; success of, 23

Epic Records, 53–54

EPS 16+, 15

Erick Sermon, 89

"Fame" (GZA/Genius), 163

"Far Cry" (Marvin Gaye), 107

"Faster Blade" (Raekwon), 59

"Films" (Gary Numan), 216

"Fish" (Ghostface, Raekwon, Cappadonna), 60–61

Fishscale (Ghostface Killah), 186

Fishscale (MF DOOM contributions), 189

Fishscale and DEF JAM records, 189–90

Fisk, Carlton, 32, 193

Five Deadly Venoms, 38

Five Deadly Venoms (kung fu film), 58

The Five Deadly Venoms (Kung fu film), 136

Five Percent Nation (Nation of Gods and Earths), 3; 120 Lessons, 2; and African American youth, 3; and "A Day to God Is 1000 Years,"167; ethos, 2; and GZA/ Genius, 2; and hip-hop, 3; on "I Gotcha Back," 55; on "Older Gods," 75; and Ol' Dirty Bastard, 36; rhetoric on "Criminology," 43; rhetoric on "Rolllin' Wit You," 106; on "Snakes,"38; Supreme

Alphabet, Supreme Mathematics, 2; teachings, "North Star (Jewels),"49; terms from in hip-hop and rap, 2–3; in *Tical 2000. Judgement Day*, 88; on "Wu Revoluton," 72–73; and Wu-Tang Clan, 2

Flavor Fav, 156

"Flowers" (Raekwon, Method Man, Superb, Ghostface), 146

"The Forest" (Ghostface), 149

Forever (Wu-Tang Clan), 55

"Framed" (Kool G. Rap, Killa Sin), 164–65

Freddie Foxx aka Bumpy Knuckles, 111

Fresh (film), 45, 48–49, 53

"Friction" (Inspectah Deck, Masta Killah), 101

Fruikwan, 28

Frusciante, John, 206

"Fuck What You Think" (posse cut), 97

Fugees, 65

Funk Master Flex, 11

Geffen Records, 27, 56

"Get Out of My Life, Woman" (Lee Dorsey), 76

Get Rich or Die Trying (50 Cent), 50

"Get Them Out Ya Way Pa" (Raekwon, U-God, Masta Killa), 208

"Getting High" (Guest rappers), 105

"Get Ya Weight" (Inspectah Deck), 190

"Ghetto Child" (O. V. Wright), 77

"Ghetto Superstar" (Pras and Ol' Dirty Bastard), 39

ghetto themes: "Babies," 157; "C.R.E.A.M.," 22; "Investigative

Reports," 55; *Ironman*, 57; *Liquid Swords*, 57; *Only Built 4 Cuban Linx*, 57

"Ghost Deini" (Ghostface Killah), 114

Ghostdini: Wizard of Poetry in Emerald City (Ghostface), 222

Ghost Dog: The Way of the Samurai: The Album (soundtrack), xiii, 141

Ghostdog: Way of the Samurai (RZA, Jarmusch), 166

"Ghostface" (Ghostface), 176

Ghostface Killah, xi; "260," 59; "After the Laughter," 23; aggressive sound of, 57; "All That I Got Is You" (Ghostface), 62–63; on being an MC, 175–76; and Beyonce in performance, 174; "Bring the Ruckus," 18; "Brooklyn Zoo II (Tiger Crane)," 38; "Can It All be So Simple," 20; "Can It Be All So Simple (Remix), 45; comments on *Ironman*, 64; "Criminology," 43; with Def Jam Records, 174; as executive producer of *Enter the Wu-Tang*, 57; "Fish," 61; "Glaciers of Ice" (*Raekwon* with *Raekwon* and Masta Killah), 42; gun charges, 86; gunfight in Philadelphia, 58; "Heaven & Hell" Raekwon and Ghostface, 48–49; "Ice Cream," 47; "Ice Water," 46; "Iron Maiden," 58; *Ironman*, 57; legal troubles, 112; as lyricist, 20; as MC, 203; and Mike Caruso, 154; musical output, 2006, 196; and Notorious B.I.G., 45–46; "Older Gods" (Raekwon, Ghostface), 75; *Only Built 4 Cuban Linx*, 40; *Only Built 4 Cuban Linx*, 57; popularity of, 145; promoting *Big Doe Rehab*, 205; in "Protect Ya Neck,"10; and Raekwon, 7, 20; with *Raekwon* on "Can It Be All so Simple," 40; "Rainy Dayz," 44; rap artist hierarchy and *Only Built 4 Cuban Linx*, 49; recording *Only Built 4 Cuban Linx*, 41; release date conflict with Wu-Tang Clan, 203, 206; rhyme style, 114; solo opportunity, 58; "The Soul Controller" (Ghostface), 63–64; "Spot Rusherz" (Ghostface, Raekwon), 47; in Steubenville, Ohio, 8; "Striving for Perfection" (with Raekwon), 41, 42; *Supreme Clientele*, xiii, 88; as Wally champ, 123; "Wisdom Body" (Ghostface), 46–47; writing talent, 23; "Wu Gambinos," 48; "Wu-Tang: 7th Chamber," 20; as Wu-Tang Clan's most dependable artist, 186–87

Ghostface Killah, and RZA, 5

Ghostface rift with RZA, 111

Ghostface and RZA in Africa, 112

"Ghost Showers" (Ghostface, Maadam Majestic), 148

"Girl Samurai Lullaby" (Rash Digga), 217

"Giving Up" (Gladys Knight & The Pips), 80

"Glaciers of Ice" (*Raekwon* with Ghostface and Masta Killah), 42, 46

"The Glide" (Raekwon, U-God, La the Darkman, Method Man), 193

"God is Love" (Cappadonna and Killa priest), 218

"Goin' Down" (Ol' Dirty Bastard), 37

"Gold" (GZA/Genius), 52–53

Golden Arms, 106–7. *See also* U-God

Golden Arms Redemption (U-God), xiii, 88, 98–99; 106; reception for, 108; weaknesses in, 107–8

"Good" (Ghostface Killah), 194

"Good Knight" (RZA), 215

"Good Morning, Heartache" (Billie Holiday), 105–6

"Good Morning, Heartache" (Ol' Dirty Bastard), 105–6

"Gotcha Back" (GZA/Geniiius), 53

"Gotta Find a New World" (Al Green), 58

Gotti, Irv, 103, 105

"Got Your Money" (Ol' Dirty Bastard), 104

"The Grain" (Ghostface Killah), 114–15

Grandmasters (DJ Muggs vs. GZA), 185–86

Grant, Oli, 124

Gravediggaz project *6 Feet Deep*, 28

"Gravel Pit" (RZA, Method Man, Ghostface, U-God, Raekwon, Paulisa Morgan), 139

Green is Blues (Al Green and Willie Mitchell), 58

"Grid Iron Rap" (Method Man with True Master), 92

"Grits" (RZA), 167

"Groovin' " (Willie Mitchell), 51, 54

"The Grunge" (Bobby Digital), 166

"Guillotine (Swords)" (Inspector Deck, Ghostface, Raekwon and GZA), 45

"Gun Will Go" (Raekwon, Method Man, Masta Killa, Sunny Valentine), 209

"Gypsy Woman" (Persuasions), 207

GZA/Genius, xi; vs. 50 Cent, 216; in All in Together, 3–4; *Beneath the Surface*, xiii, 88; "Bring the Ruckus," 18; on Cold Chillin' Records, 4; conflict with 50 Cent, 220; distance from *Iron Flag recording*, 154; Geffen Records, 27; as gifted rap veteran, 50–51; "Gold" (GZA/Genius), 52–53; "Hells Wind Staff/Killa Hills 10304" (GZA/Genius), 55; "I Gotcha Back" (GZA/Genius), 55; as Justice, 2; "Living in the World Today" (GZA/Genius and Method Man), 52; *Liquid Swords*, xi, 28, 50; *Liquid Swords* album cover, 51; and Muggs, 186; "Older Gods" (Raekwon, Ghostface), 75; "Protect Ya Neck" (Wu-Tang Clan), 10, 56; rhyming technique, 53; and RZA, 2; RZA and Ol' Dirty Bastard, 1; "Shame on a Nigga," 19; in Staten Island. *See also* Price, Gary "Swordsman" (GZA/Genius), 55; *Words from a Genius*, 4, 50. *See also* Price, Gary

GZA Productions, 55

"Handwriting on the Wall" (RZA and Rass Kass), 96

"Harbor Masters" (RZA, Ghostface, AZ, Inspectah Deck), 219

"Hard Times" (Baby Huey, Ghostface, guests), 116

"Harlem World" (Ol' Dirty Bastard), 39

Harrison, Dhani, 206

Hassan aka Phantom of the Beats, 164

Havoc (Mobb Deep), 89

Hayes, Isaac: influence on Wu-Tang Clan, 81; *The W*, 81

"The Heart Gently Weeps," 205–6, 208

"Heaterz" (True Master), 80

"Heaven & Hell" Raekwon and Ghostface, 48–49

"For Heaven's Sake" (Wu-Tang Clan), 74

"Hells Wind Staff/Killa Hills 10304" (GZA/Genius), 55

"Hellz Wind Staff" (Wu-Tang Clan), 80

"As High as Wu-Tang Get" (Ol' Dirty Bastard, GZA/Genius, Method Man), 74

"The Hilton" (Ghostface and Raekwon), 149

hip-hop: changes in hip-hop landscape, 158; and Five Percent Nation, 2–3; growth of influence, 159; role of sampling, 159–60; vernacular in, 3; West Coast prominence, 17–18, 64–65; Wu-Tang Clan and East Coast rise, 65

hip-hop artists' effect on culture, ix–x

"Hip Hug-Her" (Booker T & The MGs), 35

"Hippa to Da Hoppa" (Ol' Dirty Bastard), 36

Hi-Tek, 195

"Hit or Miss" (Bo Diddley), 32

"In the Hole" (Bar Keys), 52

"Holla" (Ghostface), 175

"Hollow Bones" (Raekwon, Inspectah Deck, Ghostface), 136

"Hollow Bones" and insider slang, 134–35

"Holocaust (Silkworm)" (RZA, Ghostface, Holocaust, Dr. Doom), 96

"In the Hood" (Wu-Tang Clan and Suga Bang Bang), 155

"Hood Rats" (RZA), 167

"Hope That We Can Be Together Soon" (Harold Melvin and the Blue Notes), 148

Hot Buttered Soul (Isaac Hayes), 138

"House of Fly Diggers" (posse cut), 221

Hugo, Chad, 103–4

"I Can't Go To Sleep" (Ghostface, RZA), 138

"I Can't Sleep" (Wu-Tang Clan), 206

"Ice," 149

"Ice Cream" (Ghostface, Raekwon, Cappadonna), 47

"Ice Cream Pt. 2" (Ice Water Inc, Method Man, Cappadonna), 170

"Ice Water" (Ghostface, Raekwon, Cappadonna), 46

Ice Water Inc., ix, 168, 169

"I'd Be So Happy" (Three Dog Night), 55

"If You Think It (You May as Well Do It)" (Emotions), 46

A.I.G. (Allah Wise, Darkim Be Allah), 128

"I Gets My Thang in Action" (Method Man), 32

"I Gotcha Back" (GZA/Genius), 55

"I Go Through Life" (Wu-Tang Clan), 201

"I Keep Asking You Questions" (Black Ivory), 43

"I Like It" (The Emotions), 35

"I'll Be There for You/You're All I Need to Get By" (Method Man), 30–31

"I'll Do Anything for You" (Denroy Morgan), 91

"Ill Figures" (RZA, Raekwon, Kool G Rap), 219

"I'll Never Do You Wrong" (Joe Tex), 38

"I Love You More than You'll Ever Know" (Blood, Sweat and Tears), 76

"I'm Afraid the Masquerade is Over" (David Porter), 52

"I'm His Wife, You're Just His Friend" (Ann Sexton), 52

Immobilarity (Raekwon), xiii, 88; critique, 109; Godfather III as inspiration, 109; pressure from *Only Built 4 Cuban Linx.*, 108; *Reception*, 110

"Impossible" (Wu-Tang Gang), 77

"Incarcerated Blow," 43

"Incarcerated Scarfaces" (Raekwon), 44

Industry Shakedown (Freddie Foxx aka Bumpy Knuckles), 111

The Infinite Archatechz, 110

Inspectah Deck, xi; "Bring the Ruckus," 18; "Cold World" (Inspectah Deck), 53; on " C.R.E.A.M.," 22; early life, 7; producer, "Visionz," 74; production, "Kiss of a Black Widow," 97; production, *Uncontrolled Substances*, 101; "Protect Ya Neck," 9; sound production, *Wu-Tang Clan Forever*, 74; *Uncontrolled Substance*, xiii, 88, 98–99; *Wu-Tang Clan Forever*, 73

Internet and democratization of music industry, xiv–xv

"Intro" on *Return to 36 Chambers (The Dirty Version)* Ol' Dirty Bastard, 35

"Intro" on *RZA as Bobby Digital in Stereo* (RZA), 93

"Investigative Reports," 55

"Investigative Reports" (GZA/Genius,Ghostface, Raekwon, U-God), 55

Iron Flag (Wu-Tang Clan), 139, 158, 160; inclusion of outside producers, 156; Kung-fu dialogue in, 158; as most complete group album, 157; reception for, 160

"Iron God Chamber" (RZA, U-God, Inspectah Deck), 192

"Iron Maiden" (Ghostface with Raekwon and Cappadonna), 58

Ironman (Ghostface Killah), xi, 46, 56, 57

"Iron's Theme" (ufnknown vocalist), 117

"Is It Because I'm Black" (Syl Johnson), 136

Islord, 96, 97

"It's Yourz" (Wu-Tang Clan), 76

"It's a New Day" (Skull Snaps), 36

"It's Yours" (Wu-Tang Gang), 76

"I Want Pussy" (Ol' Dirty Bastard), 105

"I Will Survive" (Gloria Gaynor), 32

"Jah World" (Ghostface, RZA, Junior Reid), 140

Jay Dee/J Dilla, 189

Jay-Z, 220

J. Dilla, 220, 221

Johnny Blaze, 54. *See also* Method Man

"Josephine,"195
"Judgement Day" (Method Man), 89
Juice Crew, 4
"The Juks" (Ghostface, Superb, Trife), 149
"Jury" (Raekwon), 109
Just Blaze, 160

"Keisha's House" (Ghostface), 176
Kelis, 104
"Killa Beez," 19
"Killa Lipstick" (Ghostface Killah), 204
Killa Priest: "Snakes," 38; solo career, 126; work with RZA, 87
Killarmy, 126
Kill Bill series (films) (RZA, Tarantino), 166
Kill Bill Vol 1 &2 (RZA), xiv
Kill Bill Vol. 1 and Vol. 2 Original Soundtracks, 166
The Killer (film) (John Wu), 40–41, 43
Kinetic 9, 97
King Tech, 97
"Kiss of a Black Widow" (RZA, Ol' Dirty Bastard), 96
"Knock Knock" (GZA/Genius), 163
"Knowledge God" (Raekwon), 42
Koch Records (*The Movement*), 164
"Konichiwa Bitches" (Method man), 193
Kool G. Rap, 217
Kung-fu audio: "Duck Seazon" (Wu-Tang Clan), 80; on "Hellz Wind Staff," 80
Kung fu dialogue on "Mantis," 96
kung fu in "Hippa to Da Hoppa," 36

"Lab Drunk" (RZA), 97
"Labels" (GZA/Genius), 53–54
Large Professor, 218

"La Rhumba" (RZA), 143
"Last Night a DJ Save My Life" (Indeep), 91
La the Darkman, 193
Legend of the Liquid Sword (GZA/Genius): Allen Mathematics, GZA, Arabian Knight, producers, 163; reception for, 164
"Let It Be Me" (Linda Jones), 223
"Let My Niggas Live" (Nas), 138
"Let's Ride" (Ginuwine), 194
The Lex Diamond Story, 170
The Lex Diamond Story (Raekwon), 168
Life After Death (Notorious B.I.G), 82
"Life Changes" (formerly "I Go Through Life") (posse cut), 210
"Life Is a Movie" (GZA/Genius), 216
Lil Mo, 106
"A Lil Story" (Inspectah Deck), 190
Lil Wayne's Young Money, 224
Liquid Swords (GZA/Genius), xi, 28, 50–51, 56
"Liquid Swords" (RZA), 51
Liquid Swords Entertainment, 126
"Liquid Swords" RZA sampling on, 51
Liquid words Entertainment, 100
"Little Ghetto Boy" (Donny Hathaway), 76
"Little Ghetto Boys" (Raekwon), 77
"Living in the World Today" (GZA/Genius and Method Man), 52
Lone Wolf and Cub Japanese film series, 51
"As Long As I've Got You" (Charmels), 55
"Looking Out My Window" (Tom Jones), 167
Lord Superb, 110

Loud Records, 13, 27, 101, 154, 168, 201

"Love Jones" (Brighter Side of Darkness), 95

"Love Jones" (RZA), 95

Lovell, Maati, 86

"Love Session" (Ruff Endz), 149

Made in Brooklyn (Masta Killa), 191–92

"Malcolm" (Ghostface), 117

The Manifesto (Inspectah Deck), 223

"Mantis" (RZA and Masta Killa), 95–96

"Marcia in LA" (Alzati spia), 208

"Maria," 75

Marl, Marley, 15

"Marvel" (RZA, Ghostface), 64

Masta Killa, xi, 19; *The Big Doe Rehab*, 204; on confusion in hip-hop world, 72–73; "Da Mystery of Chessboxin'," 21; "Glaciers of Ice" (*Raekwon* with Ghostface and *Raekwon*), 42; "Mantis," 95–96; musical output, 2006, 196; "Snakes," 38; as team player, 181–82; "Wu Gambinos," 48

Master Killer (Chambers of Shaolin) (Shaw Brothers film), 17

Mathematics: producer, "Pencil," 215; producer, *Pro-Tools*, 216; producer, "Stick Me for My Riches," 209; as Wu-Tang Clan's DJ, 100. *See also* Allah Mathematics

"Maxine," 146

"Mechanical Man" (Jerry Butler), 29

"Mercy, Mercy, Mercy" (Willie Mitchell), 51

"Metal Lungies" (Ghostface, et al.), 176

Method Man, xi, xiii

Method Man: assault charges, 86; *The Big Doe Rehab*, 204; *Blackout!* 99; "Bring the Pain," 30; cameo performances, 177–78; on criticism of *Tical 2000: Judgement Daqy*, 92; "Da Mystery of Chessboxin'," 21; with D'Angelo, 90; and Def Jam label, 27, 178; "Dirty Dancin' " (Ol' Dirty Bastard and Method Man), 39; early life, 7; emergence of, xi; "Ice Cream," 47; "I Gets My Thang in Action" (Method Man), 32–33; as individual star, xi; "Living in the World Today" (GZA/Genius and Method Man), 52; "Method Man," 14; "Meth vs. Chef" (Method Man and Raekwon), 32; musical output, 2006, 196; opinion of *Tical*, 28–33; "P.L.O. Style" (Method Man), 32; production, "Judgment Day," 89; "Protect Ya Neck," 10; "Raw Hide" (Ol' Dirty Bastard), 36; with Redman, xiii; "Release Yo' Delf" (Method Man), 32; rhymes' success, 31; and RZA, 5; "Shame on a Nigga," 18; solo career, 34; as soloist, 27; song creation, 90; street hustler life, 33; "Sub Crazy" (Method Man), 32; successes of, 22; *Tical*, xi, 28; *Tical 2000*, xiii, 98; *Tical 2000: Judgement Day*, 88; *Tical 2000: Judgement Day* (Method Man), xii; use of double entendres, sarcasm, 33; "Wu Gambinos," 48; as Wu-Tang Clan's first star, 14

"Method Man" (Method Man), 22, 35

"Method Man (Remix),'' 33

"Meth vs. Chef" (Method Man and Raekwon), 31–32, 45

"Meth vs. Chef 2" (Method Man, Ghostface, Raekwon), 223

MF DOOM, 189, 195

"The M.G.M" (Ghostface and Raekwon), 79

"Mighty healthy" (Ghostface), 112

"Mighty Healthy" (Ghostface Killah), 116

"Miguel Sanchez" (Trife, Sun God), 195

"Miranda" (Method Man, Ghostface, Raekwon), 223

misogyny: "Cracker Jack" (Ol' Dirty Bastard), 106; "Dog Shit" (Ol' Dirty Bastard), 79; "Maria" (Ol' Dirty Bastard), 75; "Marvel" (RZA, Ghostface), 64; "Wildflower" (Ghostface), 58–59

"The Missing Watch" (Ghostface), 168

"Missing Watch" (Polite), 170

Mitchell, Willie, 146–47

"The Monument" (GAZ, Ghostface, RZA), 139

More Fish (Ghostface Killah), 194

Morricone, Ennio, 208

"Motherless Child" (O. V. Wright version), 62

"Motherless Child" (Raekwon, Ghostface), 62

"The Motto" (Method Man), 181

The Movement (Inspectah Deck), 164

"Movers and Shakers" (Inspectah Deck), 101

"Mr. Sandman" (Chordettes), 33

Mr. Xcitement (U-God), 185

Muggs and GZA/Genius, 186

Murdoc, 38

Music from the Motion Picture Ghost Dog: The Way of the Samurai (RZA), 166

"My Guitar" (Ghostface), 206

"My Guitar Gently Weeps" (The Beatles), 206

"My Hero is a Gun" (*Mahogony Original Soundtrack)*, 114

"My Lovin is Digi" (RZA), 96

MySpace page, 206

"Naked Truth" (Ghostface), 176

Nas, 65

Nature Sound Records, 192

"Nautilus" (Bob James), 61, 208

Neptunes, 103

"Never Be the Same Again" (Carl Thomas, Ghostface), 145–47

"Never Can Say Goodbye" (Force MDs), 61

"New Classic," 218

"New Wu" ("Wu Ooh") (Raekwon, Method Man, Ghostface), 220

Next Plateau Records, 54

"Nigga Please" (Ol' Dirty Bastard), 105

Nigga Please (Ol' Dirty Bastard), xiii, 88, 98, 102: producers, 103; reception for, 106

Ninjaman, 30

"No More Tears (enough is enough)" (Barbara Streisand and Donna Summer), 44

"North Star (Jewels)" (Ol' Dirty Bastard as Papa Wu), 49

"North Star (Jewels)" (Raekwon), 49

No Said Date (Masta Killa), 181–83

"No Said Date" (Masta Killa), 182

Notorious B.I.G., 45, 65, 72

No Way Out (Puff Daddy & The Family/Diddy), 82
"Nutmeg" (Ghostface Killah), 113
N-word and *Only Built 4 Cuban Linx.*, 41
"NYC Everything" (RZA and Method Man), 95

Odadjian, Shavo, 208, 217
"O Day" (RZA), 215
ODB. *See* Ol´Dirty Bastard
Okazaki, Takashi, 202
Ol' Dirty Bastard, xi, 37, 79; All in Together, 3–4; as Ason Unique, 36; "Baby Come On" (Ol' Dirty Bastard), 35; "Brooklyn Zoo" (Ol' Dirty Bastard), 35–36; "Brooklyn Zoo II (Tiger Crane)," 38; cash ruling, 36; child support charges, 86; as clown prince of Wu-Tang Clan, 34; continueing legal troubles, 154; "Cuttin' Headz" (Ol' Dirty Bastard and RZA), 38–39; "Damage" (with RZA), 36; death of, 106, 173, 184; difficulties participating in Wu-Tang Clan, 141; as Dirt McGirt, 173; "Dirty Dancin' " (Ol' Dirty Bastard and Method Man), 39; "Dog Shit" (Ol' Dirty Bastard), 79; "Don't U Know" (Ol' Dirty Bastard), 36–37; "Drunk Game (Sweet Sugar Pie)" (Ol' Dirty Bastard), 37; Elektra Records, 27; emergence of, xi; "Fantasy Remix" with Mariah Carey, 39; "Goin' Down" (Ol' Dirty Bastard), 37; at Grammy Awards, 1998, 86; GZA/Genius and RZA, 1; "Harlem World" (Ol' Dirty Bastard), 39; heroics, 86;

"As High as Wu-Tang Get" (Ol' Dirty Bastard), 74; "Hippa to Da Hoppa" (Ol' Dirty Bastard), 36; incarceration and mental health problems, xiii, 36, 137, 173; increasing paranoia, 105; as individual star, xi; and "Intro" to *Return to 36 Chambers (The Dirty Version)*, 35; legal problems, xiii, 133; MC skills, 36; name changing, 102; *Nigga Please*, 88, 98, 102; as "Osirus," 185; as Papa Wu, "North Star (Jewels)," 49; post-psychiatric treatment center efforts, 183; in "Protect Ya Neck," 10; "Raw Hide" (Ol' Dirty Bastard), 36; relations with Wu-Tang Clan members, 184; *Return of the 36 Chambers (The Dirty Version)*, xi; *Return to the 36 Chambers (The Dirty Version)*, 28, 34, 39; rhyming skills, 35–36; run-ins with law enforcement, 103; self-indulgence, *Return to 36 Chambers (The Dirty Version)*, 36–37; on "Shame on a Nigga,"18–19; "Shimmy Shimmy Ya" (Ol' Dirty Bastard), 35; "Snakes" (posse cut), 37–38; "Somewhere Over the Rainbow," 37; as the Specialist, 3–4; in Staten Island, 1; "The Stomp" (Ol' Dirty Bastard), 37; substance abuse problems, 103; towards end of life, 80; troubles following, 34
"Older Gods" (Raekwon, Ghostface, GZA), 75
Ol' Dirty Bastard, *Nigga Please*, xiii
"Old Man" (Masta Killa, RZA, Ol' Dirty Bastard), 182
"One" (Ghostface Killah), 113

"One Blood Under W" (Masta Killa), 137

"One Way Street" (Ann Peebles), 101

Only Built 4 Cuban Linx.Pt. II (Raekwon) xiv, 211, 219–20: Dr. Dre tracks, 220; production duration, 220; reception for, 221–22; Wu-Tang Clan characteristics, 220–21

Only Built 4 Cuban Linx (Raekwon), xiii, 28, 41; reception for, 49–50; and RZA, 49. *See also Only Built 4 Cuban Linx.*; "The Purple Tape"

"Ooh, I Love You Rakeem" (RZA as Prince Rakeem), 4–5

Osirus (Ol' Dirty Bastard), 73, 184–85

Osirus(Ol' Dirty Bastard), 184–85

"Our Dreams" (Wu-Tang Clan), 227; RZA, producer, 223

OutKast, 65

"Over" (Ghostface), 175

"Pa-blow Escablow" (Ice Water Inc), 170

"Paisley Darts" (Cappaadonna, Trife, Raekwon, Sun God, Method Man), 204

"Papa Was Too" (Joe Tex), 32, 38

Papa Wu. *See* Ol'Dirty Bastard

"Paper Plate" (GZA/Genius), 216

"Pass the bone" (GZA/Genius and RZA), 4

P. C. (Paulie Caskets), 169

"Pencil" (RZA, Masta Killa), 215

"Penny Lover" (Lionel Richie), 109

"Perfect World" (Method Man), 91

"Phone Tap" (The Firm), 97

"Phone Time" (Capone-N-Noreaga), 97

The Pillage (Cappadonna), 60, 101

platinum-selling albums: *Enter the Wu-Tang (36 Chambers)*, xi; *Ironman* (Ghostface), xi; *Tical*, xi; *Tical* (Method Man), 28; *Tical 2000*, xiii; *The W*, xiii; *Wu-Tan Clan Forever*, 82; *Wu-Tang Forever*, xii

"P.L.O. Style" (Method Man), 32

"Poisonous Darts" (Ghostface), 59, 60

Polite, 169–70

Polluted Water (Ice Water Inc.), 169

Popa Wu: misogyny, 75–76; on "Wu Revolution," 72–73

"Pop Shots" (Ol' Dirty Bastard), 185

posse cuts as procedural: "Assassination Day," 60; "Winter Warz," 60; "Wu Gambinos," 60

"Presidential MC" (Raekwon, RZA), 193

The Pretty Toney Album (Ghostface Killah), 174, 176–77

Price, Gary. *See also* GZA/Genius

Price, Sean, 219

Prince Paul, 15

Prince Paul Gravediggaz project, 28

Prince Rakeem (RZA as), 4

Prodigal Sun, 38, 163

"The Projects" (Ghostface and Raekwon), 78

"Project Talk" (RZA), 97

"Protect Ya Neck" (GZA/Genius verse), 56

"Protect Ya Neck (The Jump Off)" (GZA), 138

"Protect Ya Neck (The Jump Off)" (Wu-Tang Clan), 135–36

"Protect Ya Neck" (Wu-Tang Clan), 9–11, 13–14, 35

"Protect Ya Neck II The Zoo"
(Brooklyn Zu, et al.), 38
Pro-Tools (GZA/Genius),
214, 215
Pro-Tools (RZA, GZA/Genius)
reception for, 216–17
"Publicity" (GZA/Genius), 100
"Puff Daddy Mix" (Sean "Puffy"
Combs), 30
"the purple tape," 45
"purple tape," 49
"The Purple Tape," 42. *See also*
Only Built 4 Cuban Linx.
"Push" (Ghostface, Missy Elliott),
176
Q-Tip, 202, 217
Qu'Ran Goodman, 90

"Radioactive (Four Assassins)"
(GZA, Raekwon, Method Man,
Masta Killa), 157
Raekwon: "260," 59; at Aftermath
Entertainment, 202–3; "Bring the
Ruckus," 18; "Can It Be All So
Simple," 20; "Can It Be All So
Simple (Remix)" (Ghostface and
Raekwon), 45; "The Closing"
(Raekwon), 81; collaboration with
Ghostface Killah, 20; "
C.R.E.A.M.," 21, 22; on creating
and writing, 42; "Criminology,"
43; discussing *Only Built 4 Cuban
Linx.*, 41; "Faster Blade"
(Raekwon), 59; "Fish," 61; and
Ghostface Killah, 7; with
Ghostface Killah on "Can It Be
All So Simple," 40; "Glaciers of
Ice" (*Raekwon* with Ghostface
and Masta Killah), 42; "Heaven &
Hell" Raekwon and Ghostface,
48–49; on "Ice Cream," 47; "Ice

Water," 46; *Immobilarity*, xiii, 88,
99; "Incarcerated Surfaces," 44;
"Knowledge God" (*Raekwon*), 42;
on the language of rap, 44; leaving
drugs behind, 108; "Little Ghetto
Boys" (Raekwon), 77; on "Meth
vs. Chef" (Method Man), 40;
"Meth vs. Chef" (Method Man
and Raekwon), 32; need for radio-
friendly material, 145; "North
Star (Jewels)," 49; and Notorious
B.I.G., 45–46; "Older Gods"
(Raekwon, Ghostface), 75; *Only
Built 4 Cuban Linx*, xi, xiii, 28; on
Only Built 4 Cuban Linx, 40; *Only
Built 4 Cuban Linx Pt II*, xiv; in
"Protect Ya Neck," 9–10; "Rainy
Dayz," 44; rap artist hierarchy and
Only Built 4 Cuban Linx., 49; on
"Raw Hide" (Ol' Dirty Bastard),
36, 40; recording *Only Built 4
Cuban Linx.*, 41; rift with RZA,
111; on "Shame on a Nigga," 18;
"Spot Rusherz" (Ghostface,
Raekwon), 47; "Striving for
Perfection" (with Ghostface
Killah), 41, 42; on , 204; on "Wu
Gambinos," 48; on "Wu-Tang: 7th
Chamber," 20. *See also* Raekwon
Rage Against the Machine, 85–86
Rah Digga, 217
"In the Rain" (The Dramatics), 53
"Rainy Dayz" (Raekwon and
Ghostface), 44
Ranch Crew, 52
Rapper Superb, 114
Rass Kass, 96
"Raw Hide" (Ol' Dirty Bastard), 36
"Razor Sharp Mix" (RZA), 30–31
Razor Sharp Records, 44, 57, 60–61,
107, 126

"Real Life" (Raekwon), 109
Reasonable Doubt (Jay-Z), 50
"Redbull" (Redman, Method Man, Inspectah Deck, Raekwon), 136
Redman, xiii, 195
"Release Yo' Delf" (Method Man), 30, 32
Remedy, 128
The Resident Patient (Inspectah Deck), 190
"Retro-Godfather" (Method Man), 91
Return to 36 Chambers (The Dirty Version), 34–36
Return to the 36 Chambers (Wu-Tang Clan) release of, xi
Return to the 36 Chambers: The Dirty Version, xi, 39
Return to the 36 Chambers: The Dirty Version (Ol' Dirty Bastard), 28
"Reunited" (Wu-Tang clan), 65, 73
The Revelations, 219
Reynoso, Jose "Choco," 166
Rifkind, Steve, xiv, 201
"Riot" (Blackbyrds), 62
"Robbery" (Ice Water Inc.), 170
Roc-a-Fella Records, 173
Rock, Chris, 103
Rock, Pete, 188
"Rocket Love" (Stevie Wonder), 53
Rollie Fingers. *See* Inspectah Deck
"Rollin' Wit You" (Ol' Dirty Bastard), 104–5
Ronson, Mark, 195
The Roots, 86
Royal Fam (Timbo King, et al.), 128
Rugged Monk, 215
"Rules" (Wu-Tang Clan), 155
"Rumble" (posse cut), 107

"Run" (Ghostface with RZA producer), 174
"Run 4 Cover," 141
Rush Associated Labels, 54
"Rushing elephants," 208
Russell Jones, 39. *See also* Ol´Dirty Bastard
Ryman, Ethan, 37
RZA, x, xii, 55; absence from *Immobilarity* (Raekwon), 109–10; absence on *The Lex Diamond Story*, 169; "After the Laughter," 23; in All in Together, 3–4; "American Gangster" (film), 212; architect of Wu-Tang Clan, x–xi; as Bobby Boulders, 139; as Bobby Digital, xii, 92; *Bobby Digital in Stereo*, xii–xiii, 98; "Can It All be So Simple," 20; "Clan in da Front," 19; classic albums, xii; comments on *Wu-Tang Clan Forever*, 81; contributions to "Break Ups 2 Make Up,"91; control of Clan's solo contracts, 27–28; coproducer of "The Stomp," 37; core philosophy of principles, 5; and "C.R.E.A.M.," 21–22; criticism of other hip-hop producers, emcees, 76–77; "Cuttin' Headz" (Ol' Dirty Bastard and RZA), 38–39; "Damage" (with Ol' Dirty Bastard), 36–37; decline of quality, 129; as dictator of Wu-Tang clan, 8; disputes with U-God, 185; early life, 1; executive producer, *Wu-Tang Chamber Music*, 218–19; and Five Percent Nation's 120 lessons, 3; five year plan, xii; Godfather influence, 224; Gravediggaz project, 28;

grooming artists, 214–15; GZA/ Genius and Ol' Dirty Bastard, 1; "Hells Wind Staff/Killa Hills 10304" (GZA/Genius), 55; and individual members' demands, 87; and individual solo deals, 13; initial failure, 5; instrumental. "Retro-Godfather,"91; instrumental sounds, *Only Built 4 Cuban Linx*, 41; *Ironman* production, 57; Kung Fu film influence, 1–2; legacy, 224–26; "Liquid Swords" (RZA), 51–52; *Liquid Swords* production, 56; loass of creative control, 72; "Mantis," 95–96; marketing Wu-Tang Clan merchandise, 47–48; as MC, 95; misogyny, 76; movie scores, xiv, 166; music theory student, 86, 129; on *No Said Date*, 182; "NYC Everything" (RZA and Method Man), 95; *Only Built 4 Cuban Linx*, 56; *Only Built 4 Cuban Linx Pt. II*, 220; participation in 1999 recordings, 99; as Prince Rakeem, 4; as producer, xiii; producer, *Bulletproof Wallets*, 146; producer, "It's Yours," 76; producer, "Life is a Movie, 216; producer, *Return to 36 Chambers (The Dirty Version)*, 34; producer, *The Wu*, 135; producer, *Uncontrolled substance*, 101; as producer vs. rapper, 215; production, *Bobby Digital in Stereo*, 97; production, "Impossible," 77; production, "It's Yourz," 76; production, *Nigga Please*, 105; on production motives, 56–57; production on "*4:21. The Day After*, 193; production role, later

albums, 129; production sensibilities, *Only Built 4 Cuban Linx*, 41; "Protect Ya Neck," 10; as rapper, 95; relationship changes with Wu-Tang Clan, 87–88; relationship with U-God, 107; romantic lyrics, 95; "Rough Cut" on *Legend of the Liquid Sword*, 163; *RZA as Bobby Digital in Stereo*, 88; as The Rzarector, 28; RZA samples on "Retro-Godfather,"91; samples, "retro-Godfather," 91; samples on "Rainy Dayz," 44; "Snakes," 38; sonic aesthetic development, 211; sound engineering, *Only Built 4 Cuban Linx*, 50; sound engineering on "Cold World," 53; sound engineering on "Duel of the Iron Mic," 52; sound engineering on "Shadowboxing,"54–55; and sound production, 15, 20; sound production, "All That I Got Is You," 63; sound production, *Ironman*, 64; sound production, "Reunited," 73; sound production, "The Soul Controller," 64; sound production, *Tical 2000: Judgment Day*, 89; sound production, use of keyboards for, 73; sound production by, 35; sound production influence on hip-hop, 65; sound production on "Box in Hand" on *Ironman*, 61; sound production on "Daytona 500," 61; sound production on "Faster Blade," 59; sound production on "Ice Water," 46; sound production on "Motherless Child," 62; sound production on "Verbal Intercourse,"46, 59, 61; soundtrack, scoring work, 142, 1225; sound use on "Knowledge God," 42; in Steubenville, Ohio, 5, 8; string samples, *Wu-Tang Forever*, 81; as student of music theory, 73, 91; switch from drum machine to keyboard, 15; and *Tical*, 29; track, "Gold" (GZA/Genius), 53; treatment of women themes, 97; use of live musicians, 74; use of *The Killer* (film) score on *Only Built 4 Cuban Linx*, 40–41; waning influence, 112; work with Wu-Tang Clan affiliates, 86–87; on "Wu Gambinos," 48; on "Wu-Tang Clan Ain't Nuthin ta F' Wit," 21; on *Wu-Tang Clan Forever*, 73; and Wu-Tang Clan's artistic success, xii; and Wu-Tang Clan's success, xii. *See also* Diggs, Robert Fitzgerald

RZA and Ghostface in Africa, 112

RZA as Bobby Digital in Stereo, 88; digital orchestra in, 93; "Intro," 93

RZA as Bobby Digital in Stereo (RZA): and music theory, 93; as producer, 93

RZA boutique labels, 126

RZA on *Supreme Clientele*, 114–15

RZA presents Afro-Samurai: The Album, 202

RZA presents Wu-Tang Killa Bees: The Swarm, 112

RZA productions: "Long Kiss Goodnight" (Notorious B.I.G.), 125; "Stand Up" (Ghostface), 125; "Tres Leches (Triboro Trilogy)" (Inspectah Deck), 125

the Rzarector (RZA), 28

RZA rift with Ghostface, 111

RZA rift with Raekwon, 111

RZA rift with U-God, 111

RZA vs. Bobby Digital, 166

RZA vs. Bobby Digital battle, 143–44

Sadat X, 219

sample fees, 73

samples clearance issues, 146, 188, 206

sampling, 15, 159–60

Sanctuary Records (*Birth of a Prince*), 165

"Saturday Night" (Ghostface Killah), 114

"Say," 192–93

"Scarface"(film) (Brian de Palma), 43

"School" (Masta Killa, RZA), 182

Sean "Diddy" ("Puffy") Combs, 82

Sean "Diddy" ("Puffy") Combs Bad Boy artists, x

"Second Coming" (Tekitha), 81

"See the Joy" (RZA), 167

Seijen, Thea van, 217

September 11, 2001, 155

Sermon, Erick, 192

"Severe Punishment" (posse cut), 75

"Sexcapades" (Easy Mobee and RZA as Prince Rakeem), 5

Shabazz, Melquan, 4

"Shadowboxing" (GZA/Genius and Method Man), 54

"Shakey Dog starring Lolita" (Raekwon), 204

Shallah Raaekwan, 40. *See also* Raekwon

"Shame on a Nigga" (Wu-Tang Clan), 18–19

Shaolin and Wu-Tang (kung-fu film), 2, 207

Shaolin vs. Lama (kung-fu film), 54

Shaolin vs. Wu-Tang (Raekwon), 223

Sheek Louch, 176, 195

"Shimmy Shimmy Ya" (Ol' Dirty Bastard), 35

Shogun Assassin (Japanese *jidaigeki* film), 51

Shorti Shit Stain, 38

"Shorty Right There" (Streetlife), 164–65

Shyheim the Rugged Child, 15, 19, 79

"Slow Grind African" (RZA), 94–95

"Slow Grind French" (RZA), 94, 96

"Slow Grind Italian" (RZA), 94, 96

Smith, Clarence (Clarence 13X), 2, 3

"Smith Brothers" (Raekwon), 169

"Snakes" (Ol' Dirty Bastard, posse cut), 37–38

"Sneakers" (Raekwon), 109

"Sneakin' in the Back" (Tom Scott), 79

Snoop Dogg, 17–18, 64

"Snowbound" (Sarah Vaughn), 33

"So Many Things to Say" (Lauryn Hill), 193

"Somewhere Over the Rainbos" (Ol' Dirty Bastard), 37

Sommers, Jamie, 96, 97, 128

"The Soul Controller" (Ghostface), 63–64

"Soul Power (Black Jungle)" Wu-Tang Clan and Flavor Fav, 156

The Soul Zodiac (Cannonball Adderly), 53

South Bronx, ix

"Speak Softly Love" (The Professionals), 220

"Spot Rusherz" (Ghostface, Raekwon), 47

SRC Records, xiv

SRC Records (Universal Motown Records), 201

"Star Children" (Mighty Ryeders), 95

Starks, Tony. *See* Ghostface Killah

"Starter" (Sunny Valentine, Wu-Tang Clan), 209

Staten Island, 9, 11; Cappadonna, 48; Cold Crush Brothers, 52; The Force MDs, 61; Ghostface's upbringing on, 63; Killla Hills (Park Hill Projects), 55; in "Motherless Child," 62; RZA's early life in, 1; and Wu-Tang Clan, 50

"Stay In Your Lane" (U-God), 107–8

"Stay True" (Ghostface Killah), 116

"Stick Me for My Riches" (Gerald Alston, Raewkon, Method Man, Inspectah Deck, RZA, GZA), 209

"Stimulation" (Method Man), 33

"The Stomp" (Ol' Dirty Bastard), 37

"Stomp da Roach" (GZA/Gemois), 218

Stone Mecca, 217

"Straight Up the Block" (Black Knightgs, Thea van Seijan), 215

"Strawberry" (Ghostface, Killa Sin), 148–49

"Street Chemistry" (Prodigal Sunn, Trife, Ghostface), 149

"Street Corner" (GZA, Inspectah Deck, U-God), 192

Streetlife, 193

"Striving for Perfection" (Raekwon and Ghostface), 41, 42

"Stroke of Death" (Ghostface, Solomon Childs, RZA), 116–17
"Stroke of Death" (RZA Produced), 116
Stumik, 169
Styles Pon, 176
"Sub Crazy" (Method Man), 32
Suga Bang Bang, 202, 217
"The Sun" (RZA; Raekwon, Slick Rick), 147
Sun God, 195
"Sunlight" (RZA), 209
"Sunshower" (RZA), 81
Sunz of Man, 36–37, 38, 126
"Supa GFK" (Ghostface Killah), 204–5
Supreme Clientele: reception, 118–19; and rescue of Wu-Tang Clan, 119
Supreme Clientele (Ghostface Killah), xiii, 88, 133; release troubles, 112; RZA and keyboard-sample balance, 141; RZA influence, 113
Supreme Clientele (Ghostface Killah), 88
Supreme Mathematics on "1112," 99
"Suspect Chin Music" (Method Man and Streetlife), 91
"Swordsman" (GZA/Genius), 55
"Synthetic Substitution" (Bliss), 18, 19, 39
System of the Down, 208, 217

"Take it Back" (Raaekwon, Inspectah Deck, Ghostface, U-God), 208
"Take me to the Mardi Gras" (Bob James), 146
Tañob Lweño, 202

The Tao of Wu (RZA), 9, 93
Tao of Wu (RZA), 50
"Tar Pit" (U-God, Cappadonna, Streetlife, George Clinton), 210
"Tearz" (Wu-Tang Clan), 11, 22
"Teddy Skit" (Superb, Ghostface), 148
Teddy Ted & J. Serbe, 218
Tekitha, 77; "Impossible," 77; "Second Coming," 81; work with RZA, 87
"Terri's Tune" (David Axelrod), 101
"Terrorists" (RZA; et. al.), 96
Thea van Seijen, 215
"Theodore" (Ghostface and Theodore Unit), 148
Theodore Unit, 148, 188, 195, 204
"This Is Something for the Radio" (Biz Markie), 148
Thomas, Carl, 145–46
Tical (Method Man), xi, 28–29, 30–31
"Tical" (Method Man and RZA), 29
Tical 0: The Prequel (Method Man), 177, 178–81; problems with, 178–80; vs. *Tical*, 178
Tical 2000 (Method Man), 98
Tical 2000: Judgement Day (Method Man), xii, 88; debut, 89–90; Five Percent Nation (Nation of Gods and Earths (Five Percent Nation), 88; outros, 89; skits, 91; sound production, 89
Timbo King, 96
"A Time to Love" (Earl Klugh's acoustic guitar), 47
"Time Without End" (Bel Canto), 37
Tommy Boy Records, 4, 5
Too Poetic, 28
"Torture" (Method Man with True Master), 92

Trackmasters, 89, 90

"Train Trussle" (Ghostface), 218

The Trials and Tribulations of Russell Jones (Ol' Dirty Bastard), 173

Trife Da God, 204

Trife Diesel, 148, 188, 195

Triflyn, 110

"Triumph" (posse), 73, 77

"Trouble, Heartaches & Sadness" (Peebles), 54–55

True Master, 19, 61, 126; producer, "Biscuits" (Ghostface), 175; producer, "Dat Gangsta," 107; producer, "La Rhumbaa," 143; producer, *Pro-Tools*, 216; producer, "The M.G.M.," 79; producer, "Ya'll Been Warned," 156; production of "Brooklyn Zoo," 35; sound production, *Tical 2000: Judgment Day*, 89, 91; sound production, *Wu-Tang Clan Forever*, 74

Tupac Shakkur, 65, 72, 73

"Turbo Charge" (U-God), 108

"The Turn" (RZA), 181

"Tush" (Ghostface, Missy Elliott), 176

Twiz, 148

U-God, xi; *The Big Doe Rehab*, 204; "Da Mystery of Chessboxin'," 21; disputes with RZA, 185; *Dopium*, 218; early life, 7; *Enter the Wu-Tang (36 Chambers)*, 21; *Golden Arms Redemption*, xiii, 88; *Golden Arms Redemption* (U-God), 98–99; lack of demand for solo album from, 107; *Only Built 4 Cuban Linx.*, 42; and prison, 21; "Protect Ya Neck," 10, 21; relationship with RZA,

107; as soloist on Wu-Tang Clan cuts, 107

U-God rift with RZA, 111

U-Godzilla Presents the Hillside Scramblers (U-God), 185

Uncontrolled Substance (Inspectah Deck), xiii, 88, 98, 100–102

Universal Records, 168

"Unpredictable" (RZA, Shavo Odadjian), 208

"Unspoken Word" (RZA), 94

Urban Icon Records (Inspectah Deck), 190

The Usual Suspects (film), 59, 64

"Verbal Intercourse" (Nas), 46

violence as theme: "Imposible," 77; "Little Ghetto Boys," 77

"Visionz" (Method Man, Raekwon, Masta Killah, Inspectah Deck, Ghostface), 74

Voodoo (D'Angelo, Method Man), 90

"The W" (Ghostface, RZA, Raekwon, busta Rhymes, GZA), 139

The W (guest stars), 137

The W (Wu-Tang Clan), xiii; problems with, 143; reception for, 140; RZA, producer, 135; vs. *Wu-Tang Forever*, 133–34

"Walking Through the Darkness" (Ghostface, Tekitha), 149

"Walk on By" (Isaac Hayes), 138

"Wang Dang Doodle" (Koko Taylor), 44

"Warm and Tender" (Johnny Mathis), 210

"Warp Factor II" (Vince Montana), 91

"The Watch" (Ghostface, Raekwon), 147, 168–69

"The Way We Were/Try to
  Remember" (Gladys Knight and
  the Pips), 20, 45
"Weak Spot" (RZA, Raekwon,
  GZA), 210
"We Celebrate" (Ghostface
  Killah), 204
"Welcome Home" (Ol' Dirty
  Bastard), 183–84
"We Made It" (Carlos Broady-
  produced), 116
"We Made It" (Superb, Chip Banks,
  Hell Razah, Ghostface), 116
"We Pop" (Bobby Digital), 166–67
"We're Almost There" (Michael
  Jackson), 223
West, Kanye, 160
West Coast prominence of hip-hop
  groups, 65
"Whar" (Ghostface, Kool G. Rap),
  217
"What the Blood Clot" (Method
  Man), 31
"What Would I do"
  (Ernie Hines), 101
"Wherever I Go" (RZA), 167
"The Whistle" (RZA), 167
"Who Got it" (Ayatolloah,
  producer), 164–65
"Who Would lYou Fuck"
  (Ghostface, et al. skit), 117
Wigs, Shawn, 195
"Wildflower" (Ghostface), 58
Williams, Pharrell, 103–4
Willie Mitchell, 58
"Windmill" (GZA; Raekwon, Masta
  Killa, Inspectah Deck, Method
  Man, Cappadonna): on "Kill Bill
  Vol. 1" (Soundtrack), 210; RZA,
  sound production, 210
"Winter Warz" (posse cut), 60

"Wisdom Body" (Ghostface), 46–47
"Wolves," 209
women, treatment of and RZA, 97
"Woodrow the Basehead Skit"
  (Ghostface Killah), 116
"Word on the Street" (Inspectah
  Deck), 101
Words from a Genius (GZA/
  Genius), 4, 50
Wu, John, 41
"Wu-Banga 101" (GZA, Cappa-
  donna, Raekwon, Masta Killah,
  Ghostface), 118
"Wu-Delfonics," 62
Wu-Elements, 112, 126
"Wu Gambinos" (Method Man,
  Raekwon, RZA, Masta Killa,
  Ghostface), 48
"Wu Gambinos" (posse cut), 48
Wu-Gambinos as Wu-Tang Clan's
  mafia alternate names, 48
Wu Gambinos on *Only Built 4
  Cuban Linx.*, 48
The Wu-Massacre (Def Jam Wu-Tan
  Clan members), 222–23
"Wu Revolution" (Wu-Tang Clan),
  72–73
"Wu-Revolution" and misogynsm, 75
Wu-Syndicate (The Syndicate),
  128, 129
Wu Tan Forever (Wu-Tang Clan),
  72–73
"Wu Tang: 7th Chamber" (Wu-Tang
  Clan), 20
"Wu-Tang: 7th Chamber, Pt.," 23
Wu-Tang Chamber Music (Wu-Tang
  Clan), 218–19
Wu-Tang Clan, 32, 65; *8 Diagrams*,
  xiv; albums' performance, 2003,
  170–71; appeal, 225; August 2006
  Tour, 192; beginnings, x; brand

expansion, xii; business savvy, 226; "Cash Still Rules/Scary Hours (Still Don't Nothing Move But the Money)" (Wu-Tang Clan), 74; changes in hip-hop landscape, 158; changes to group personality, 72; and Clan-owned imprints, 57; classic albums, xii; conflict over avant-garde vs. basic approach, 211–12; consistency, 39; contract terms, 13; creative control, 13; declining quality, 129–30; from dictatorship to democracy, 141; disunity, 226–27; early albusm, xi; and East Coast hip-hop, 65; vs. East Coast rivals, 65; eclipse in hip-hop world, 159; end of five year plan, 85; expanding audience demographics, 85–86; fading influence, 196; Five Percent Nation (Nation of Gods and Earths rhetoric), 2–3; five-year plan, xii, 8–9; getting together, 8; group dynamics problems, xiv; "For Heaven's Sake" (Wu-Tang Clan), 74; vs. hip-hop peers, 133; as hip-hop trendsetters, xi; and individual albums, 59; individual member use of RZA beat, 32; and individual solo deals, 13; *Iron Flag*, xiii; legal troubles, 86; lyrics and Five Percent Nation, 2–3; master plan, 27; members, xi, 7; members as solo stars, 27; misogynistic lyrics, 37; moral dichotomy, 76; move to California, 73; vs. Notorious B.I.G., 45; post *8 Diagrams* tour without RZA, 213; products: Wu-Wear clothing, 73; public conflicts and dysfunction, 206–7; qualities, xi; Rage Against the Machine tour, 86; rapping, 54; Rebirth Tour, USA, 227; rebuilding efforts, 153–54; recording after September 11, 2001, 154; recording in California, 133; release from contracts with RZA, 173–74; reputation and *Only Built 4 Cuban Linx*, 49–50; reunion, 186; rift, 110–11; RZA and artistic success of, xii; RZA as dictatorship, 8; significance of *Tical*, 34; solo albums, 27–28; start of reign of, 56; and Staten Island, 9, 11; status of, xiv–xv; style, 23; and success of hip-hop, 85; tour in 2007, 203; and underground hip-hop, 159; United Kingdom tour, 227; unofficially disbanded, 86; as virtual corporation, 125; *Wu-Tang Forever*, xii. *See also* RZA

"Wu-Tang Clan Ain't Nuthin ta F' Wit," 21

Wu-Tang Clan as actors: *American Gangster*, 125; *Black and White* (film), 124; *Derailed* (film), 125; RZA, GZA in *Coffee and Cigarettes* (Jim Jarmusch), 124–25; *The Wire* (HBO), 124

Wu-Tang Clan brand marketability: Clarks Wallabee Shoes, 123; "Ice Cream" for marketing, 47–48; synbergy between music, brand, 124; Wu-Wear Clothing Inc., 124; "Wu-Wear: Garment Renaissance" (RZA), 124

Wu-Tang Clan cameos, 125

Wu-Tang Clan Forever (Wu-Tang Clan): bestselling album, 160; success of, 82, 85

Wu-Tang Clan kung fu video, 124

Wu-Tang Clan mentees, 128–29

Wu-Tang comic book line, 124
Wu-Tang International, 129
*Wu-Tang Killa Bees: The Swarm,
    Vol.1*, 127–28
"A Wu-Tang Life" (clothing line
    with A-Life), 224
Wu-Tang Manual, 8; on being
    digital, 93; on "Bring the
    motherfucking ruckus! " 18
Wu-Tang Manual (RZA), 225
Wu-Tang Music Group, 218
Wu-Tang Productions: first home, 8;
    "Protect Ya Neck" (Wu-Tang
    Clan), 13
Wu-Tang Records, 126; "Protect Ya
    Neck" (Wu-Tang Clan), 10
Wu-Wear clothing, 73
Wu-Wear Clothing Inc, 124
"Wu-Wear: Garment Renaissance"
    (RZA), 124
"Wyld in da Club" (Ice Water Inc.), 170

"Yae Yo" (Raekwon), 109
"Ya'll Been Warned" (Wu-Tang
    Clan), 156–57
"You Can't Stop Me Now" (RZA,
    Inspectah Deck), 214
"You Don't Want to Fuck With Me"
    (Ol' Dirty Bastard), 105
"You Know I'm No Good" (Amy
    Winehouse), 195
"You'll Never Know" (RZA), 167
Young Jeezy "The Snowman, " 187
"You Ought to Be with Me" (Al
    Green), 59
"You Play Too Much"
    (Chris Rock), 91
"You're All I Need to Get By"
    (Gaye and Terrell), 30
"You're Getting Too Smart" (The
    Detroit Emeralds), 43–44

Zu Keeper, 38

About the Author

ALVIN BLANCO is a writer and editor. He received a BA in African and African American Studies and Psychology from the University of Virginia. A former Features Editor at AllHipHop.com, over the past decade his work has appeared in *Vibe, Spin, XXL, The Source, Village Voice*, and many other notable publications.